The Muvipix.com Guide to
Adobe Photoshop
Elements 2019

Steve Grisetti

The tools in Adobe's amazing photo editing program, and how to use them to create great-looking photos on your personal computer.

About Muvipix.com

Muvipix.com was created to offer support and community to amateur and semi-professional videomakers. Registration is free, and that gets you access to the world's friendliest, most helpful forum and lots of ad-free space for displaying your work. On the products page, you'll find dozens of free tips, tutorials, motion backgrounds, DVD templates, sound effects, royalty-free music and stock video clips. For a small annual subscription fee that we use to keep the site running, you'll have unlimited downloads from the ever-growing library of support materials and media.

We invite you to drop by and visit our thriving community. It costs absolutely nothing – and we'd love to have you join the neighborhood!

http://Muvipix.com

About the author

Steve Grisetti holds a master's degree in Telecommunications from Ohio University and spent several years working in the motion picture and television industry in Los Angeles. A veteran user of several video editing programs and systems, Steve is the co-founder of Muvipix.com, a help and support site for amateur and semi-professional videomakers. A professional graphic designer and video freelancer, he has taught classes in Photoshop, lectured on design and even created classes for lynda.com. He lives in suburban Milwaukee.

Other books by Steve Grisetti

Adobe Premiere Elements 2.0 In a Snap (with Chuck Engels)
Cool Tricks & Hot Tips for Adobe Premiere Elements
The Muvipix.com Guide to DVD Architect
The Muvipix.com Guides to Vegas Movie Studio HD 10 and 11
The Muvipix.com Guide to Sony Movie Studio 12 and 13
The Muvipix.com Guide to Vegas Movie Studio 14 and 15
The Muvipix.com Guide to CyberLink PowerDirector 12, 13, 14, 15 and 16
The Muvipix.com Guides to Adobe Premiere Elements 7, 8, 9, 10, 11, 12, 13, 14, 15 and 2018
The Muvipix.com Guides to Photoshop Elements & Premiere Elements 7, 8 , 9 , 10, 11, 12, 13, 14 and 15
The Muvipix.com Guide to Photoshop Elements 2018

An Introduction

Adobe continues to add helpful features to its best-selling photo editing software. It has also added to its library of Guided Edits, step-by-step instructions for creating cool new photo effects.

Among the new Guided Edits is a Meme Maker, which uses templates to create graphics for sharing on social media, as well as a tool for adding a graphic and text overlays to your pictures.

You'll also find Guided Edits for making your photos look like artists' sketches as well as very cool tool for dropping photos into text shapes and titles.

Adobe has also completely redesigned the program's welcome screen. Now called the Elements Hub, this screen not only serves as a launchpad for your Elements programs and projects, but it also provides a search tool for finding help and tutorials for practically any image editing task.

Additionally, the Hub generates Auto Creations – slideshows and movies automatically created from your photo and video files by the Organizer, Photoshop Elements and, if it's installed, Premiere Elements while you're busy doing other things.

We'll show you how to use all of these new tools and we'll throw in a couple of tips to keep your work flowing smoothly along the way.

We also hope, if you've got any questions, you'll feel free to drop by our web site, Muvipix.com, and check out our library of tips and tutorials. And, if you've got any questions, please feel free to ask them on our free Community Forum. We love helping people out.

Muvipix.com was created in 2006 as a community and a learning center for videomakers at a variety of levels. Our community includes everyone from amateurs and hobbyists to semi-pros, professionals and even people with broadcast experience. You won't find more knowledgeable, helpful people anywhere else on the Web. I very much encourage you to drop by our forums and say hello. At the very least, you'll make some new friends. And it's rare that there's a question posted that isn't quickly and enthusiastically answered.

Our learning center consists of video tutorials, tips and, of course, books. But we also offer a wealth of support in the form of custom-created DVD and BluRay disc menus, motion background videos, licensed music and even stock footage. Much of it is absolutely free – and there's even more available for those who purchase one of our affordable site subscriptions.

Our goal has always been to help people get up to speed making great videos and, once they're there, to provide them with the inspiration and means to get better and better at doing so.

Why? Because we know making movies and taking great pictures is a heck of a lot of fun – and we want to share that fun with everyone!

Our books, then, are a manifestation of that goal. And my hope for you is that this book helps *you* get up to speed. I think you'll find that once you learn the basics, making movies on your home computer is a lot more fun than you ever imagined! And you may even amaze yourself with the results in the process.

Thanks for supporting Muvipix.com, and happy moviemaking!

Steve
http://Muvipix.com

The Muvipix.com Guide to Adobe Photoshop Elements 2019

Part I: Photoshop Elements Basics

Chapter 1

Things You Need to Know 3
Principles of photo and graphics editing

Pixels	4
Resolution	5
Raster vs. vector graphics	7
Image Size vs. Canvas Size	8
Selections	9
Layers	9
Alpha	10
RGB Color	10
The Tool Options Bin	11
What is a native PSD file?	12

Chapter 2

Get to Know Photoshop Elements 2019 13
What's what and what it does

The Elements Hub	14
Auto Creations	14
The Editor workspace	15
The Expert Edit Workspace	16
Guides and Rulers	18
The Toolbox	18
The Panel Bin	18
The Photo Bin	20
What's new in Photoshop Elements 2019?	21
Need some Basic Training?	23

Table of Contents

Part II: Quick and Guided Photo Editing

Chapter 3

Quick Fixes 27

Easy ways to touch up photos

The Quick Fix Toolbox	29
Adjustments, Effects, Textures and Frames	30
Make Quick Adjustments	30
Add Quick Effects	31
Organizer Instant Fixes	31
Apply Quick Textures	32
Add Quick Frames	32
Finalize your Quick Fix	32

Chapter 4

Guided Edits... 33

Photo adjustments and cool tricks, one step at a time

Basics	35
Color Guided Edits	36
Black & White Edits	36
Fun Edits	36
The Meme Maker Guided Edit	38
The Multi-Photo Text Guided Edit	39
The Double Exposure Guided Edit	40
The Painterly Guided Edit effect	42
The "Out of Bounds" Guided Edit effect	43
Create a Picture Stack	46
Create a Puzzle Effect	46
Special Edits	48
The Depth of Field Guided Edit	49
The Text and Border Overlay Guided Edit	50
Photomerge Guided Edits	52
Paste between photos with Photomerge Compose	52
Combine the best-lit elements from two photos with Photomerge Exposure	54
Manually align your photos for Photomerging	56
Combine photos with Photomerge Panorama	57
The Actions panel	59

Part III: The Expert Photo Editing Workspace

Chapter 5
Get to Know the Photoshop
Elements Toolbox 63
Your main photo editing toolkit

The Tool Options	64
The Color Picker	65
The Eyedropper/Sampler Tool	66
The Color Swatch panel	66
Additional Foreground/Background Color options	67
The Zoom Tool	67
The Hand Tool	67
The Move Tool	67
Making Selections	68
The Marquee Selection Tools	69
Feathering	69
Lasso Selection Tools	70
Quick Selection Tools	71
The Refine Selection Brush and Push tool	72
The Refine Selection Brush Edge Selector	73
Eye Tools	
The Red Eye Removal Tool	74
Open Closed Eyes	74
The Spot Healing Brush Tool	75
What is Anti-Aliasing?	75
Content Aware Fill	76
The Healing Brush Tools	76
The Smart Brush Tools	77
The Clone Stamp Tool	78
The Pattern Stamp Tool	78
Blur, Smudge and Sharpen	79
The Sponge, Dodge and Burn Tools	80
The Brush Tools	81
The Impressionist Brush	81
The Color Replacement Brush	81
Brush settings and options	82
Eraser Tools	83
The Eraser	83
The Background Eraser Tool	83
The Magic Eraser Tool	84
Advanced brush tool settings	84

Table of Contents

The Paint Bucket (Fill) Tool 85
The Gradient Tool 85
The Shape Tools 86
Typing Tools 88
The Pencil Tool 88
Cropping Tools 88
  The Crop Tool 89
  The Cookie Cutter Tool 90
  The Perspective Crop Tool 91
The Recompose Tool 92
The Content Aware Move Tool 94
The Straighten Tool 95

Chapter 6

Select and Isolate Areas in Your Photos 97
Working with selections

Why select and isolate? 98
Feathering 99
The Select menu 100
Refine the edge of your selection 101
  Edge Detection 101
  Refine Edge Adjustments 102
Use a selection to protect an area 104
Cut and paste a selection into another photo 104
Fill or stroke a selection 107

Chapter 7

Resize Your Images 109
Image and canvas sizes

Image Size vs. Canvas Size 110
Image Resizing 112
Canvas Resizing 114

Chapter 8

Correct Color and Lighting 117
Adjust and clean up your images

Auto Fixes 118
Control what gets changed 119
Auto Smart Tone 120
Adjust Color 121
  Remove Color Cast 121
  Adjust Hue/Saturation 122

Remove Color   122
Replace Color   122
Adjust Color Curves   123
Adjust Color for Skin Tone   123
Defringe Layer   123
Adjust Lighting   124
Brightness/Contrast   124
Shadows/Highlights   124
Levels   125
Convert to Black and White   126
Haze Removal   126
Adjust Sharpness   127
Unsharp Mask   127
Adjust Facial Features   128
Shake Reduction   129
Adjustment Layers   129
Use Levels to color correct a photo   131

Chapter 9
Work With Photoshop Elements Layers 133
Stacks of images

How layers work   134
Select a layer to edit   135
The Layers panel   136
Simplify or Flatten a Layer   138
Copy layers from one image file to another   139
Add transparency with Layer Masks   140
Create non-square graphics   141

Chapter 10
Create and Edit Text 145
Typing, sizing, coloring and shaping

The Type Tools   146
Re-edit a text layer   147
The Type Tool Options Bin   148
Shape and resize your text   150
Other transform options   151
Type on a Selection, Shape or Path   151
Type Text on a Selection   151
Type Text on a Shape   152
Type Text on a Custom Path   152

Table of Contents

Chapter 11

Add Photo Effects and Filters..........................153
Use Photoshop Elements' special effects

The Filter/Adjustments menu	154
The Filter Gallery	156
The Effects, Filters and Styles panels	157
The Effects panel	158
The Filters panel	159
Render Filters, a close-up	160
The Styles panel	162
Graphics	164

Part IV: Advanced Photo Editing

Chapter 12

Photoshop Elements Tricks..............................167
Have fun with your photos

Swap out a face	168
Swap out a background	171
Remove warts and blemishes	173
Remove big things from your photos	174
Add things to your photos	175

Chapter 13

Advanced Photo Editing Tools.......................177
Photoshop Elements extras

Scan your photos	178
Screen captures	180
Divide Scanned Photos	181
Why you should clear your camera's memory regularly	182
Download photos from your digital camera	182
Edit in Camera RAW	184
Process Multiple Files	186
Create Premiere Elements Movie Menu templates in Photoshop Elements	187
Photoshop Elements Preferences and Presets	199
New File presets	200

Chapter 14
Learn About Your Photoshop Elements File..201
Important information on your Photoshop Elements file window

The Info Bar	202
Why does a "100% zoom" video fill only part of my computer screen?	203
The Status Bar	205
The Info panel	206
File Info	207

Part V: The Elements Organizer

Chapter 15
Manage Your Files with the Organizer.......211
Getting to Know the Media Browser

Adaptive Grid vs. Details View	213
Auto Curate	214
The Media Browser area	214
The Organizer Catalog	215
The Back or All Media buttons	215
Manually add to and update your Organizer Catalog	216
Import media files into your Catalog	216
Resync media in or remove media from your Catalog	216
Switch between Album and Folder Views	217
Managed, Unmanaged and Watched Folders	218
What is metadata?	218
Add your own Metadata	220
Auto Analyze your media	220
Search your catalog using Filters	222
Assign your media files to Albums	223
Manage your files with Keyword Tags	224
Find People in your files	225
Add People to Groups	227
Manage your photos by Place	227
Manage your media files by Date or Event	229
Instant Fix a photo	230

Table of Contents

Chapter 16

Create Fun Pieces 233

The Organizer's project templates

Create an Organizer Slideshow	234
Create Photo Prints	237
Print Individual Prints on your local printer	237
Print a Picture Package or Contact Sheet on your local printer	238
Create a Photo Book	238
Create a Greeting Card	241
Create a Photo Calendar	242
Create a Photo Collage	243
Create an InstantMovie	244
Create a Video Story	244
Create a Video Collage	244
Create a DVD with Menu	244
Create a CD Jacket	244
Create a DVD Jacket	244
Print a CD/DVD Label	245

Chapter 17

Share Your Photos and Videos 247

The Organizer's output tools

Share your photos via e-mail	248
Share your photos on Flickr	249
Set up e-mail sharing for the Elements Organizer	250
Share your photos on Twitter	250
Share your video on Vimeo	250
Share your video on YouTube	250
Create an Elements Organizer Contact Book	251
Burn a Video DVD	251
Share as a PDF Slide Show	251

Part I

Photoshop Elements Basics

Pixels & Resolution

Raster vs. Vector Graphics

Image Size vs. Canvas Size

Selection

Layers & Alpha

RGB Colors

The Option Bar

Native PSD files

Chapter 1

Things You Need to Know
Principles of photo and graphics editing

Photoshop Elements is a surprisingly powerful photo and graphics editor that borrows a large number of tools from its big brother, Photoshop, the industry standard for photo and graphics work. In fact, both programs can even open and edit the same types of files.

The few limitations Elements does have, in fact, might well be things you'll never even miss (unless you're preparing files that will ultimately go onto a printing press).

But before we go too deeply into the tools in this fine program, there are a couple of basic principles you'll need to understand.

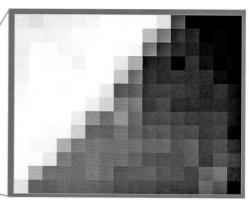

The building blocks of all digital photos are rectangular (usually square) blocks of color known as pixels.

Pixels

Pixels are the building blocks of all digital graphics and photos. Whether you can see them or not, all digital photos as well as photos and graphics created in Photoshop Elements are made up of these little squares of color. Even a tremendously rich, detailed digital photograph, if you blew it up large enough, would reveal itself to be little more than thousands (or millions) of little squares of solid color, each one some mixture of red, green and blue.

This is easier to see on a low-resolution image, such as a graphic created for a web site. Zoom in as far as Photoshop Elements will let you go and you'll soon see that even the apparently smoothest gradation of color is actually made up of little blocks of solid color.

An understanding of pixels is vital to developing a deeper understanding of how Photoshop Elements works. In order to fully comprehend how virtually any tool does what it does or how any setting affects your image – or how to measure the relative size of your images – you must learn to see your images not merely as pictures of people, animals and places but as compositions of thousands and thousands of little blocks of color.

Non-square pixels – and more than you probably want to know

Like all digital photo devices, video camcorders paint their on-screen images with pixels. But, unlike in a digital photograph, video pixels in some video formats often aren't square blocks of color – they're rectangular.

Even more confusing, the shapes of these rectangular pixels vary depending on the nature of the medium.

Standard definition NTSC, the television and video format used in North America and Japan until fairly recently, used pixels that are only 90% as wide as they are tall.

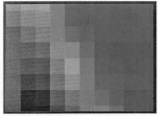
Square (photograph) pixels

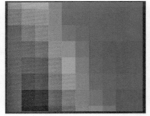
Narrower NTSC non-square 4:3 pixels

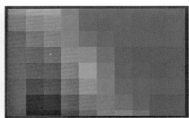
Wider NTSC non-square 16:9 pixels

Standard definition PAL, the TV format that was used in most of Europe, used pixels that were 107% as wide as they are tall. Because of this, a 720x480 pixel NTSC image and a 720x576 pixel PAL image both produced a video frame that was in the same proportion – a 4:3 ratio!

Widescreen standard definition TV used the same number of pixels to create a video frame as standard TV. The pixels were just proportioned differently. (The pixels were 120% as wide as they are tall in NTSC and 142% as wide as they are tall in PAL.) In other words, there are exactly the same number of pixels in a 4:3 video frame as there are in a 16:9 video image, as illustrated above.

Even some high-definition video camcorders use non-square pixels. In 1440x1080 hi-def TV, the pixels are 133% as wide as they are tall, so 1440x1080 pixel image produces a 16:9 image. (Though more and more hi-def camcorders are also shooting in 1920x1080, a square pixel format.)

All of this is related to technology dating back to the origins of television. And, unless you're creating graphics for video, it pretty much falls into the "nice to know" rather than "need to know" category. But it *is* nice to know – in case anyone ever asks you why a 720x480 video file becomes a 640x480 web video.

In most cases, as you're designing artwork for your videos, you won't need to concern yourself with whether your pixels are square non-square. This is because Premiere Elements will automatically adapt your square pixel images to the non-square pixel video environment. Just use these **square pixel** equivalents for creating full-screen graphics and photos:

Standard Definition 4:3 NTSC video	640x480 pixels
Widescreen Standard Def NTSC video	855x480 pixels
Standard Definition 4:3 PAL video	768x576 pixels
Widescreen Standard Def PAL video	1024x576 pixels
High Definition 16:9 video	1920x1080 pixels
UHD 4K video	3480x2160 pixels

Resolution

Resolution means, basically, how many of these pixels are crammed into how much space. Standard definition video, like images created for the Internet, doesn't require a particularly high resolution image. Print, on the other hand, can require a pixel density of two to four times that of an on-screen image.

High resolution photo

Same size photo, at much lower resolution (fewer pixels per inch)

Just as digital photos are made up of pixels, printed images are made up of little dots of color or ink. A good, press-worthy image may need 300 dots of color per inch (or more) in order to appear to the eye as a smooth color image. Home printed pieces, like the kind you'd print off your desktop printer, can have as few as 150 dots or pixels per inch. Graphics that will be used on-screen (for the Web or in a video) are about 72 pixels per inch. This is why, if you download a graphic from a web site and print it out, you'll often find that the picture prints fuzzy, jagged or "pixelated."

In order to get a good, high-resolution print-out of a 4"x3" photo, you'd need a photo that measures as much as 1200 pixels wide and 900 pixels tall. That's a lot of pixels when you consider that a standard definition TV frame measures only 640 x 480 square pixels. In other words, that 1200 x 900 photo you used for your print-out has four times as many pixels as an equivalent full-screen image on a standard definition TV set!

And that's why we say video is a relatively low-resolution medium. High-definition video needs a bit more image data (1920 x 1080 pixels) – but still only a fraction of what print artwork requires (and less than half of the resolution produced by a 5 megapixel digital still camera).

Video images are measured in pixels. In other words, as you're working on images for your videos, their dimensions, in pixels, are the only relevant measurement.

The measurements of any graphics and photos you prepare for video are *never* expressed in inches or centimeters. Even the resolution of your images, in terms of pixels per inch, isn't really relevant.

Why doesn't linear measurement (like inches and centimeters) matter in the world of video graphics? Well, basically, it's because you never know the size of the TV your video is going to be shown on!

TVs and computer monitors come in a variety of sizes and screen settings. A graphic may appear to be 2 inches across on a 17" computer monitor, 4 inches across on a 22" TV set and 30" across on a big screen TV! But the graphic itself is always the same number of *pixels* in size. Those pixels are as large or as small as the screen you're viewing them on.

So, when you're creating your graphics for video (or for the web), always think in terms of measurements in pixels. That's the only constant measurement in on-screen graphics.

Just for the sake of convenience, most people still do use 72 ppi (pixels per inch) as their resolution setting when creating their on-screen graphics. But ultimately the resolution setting makes no difference in this case. When you create an image for video or for the Web, a 640x480 pixel image is still the same size whether it's 72 ppi or 600 ppi.

Raster vs. vector graphics

All computer-created graphics fit into one of two categories – raster graphics or vector graphics – each behaving in its own unique way.

Raster graphics are graphics or photos that are composed of pixels. Digital photos and videos are both composed of pixels. The graphics files you'll be working with and importing into Premiere Elements will be composed of pixels. And, as we've discussed, all raster art requires a certain density of pixels – or resolution – in order for those pixels to be perceived as a smooth blend of colors. If you stretch or enlarge a photograph so much that its pixels show, it will appear jagged and blurry.

Vector graphics, on the other hand, are defined not by pixels but by shape, outlines and fill colors. Programs like Adobe Illustrator, for instance, create graphics in vector. Vector graphics can be as simple as a square or a circle or nearly as complicated as a photograph.

But vector graphics, because they are defined by *outlines and fill colors rather than pixels*, don't have any resolution. They can be resized indefinitely – even scaled to many times their original size – without breaking up into pixels. They remain simply outlines and fills. If you've used a simple drawing tool, such as the one in Microsoft Word, to draw a circle or square, you've worked with vector art.

Photoshop Elements is predominantly a *raster* art program. It is generally concerned with pixels of color. However, there are a few features in the program that behave as if they were vector art:

Shapes. The **Shape Tools** in Photoshop Elements can draw a variety of useful shapes – from circles and squares to lines, arrows and splashes. The shapes it creates, however, have some unique characteristics, as you'll see once you start using them.

Like vector art, these shapes can be easily resized and stretched without concern for resolution. And, if you look at a shape layer in the **Layers** panel (as illustrated to the right), you'll notice that they don't even *look* like most Photoshop art. They also won't share their layer with any other graphics. These shapes are *pseudo vector graphics*. They have all of the editing advantages of vector graphics, and they remain as such until you output your Photoshop Elements file as a graphics file or you select the option to manually render or simplify the shape layer.

Text. We usually don't think of text as vector art, but it essentially behaves the same way. You can stretch or resize text as needed in your Photoshop Elements document without concern for resolution. The text will also remain editable until you output your Photoshop Elements document as a graphics file or you select the option to manually render or simplify the text layer.

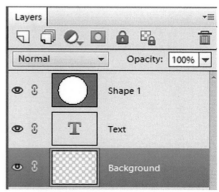

Text and shapes in Photoshop Elements, like vector art, can be resized without regard for the layer's resolution.

Once you output your Photoshop Elements file as a graphics file other than a PSD (a JPEG, TIF or GIF, for instance) or you import the file into Premiere Elements, all of the elements in your graphics file will become raster art. It all becomes pixels. And, because of that, the size (measured in pixels) of your file will determine how large the graphic or photo will be.

Image Size vs. Canvas Size

As you resize your photos or graphics files (under the **Resize** tab, as we'll discuss in **Chapter 7**), it's important to understand the difference between resizing the **Image Size** and the **Canvas Size**.

The distinction is an important one:

As illustrated below, when you resize the **Image Size**, the entire image gets bigger or smaller; when you resize the **Canvas Size**, on the other hand, the image remains the same size but you either add more space around the image or, if you size your canvas smaller, you crop the top, bottom and/or sides off the image.

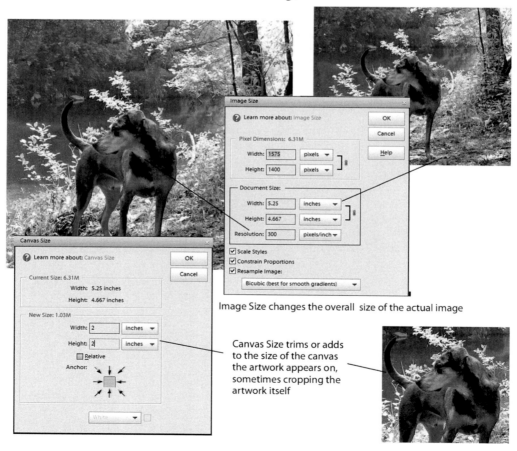

Image Size changes the overall size of the actual image

Canvas Size trims or adds to the size of the canvas the artwork appears on, sometimes cropping the artwork itself

Selections

Selection is a key concept in both Photoshop and Photoshop Elements. A number of the tools in this program are designed to enable you to select – or isolate – areas of your photo or image file and then either remove, add to or add an effect to that area only, without affecting the rest of the image.

Because your photo or graphics work will often involve precise adjustments, understanding how to select areas of your image and then add to, remove from or refine that selection is one of the keys to accessing the program's power.

We'll spend considerable time discussing how to select areas and then use those selections in **Chapter 6, Select and Isolate Areas in Your Photos.**

Many of the tools in Photoshop Elements are designed to allow you to select and isolate areas of your photos so that effects are applied only to your selection.

Layers

The biggest difference between a native Photoshop PSD file and virtually all other photo or raster graphic formats is that PSD files can include layers. These layers can include images, text, shapes or effects – some semi-transparent, some opaque – and it's important to understand how their order affects how they interact with each other.

Think of your layers as a stack of images and other elements. The topmost layers will be entirely visible, while the layers below will be visible "behind" the upper layers or quite possibly obscured completely by them.

Layers can be rearranged. They can also be hidden or made partially transparent or even made to react to certain qualities of the layers below them. And, when the background layer is removed, you can even produce graphics that are partially transparent or non-rectangular.

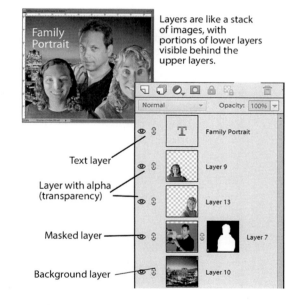

Layers are like a stack of images, with portions of lower layers visible behind the upper layers.

Text layer

Layer with alpha (transparency)

Masked layer

Background layer

Editable text is always on its own layer. Likewise, shapes, until rasterized, are always on their own layers. Layers also give you the advantage of working on your image files in portions, which you can combine, adjust and position in a variety of ways.

In addition, layers and layer groups play a vital role in creating and customizing Movie Menu templates for Premiere Elements, as we'll discuss in **Chapter 13, Advanced Photoshop Elements Tools**.

Alpha

Alpha means, essentially, transparency. However, in order for your graphics file to communicate from one program to another that an area of your image file is transparent, it needs to do so using an "alpha channel." An alpha channel is sort of like a color channel except that, in this case, the color is transparent.

Transparent GIFs and PNGs (see **Chapter 9**) use an alpha channel so that, unlike JPEGs, when used on a web site, GIF and PNG graphics can be other-than-a-square shape, allowing the background of the site to display through them.

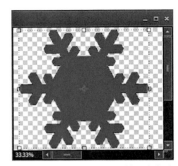

Transparency, represented by default as a checkerboard background in Photoshop Elements, can be carried with the PSD file to Premiere Elements as an "alpha" channel.

Likewise, alpha allows you to create graphics for your videos that have non-rectangular shapes or are text only, with no background.

Some graphics formats can carry alpha channels and some can not. We'll show you how to use alpha channels and which graphics file formats can carry alpha channel information in **Create non-square graphics** in **Chapter 9, Work with Photoshop Elements Layers**.

RGB Color

Virtually every graphic or photo you work with in Photoshop Elements will use either the **Grayscale** (black & white) or **RGB** color mode – meaning that every pixel in that image is a mixture of levels of red, green and blue, the three primary colors in video.

Each red, green and blue in each of those pixels is one of 256 levels of intensity, mixing together to produce a total of 16,777,216 possible color combinations. As we work with colors (**Foreground/Background Colors** in **Chapter 5, The Photoshop Elements Toolbox**), you'll see the R, the G and the B and those 256 levels of each at work.

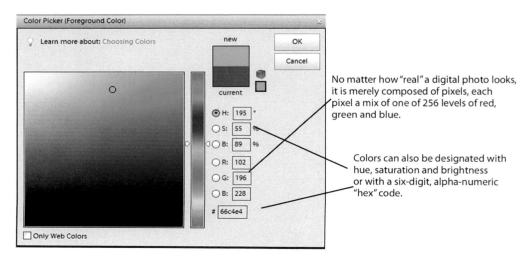

No matter how "real" a digital photo looks, it is merely composed of pixels, each pixel a mix of one of 256 levels of red, green and blue.

Colors can also be designated with hue, saturation and brightness or with a six-digit, alpha-numeric "hex" code.

The **Color Picker** (illustrated on the bottom of the facing page), which launches when you select the option to create a color, builds colors by mixing **red** (R), **green** (G) and **blue** (B) values; or by setting its **hue** (H), **saturation** (S) and **brightness** (B); or by designating the color's six-digit **Hex** value – a color format most often employed when with working with HTML and Web site design.

When the Tool Options Bin is toggled on, the space beneath the Editor will display options for whichever tool you have selected in the Toolbox.

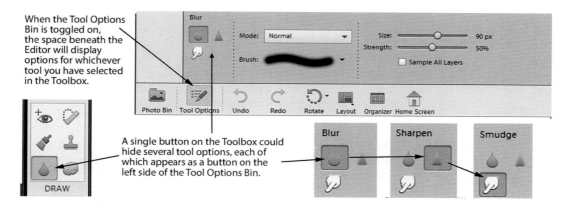

A single button on the Toolbox could hide several tool options, each of which appears as a button on the left side of the Tool Options Bin.

The Tool Options Bin

The **Tool Options Bin** shares the space below the Editor workspace with the **Photo Bin**. To view your **Tool Options** in this area, click on the button in the lower left of the interface, as illustrated above, or simply select a tool.

Virtually every tool you will use in Photoshop Elements is customizable. When you select a tool in the **Toolbox** panel, its settings and options will appear in the **Tool Options Bin**.

Even something as simple as a line drawing tool can include a myriad of options. The line drawing tool, for instance, includes settings for the width of the line and options for adding arrowheads on either or both ends.

Drop-down menus along this bar allow you to select colors and even unusual textures, like glass, plastic and chrome for your shape.

In addition to settings for each tool, the panel also includes options for switching to other tools, so that more than one tool is available under each button on the **Toolbox** panel.

In other words, as illustrated above, when the **Blur** tool is selected in the **Toolbox** panel, the left side of the **Tool Options Bin** displays not only the **Blur** tool but also the **Sharpen** and **Smudge** tools.

Most buttons on the **Toolbox** access two, three or more tools.

The **Tool Options Bin**, then, greatly extends the function and versatility of every tool. And, in **Chapter 5**, we'll discuss the many options available in this bin for each of the individual tools.

What is a native PSD file?

The basic working file for both Photoshop and Photoshop Elements is the **PSD file** (so named, of course, because that's the suffix the file is assigned on your computer).

There are unique characteristics to PSD files – namely that they can include layers, editable text and pseudo-vector shapes. (The word "native" simply means that it's in a native state, the format that all Photoshop files are saved in.)

Photoshop and Photoshop Elements can also export or save your photos and graphics files in a number of other graphics formats, from TIFs to JPEGs to GIFs to PNGs (and a dozen others). These formats, however, don't allow for re-opening layers and text for further editing, as PSDs do.

In the ancient days of technology (like, 20 years ago), Photoshop users had to export their image files to one of these graphics formats in order to import them into another program. But, as Adobe has become the leader in pretty much all facets of print and video production, it's become possible to move graphics files from program to program in their native Photoshop (PSD) state.

In other words, you can import your native PSD files directly from Photoshop Elements into your Premiere Elements project. All of the artwork becomes flattened and the shapes and text become rasterized once the file is added to your video. But any transparent areas in the PSD will remain transparent in your video (which makes them the ideal format for bringing unusually-shaped graphics into Premiere Elements, as we discuss on page 141).

Just as importantly, the original, native PSD file – including the text and layers – remains editable in Photoshop Elements. And , if you are using a PSD file in your Premiere Elements project, whenever you save the file, any updates you've made to the photo or graphics file in Photoshop Elements will automatically be reflected in your graphic in Premiere Elements.

The Welcome Screen

Quick, Guided and Expert Editing

Guides and Rulers

The Photoshop Elements Toolbox

The Panel Bin

The Photo Bin

What's New in Version 2019?

Chapter 2
Get to Know Photoshop Elements 2019
What's what and what it does

Welcome to Photoshop Elements – a terrific, affordable photo retouching application and graphics editor that just seems to get better and more feature-packed with every generation!

This is a program that seems to offer more wonderful surprises the deeper you dig into it. It provides not only the obvious tools for cleaning, stylizing and creating images, but also lots of not-so-obvious tools for managing your image files, outputting a variety of print projects and even sharing your work online.

In this chapter, we'll look at the various workspaces in Photoshop Elements – and then we'll dig deeper, looking at the tools Adobe has added in its 2019 version to make the program even more fun to use.

The Elements Hub

Whenever you launch Photoshop Elements, you'll be greeted by the **Elements Hub**, a screen offering tips, tutorials and links to your Elements programs and projects.

A key feature of the **Hub** is very intuitive help search tool. Type a brief description of what you'd like to do into the search box along the top of the screen and the **Hub** will suggest a list of related tutorials and helps (including some by yours truly!).

Another key feature of the **Elements Hub** is something Adobe calls **Auto Creations**. Whenever your computer is up and running, the Organizer's **Auto Analyzer** will be working in the background, looking for opportunities for Photoshop Elements and, if it's installed, Premiere Elements to assemble your recently saved video files and still photos into slideshows, movies and photo projects. (For more information on how the **Auto Analyzer** works, see page 220.)

Your latest **Auto Creation** will appear in the lower left of the **Elements Hub**. To see the complete set, click the **View All** button. On the screen that opens, you'll have the option of opening an **Auto Creation** in one of the Elements programs or throwing it in the trash.

To return to the **Hub** click the **Back** button at the top of the **Auto Creations** panel.

Auto Creations

Note that the **Auto Analyzer** only works when your computer is up and running. It is not able to analyze your media and Premiere Elements is not able to generate **Auto Creations** when your computer is asleep or hibernating. Also, if you have a large number of photos and/or videos on your hard drive, it may take several days for your initial set of **Auto Creations** to generate.

Menu bar   Edit Modes   Panel Bin   Create & Share Options

Toolbox

Tool Options Bin

Photo Bin

Layout

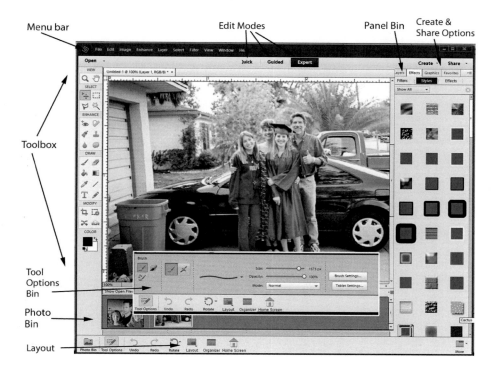

The Editor workspace

The Editor workspace in Photoshop Elements 2019 is actually *several* photo editing workspaces, each with its own set of tools and features. Its three main workspaces can be accessed by clicking on the tabs at the top center of the interface.

- In the **Quick Edit** workspace, you'll find a simplified set of tools for cleaning up or enhancing your photos. We'll show you how to use the tools in this workspace in **Chapter 3**.

- In the **Guided Edit** workspace, the program walks you, step by step, through the editing process. The **Guided Edit** tools can do some pretty advanced things too! Not only can **Guided Edits** walk you through simple clean-up of your photo, but they can also take you through some pretty high-level photo tricks, like creating a photo that seems to be standing on a reflective surface, an image with a **Tilt-Shift** effect applied and a photo in which someone seems to be popping right out of the frame! We'll show you how these cool edits work in **Chapter 4**.

- The **Expert Edit** workspace (illustrated above) includes a comprehensive photo editing and graphics creation **Toolbox**. This is likely where you'll do most of your "serious" editing. It most closely resembles the workspace in the professional version of Photoshop. Needless to say, it's the workspace most of this book is about.

Additionally, the Editor workspace shares a number of tools for creating fun photo pieces with the Elements Organizer under the **Create** and **Share** tabs in the upper right of the interface. We discuss these tools and how to use them in **Chapter 16, Create Fun Pieces** and **Chapter 17, Share Your Photos and Videos**.

By default, all open files are "docked" and appear as tabs along the top of the interface.

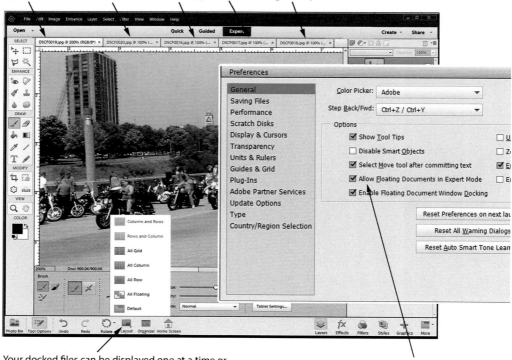

Your docked files can be displayed one at a time or in a variety of arrangements by selecting an option from the Layout menu.

The option to have Floating Windows in your Editor workspace is set in the program's Edit/Preferences.

The Expert Edit Workspace

The **Expert Edit** workspace is modeled after the interface in the professional version of Photoshop.

As illustrated at the top of the facing page, in Photoshop Elements, you have the option of displaying your open photo and image files as a single tabbed set, each photo filling the Editor workspace panel and each open file represented by a tab at the top of the workspace – or displaying your open photos as floating windows, a stack of open files that you can drag into any position around your computer desktop as you edit them.

To float your windows, you must have **Enable Floating Documents** checked on the **General** screen under **Edit/Preferences**, as in the illustration above.

The option to display your files in either mode – as well as a number of optional tabbed arrangements – is found under the **Layout** menu button.

The **Layout** menu button appears along the bottom of the interface, as seen in the illustration.

As many veteran Photoshop users know, there are advantages to displaying your photos as floating windows rather than a tabbed set.

By default, all open photos display maximized in the work panel. You can switch between your photos by clicking on the tabs along the top of the panel.

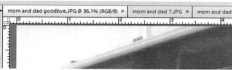

By dragging on its tab, you can undock a photo from the tabbed set and make it a floating window.

To dock or re-dock a floating window back into a tabbed set, drag it to the top of the tabbed set by its docking header (the top of the frame) until it becomes semi-transparent and a bright blue line displays around the photo. When you release your mouse button, the photo will dock with the rest of the tabbed set.

For instance, when your files are displayed as floating windows, you can copy images, portions of images and even entire layers from one image file to another simply by dragging these elements from one open file to another.

As in the illustration above, there are two ways to switch between displaying your photos as a docked, tabbed set and displaying them as floating windows:

- **Set the Layout menu to All Floating.** When you click on the **Layout** button and select **All Floating**, all of your photo files will display as floating windows.

- **Undock a photo from the tabbed set by dragging on its tab**. When you pull the photo file by its tab from the others in a tabbed set, it becomes a floating window.

Floating windows, by the way, *always float over tabbed photo files*. This means that, in order to get to the photos in your tabbed, docked set, you may have to either minimize any floating windows or drag them out of the way.

To dock or re-dock a photo into a tabbed set, simply drag the floating window by its docking header (the top of the window) to the top of the Editor workspace. When the photo file becomes semi-transparent (as illustrated above) release your mouse button and the photo will dock to the tabbed set.

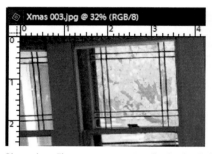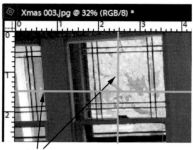

Photoshop Elements can optionally display Rulers and Guides over your image files to help you with placement and measurement of your imagery. To create a guide line, drag onto your photo from one of the rulers.

Guides and Rulers

Optionally, Photoshop Elements will display **Guides** over your image files. These horizontal and vertical lines don't show up on your final piece, of course. But they can be a great help for placing elements and text and ensuring that they are properly lined up.

The program can also display **Rulers** which, like **Guides**, can be very helpful in measuring and placing your imagery.

To display **Rulers**, select the option from the Photoshop Elements **View** menu.

To create a new **Guide**, click and drag onto your photo from one of the **Rulers** running along the tops and sides of your image files. (Drag from the **Ruler** along the top of your photo to create a horizontal guide or from the **Ruler** along the left of your photo to create a vertical guide.)

To toggle between displaying and hiding the guides on your image files, press **Ctrl+;** on a PC or ⌘**+;** on a Mac or select the option from the **View** menu.

The Toolbox

Along the left side of this workspace is the program's **Toolbox** (as illustrated on the left). The tools in this panel serve a number of functions, from selecting areas in your image file to creating graphics and text to patching and cloning areas of your images. As each tool is selected, that tool's individual settings are displayed in the **Tool Options Bin** that runs along the bottom of the editing workspace.

We'll spend considerable time getting to know the tools in the **Toolbox** and how to use their settings and options in **Chapter 5, Get to Know the Photoshop Elements Toolbox**.

The Panel Bin

To the right of the editing workspace is a column known as the **Panel Bin**, which includes a number of tools and panels that vary, depending on whether you're in **Quick Edit, Guided Edit** or **Expert** mode.

When you first open the program's Expert edit workspace, this **Panel Bin** will be in **Basic Workspace** mode. In **Basic Workspace** mode, you can view the **Layers, Effects, Filters, Styles** or **Graphics** panels in this bin by clicking on the buttons in the lower right of the program's interface.

In default Basic Workspace mode, buttons along the Action Bar access individual panels. Clicking the arrow to the right of the More button allows you to switch to Custom Workspace mode, in which more panels are available in a tabbed set.

Actions
Adjustments
Color Swatches
Favorites
Histogram
History
Info
Navigator
Custom Workspace

Layers   Effects   Filters   Styles   Graphics   More

If you click on the arrow to the right of the **More** button, you will find the option to set the **Panel Bin** to **Custom Workspace**, which opens the **Layers, Effects** and **Graphics** panels (and their respective sub-panels) in the **Panel Bin** in a tabbed set, as illustrated below

You can click and drag on any tab in the **Panel Bin** to make its panel a separate, floating panel. (It's common for experienced Photoshop Elements users to make the **Layers** panel a floating panel so that it is always available.)

Clicking directly on the **More** button will open an additional bundle of tabbed panels, including **Info, Navigation, History,** etc. These panels can likewise be accessed by clicking on the appropriate tab or, by dragging on the tab, can be made a separate, floating panel.

We take a close up look at the **Effects, Filters** and **Styles** panels in **Chapter 11,** starting on page 157.

The panels of the tabbed Panel Bin in Custom Workspace mode.

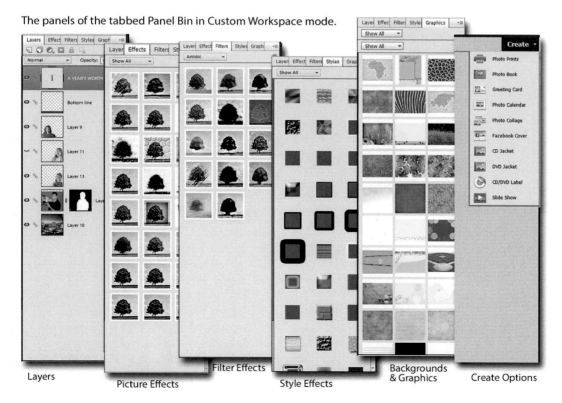

Layers   Picture Effects   Filter Effects   Style Effects   Backgrounds & Graphics   Create Options

When the Photo Bin option is selected, the area below the Editor worskpace wil display all of the photos you have open in your Photoshop Elements editor, all of the photos you have selected in the Elements Organizer's Media Browser or any photos you've saved to individual Organizer Albums.

The Photo Bin

Running along the bottom of the Editor workspace and sharing space with the **Tool Options Bin** is a small but powerful panel known as the **Photo Bin**.

When the **Photo Bin** button is selected in the lower left of the program's interface, all photos and image files you have open in your Editor workspace will appear as thumbnails in this bin.

To open a file in your **Photo Bin** in the Editor workspace, **double-click** on its thumbnail in the **Photo Bin**.

Although this is the default and most common way to use the **Photo Bin**, it is certainly not its only function. The **Photo Bin** also interfaces with a number of other workspaces.

To access and change the **Photo Bin's** display options, click on the bin's drop-down menu, which reads **Show Open Files** by default, as in the illustration above.

> **Show Open Files**. Displays, as thumbnails, all of the image files you currently have open in your **Editor** workspace.
>
> **Show Files Selected in the Organizer.** If you have both Photoshop Elements and the Elements Organizer open, and you have files selected in the Organizer's **Media Browser**, selecting this option displays those files in the **Photo Bin**. These photos or image files can then be launched in the Editor workspace by **double-clicking** on them.
>
> **Organizer Albums.** If you've created **Albums** in the Organizer (see **Chapter 15, Manage Your Files with The Organizer**), you can select the option to display the photos in a particular **Album.**

What's new in Photoshop Elements 2019?

Adobe continues to build out the world's most popular consumer photo editor with a couple of performance enhancements and several new Guided Edits.

The Elements Hub

When you first launch Photoshop Elements (or Premiere Elements), you'll be greeted by the all-new **Elements Hub**.

The **Hub** is not only a launching pad for opening your photo and video projects, but it offers you access to Adobe's latest tips and tutorials. A search box at the top of the panel can help you quickly locate tutorials for a specific task (including many by the author of this very book).

Additionally, a link on this panel opens a library of **Auto Creations**, slideshows and video projects created automatically by the Elements programs based on media identified by the **Auto Analyzer**.

We discuss the **Elements Hub** in more detail on page 14.

New Guided Edits

In Photoshop Elements 2019, Adobe continues to expand its library of **Guided Edits** – with step-by-step instructions for creating cool photo effects.

The new **Meme Creator** walks you through the process of creating photo and text graphics, perfect for posting to social media. The **Partial Sketch** shows you how to make an area of your photo look like an artist's sketch.

The **Text and Border Overlay Guided Edit** walks you through the process of creating a custom graphic overlay for your photo. **Multi-Photo Text** drops your photos into your custom text for a unique graphic composition.

We browse the entire **Guided Edits** library and focus on a couple of its coolest edits in **Chapter 4**.

New Photo Collage

The old semi-automatic **Photo Collage** tool has been completely re-designed into a workspace in which you can drop your photos into a number collage templates, giving you much more control over the look and design of your collage.

We look deeper at this cool new tool on page 243 of **Chapter 16, Create Fun Pieces.**

HEIF support

The Mac version of Photoshop Elements 2019 also includes the ability to edit the new iPhone High Efficiency Image Format (aka **.heic** files), a format using a compression system that promises smaller photo files without compromising image quality.

Need some Basic Training?

Need more help learning the basics of Photoshop Elements?

Check out my free tutorial series **Basic Training for Photoshop Elements** at Muvipix.com.

This simple, eight-part series will teach you the basics of photo resolution and show you how to adjust lighting and correct color in your photos, work with layers, add effects, scan your pictures and even share your photos and videos online. And, yes, it's absolutely free!

To see the series, just go to http://Muvipix.com and type "Basic Training for Photoshop Elements" in the product search box and then click the magnifying glass button. (We also offer Basic Training tutorials for other products, including Premiere Elements.)

And while you're there, why not drop by the Community Forum and say hi! We'd love to have you become a part of our growing city. Hope to see you there!

If you'd like to see tutorials of some of the program's latest features, check out our book page at Muvipix.com/pe2019.php.

Part II
Quick and Guided Photo Editing

Simple, Quick Fixes

The Quick Fix Toolbox

Quick Effects, Textures and Frames

Chapter 3

Quick Fixes

Easy ways to touch up photos

In addition to its more professional photo touch-up and graphic design tools, Photoshop Elements includes a number of simplified and semi-automatic tools for fixing, enhancing and adjusting your image files.

Many of these are Quick Fixes, with simplified controls and automatic functions.

The Quick Fix Work Area

View   Hand Tool   Touch-Up Tools   Set Before & After View   Quick Fix Panel Bin

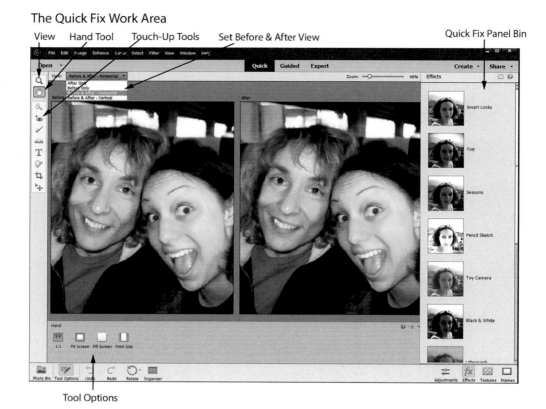

Tool Options

The Expert Editor workspace is a full-featured toolkit for fixing your photos, correcting color and creating graphic and photographic effects.

However, if you just need a simple fix – or if you're intimidated by the multitude of tools and options in the Photoshop Elements Expert workspace – the program also offers simplified **Quick Fix** tools for editing your photos and graphic files.

The **Quick Fix** workspace is launched by clicking the **Quick** tab at the top center of the Photoshop Elements interface.

To the left of the workspace is the **Quick Fix Toolbox**, described on the facing page, a simplified version of the **Expert** workspace **Toolbox**.

To the right of the workspace are simplified adjustment controls for changing the color, lighting, color temperature and sharpness of your photos. These adjustments can be made using sliders or by using the very intuitive **Quick Fix Preview** tool, as described on page 31.

A drop-down menu in the upper left of the workspace allows you to set your view as **Before Only, After Only** or **Before and After**.

To leave the **Quick Fix** workspace once you have finished applying any fixes to your image file, click the **Expert** button at the top center of the interface.

You may then choose to save the changes you've made to the image file or discard them.

The Quick Fix Toolbox

The **Quick Fix** work area includes a number of tools for viewing and manipulating your image file. The tools on the **Toolbox** to the left of the interface work similarly to their counterparts in the **Expert Editor Toolbox**. (For more information on any of these tools, see **Chapter 5, Get to Know the Photoshop Elements Toolbox**.)

The Zoom Tool (magnifying glass) controls your view.

The Hand Tool allows you to drag your image around in your viewing area.

The Quick Selection Tool selects areas on your image file for manipulation by "painting" to define the selected area. When an area is selected, any lighting or color adjustments will apply only to that selected area.

Eye Tools include a red-eye remover that fixes that annoying red reflection eyes sometimes display when you shoot with a flash in a dimly-lit room, as well as a tool for "opening" closed eyes in a photo. For more information on these features, see page 70.

The Teeth Whitener is a **Smart Brush Tool** (as discussed on page 77 of **Chapter 5, Get to Know the Photoshop Elements Toolbox**). Drag your mouse to **Quick Select** the teeth in your photo and the program will automatically bleach and brighten them for you, as illustrated below.

The Straighten Tool can be used to level out your picture (as discussed on page 95 of **Chapter 5**).

The Text Tool will add text to your photo. We discuss adding and working with text on your image files in **Chapter 10**.

The Spot Healing Brush automatically removes blemishes and other flaws using a very effective **Content Aware Fill** system. Removing a blemish is as simple as selecting this tool and then painting over the blemish, as we discuss in more detail on page 76.

The Crop Tool can be used to crop and reshape your image.

The Move Tool is used to move or drag the elements, selections or text in your image files to new positions.

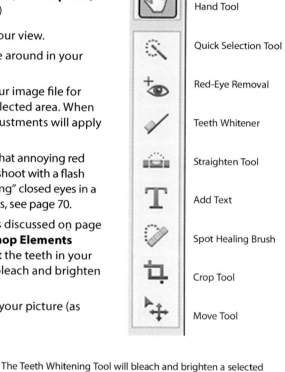

Zoom Tool

Hand Tool

Quick Selection Tool

Red-Eye Removal

Teeth Whitener

Straighten Tool

Add Text

Spot Healing Brush

Crop Tool

Move Tool

The Teeth Whitening Tool will bleach and brighten a selected area of your photo.

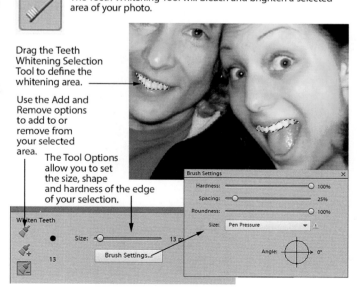

Drag the Teeth Whitening Selection Tool to define the whitening area.

Use the Add and Remove options to add to or remove from your selected area.

The Tool Options allow you to set the size, shape and hardness of the edge of your selection.

Adjustments, Effects, Textures and Frames

In addition to the cleanup and enhancement tools in the **Quick Edit** workspace, the panel bin on the right in the **Quick Fix** workspace includes libraries of **Adjustments, Effects, Textures** and **Frames.**

Switch between these option panels by clicking on the buttons in the lower right of the interface, as illustrated to the right.

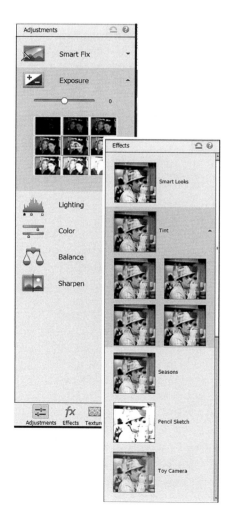

Make Quick Adjustments

The **Quick Adjustments tools** in the panel bin along the right side of the **Quick Edit** interface (activated by clicking the **Adjustments** button in the lower right of the **Quick Edit** workspace) offer easy, intuitive ways to correct and adjust the color, lighting and sharpness of your photos.

> **Smart Fix** automatically applies adjustments in brightness, contrast and sharpness.

> **Exposure** simulates the adjustments your camera makes, brightening a picture that is too dark or darkening a picture that is too light.

> **Levels** adjusts the saturation and contrast of your picture's color for either shadows, midtones or highlights.

> **Color** adjusts saturation (amount of color), hue (tint of color) and vibrance (intensity of color).

> **Balance** adjusts your photo's color temperature (more blue vs. more red) or tint.

> **Sharpness** increases the sharpness of your image.

The tools in this panel include both a slider, for increasing or decreasing intensity of the adjustment, and a **Quick Fix Preview** tool, which allows you to make an adjustment simply by clicking on one of the variations in the tic tac toe-like interface, as illustrated on the facing page. (You can even preview a change just by hovering your mouse over any of the variations.)

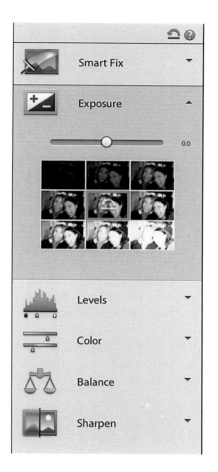

Some adjustments also include an **Auto** button for making automatic color or lighting corrections.

To undo an adjustment, click on the center square in the **Quick Fix Preview** panel or click the 🔄 **Reset** button at the top of the panel.

If you have used the **Quick Selection Tool**, as described on page 29, to select an area or areas in your photo, your adjustments will be applied only to the selected area.

Add Quick Effects

Within each of the 11 **Quick Effects** categories are looks and styles that can be applied to your photo with just a click or two.

The categories include **Smart Looks, Tints, Seasons, Pencil Sketch, Toy Camera, Black & White, Lithograph, Cross Process, Split tone, Vintage** and **Light Leak**.

When you click on any of these **Effects** categories, a sub-menu will open displaying variations of that particular look or effect.

Organizer Instant Fixes

The Elements Organizer includes its own **Instant Fix** workspace for cleaning up and adding effects to your photos. For more information on this surprisingly powerful new tool, see page 230 of **Chapter 15, Manage Your Files with the Elements Organizer.**

Apply Quick Textures

Quick Textures apply texture filters to the photo displayed in your **Quick Edit** workspace.

To apply a texture, simply **double-click** on the thumbnail displaying the effect you want to apply.

To remove a texture, apply a different **Quick Texture** or click the 🔄 **Reset** button at the top of the panel.

Add Quick Frames

Quick Frames create borders around the photo displayed in your **Quick Edit** workspace.

To add a border, simply **double-click** on the thumbnail displaying the border you want to apply.

You can create your own custom frames for this library by using the **Frame Creator Guided Edit**, as discussed on page 48.

To remove a border, apply a different **Quick Frame** or click the 🔄 **Reset** button at the top of the panel.

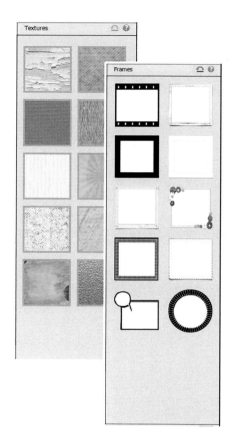

Finalize your Quick Fix

To finalize your effects, borders and/or textures and leave the **Quick Fix** workspace, click the **Expert** tab at the top center of the program's interface.

Alternatively, you can go to the **Share** menu in the upper right of the program and select an option to send your finished photo project to **Flickr** or **Twitter**.

If you open your photo project in the **Expert** workspace and look at the **Layers** panel, you will see that the program has duplicated your original photo, saved it as a new layer and applied your selected effect or border to it.

The program has done this so your **Quick Fix** is undoable. To remove a **Quick Effect, Texture** or **Frame** and revert to your original photo, simply delete this new layer.

Basic Edits

Color Edits

Black & White Edits

Fun Edits

Special Effects

Photomerge Edits

Chapter 4

Guided Edits

Photo adjustments and cool tricks, one step at a time

Guided Edits, as the name implies, are sometimes very high level photo effects made simple through wizards that walk you through each step of the process.

Guided Edits allow you to get professional-looking results with only a basic understanding of the program.

The Guided Edits library is accessed by clicking the **Guided** tab in the top center of the Photoshop Elements workspace.

Guided Edits, as the name implies, are simplified editing tools that take you step-by-step through a series of adjustments, cleaning up your image or creating special photo effects.

Photoshop Elements walks you through the entire process – explaining how each tool works, offering an automatic fix if available and then giving you the option of either keeping the changes (clicking **Done**) or rejecting the changes and returning to the main menu (**Cancel**).

If you're at all intimidated by the **Expert Edit** workspace, a **Guided Edit** may be the way to go.

The **Guided Edits** appear in six categories, each available by clicking the sub-tab at the top of the interface. Each edit's effect is illustrated with a dynamic before-and-after thumbnail.

> **Basics** clean up your photo's composition or correct its color.
>
> **Color** effects apply special effects to your photo, giving it an intriguing or surreal look.
>
> **Black & White** effects desaturate some or all of the color in your photos.
>
> **Fun Edits** create some very advanced effects, making people in your pictures, for instance, seem to pop out of the photo frame or making your photo look as though it's made from a collage of snapshots.

Special Edits create cool photo effects including vignetting, depth of field and tilt/shift.

Photomerge effects combine imagery from two or more photos to add elements to or remove elements from a scene.

Once you've finished your **Guided Edit**, your finished piece can be saved as a PSD file, edited in **Quick** or **Expert Editing** or uploaded to **Flickr** or **Twitter**.

Basics

Like the **Quick Fixes** discussed in **Chapter 3**, **Basics** are designed to offer you simple workspaces for doing color adjustments, cropping and sharpening.

Brightness and Contrast adjust the blackest and whitest levels of your photo and the contrast between them. This edit includes an **Auto Fix** adjustment button.

Correct Skin Tones is a step-by-step walkthrough of the tool described on page 123.

Crop Photo walks you through the process of trimming down or reshaping your photo.

Levels adjusts the dark, light and mid-tone levels of the red, green and blue in your photo (A similar effect to **Brightness and Contrast**). However, rather than physically changing the photo, these adjustments are made to an **Adjustment Layer** (as described on page 129).

Lighten and Darken opens tools for adjusting your photo's **Shadow**, **Highlights** and **Midtones**.

Resize Your Photos guides you through the process of optimizing the size of your photos for posting to the web or printing.

Rotate and Straighten guides you through the process of straightening a crooked photo.

Sharpen increases the contrast between pixels, sharpening the look of your photo.

The Vignette Effect makes your photo look as if it were shot with a pinhole camera, brighter in the center and darker around the sides.

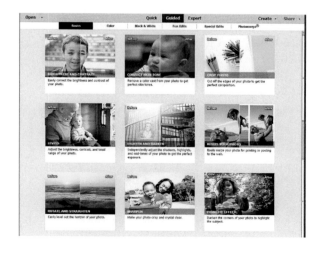

Color Guided Edits

Color edits increase or reduce the intensity or vibrance of the color in your photos.

> **Enhance Colors** offers tools for adjusting your photo's **Hue, Saturation** and **Lightness**. This edit includes an **Auto Fix** adjustment button.

> The **Lomo Camera Effect** makes your photos look as if they were shot with a LOMO, a primitive, Soviet-made camera whose weird color and exposure results have given it something of a cult following.

> **Remove Color Cast** guides you through the process of correcting the color in your photo.

> The **Saturated Film Effect** enriches the color in your photo.

Black & White Edits

Black & White edits guide you through the process of removing all or some of the color in your photos.

> **Black and White** strips the color from your photo, then enriches the black & white based on the preset you select.

> **B&W Color Pop** removes all of the color from a photo except the color you designate.

> **B&W Selection** strips the color from the areas in your photo that you designate with your **Selection Brush**.

> **High Key** washes the color out of your photo and softens its focus to give your picture an ethereal look.

> **Line Drawing** creates the effect that your photo has been hand-drawn in pencil or charcoal.

> **Low Key** increases the black levels in your photo, giving it a dark, mysterious look.

Fun Edits

The **Fun Edits** category of **Guided Edits** includes 17 fun walkthroughs for creating highly-stylized photographic effects.

> **Double-Exposure** overlays a selected area or selected person in your photo with imagery from another photo. We show you this **Guided Edit** at work on page 40.

Effects Collage breaks your photo into two, three or four panels, in one of several designs, and then applies a filter or effect to the panels.

Meme Maker creates a graphic and text composition, perfect for posting to social media. We show you this one in detail on page 38.

Multi-Photo Text is similar to the **Photo Text Guided Edit** (below) except that each letter is based on different photo. We show you how it works on page 39.

Old Fashioned Photo makes your picture look like an old black & white photo.

The **Out of Bounds Effect** lets you crop your photo, excluding certain elements, so that, say, a person's head, hand or foot extends beyond the borders of the picture. We you walk through using this cool tool beginning on page 43.

The **Painterly** guided edit walks you through the process of creating a unique texture and shape for your photo, as if the image were brushed onto a canvas. We take it for a test drive on page 42.

Partial Sketch makes an isolated area of your photo look like an artist's sketch.

Photo Text fills your text with imagery, as if the letters were cut out of your photo. **Photo Text** images can be saved as transparent PSD files and used as titles in a Premiere Elements movie!

Picture Stack breaks your photo into four, eight or twelve photos, making your picture look as if it's been pieced together from several photo segments. For more information on how to use this tool, see page 46.

Pop Art creates a colorful photo series, a la Andy Warhol's famous Marilyn Monroe portrait.

Puzzle Effect cuts your photo into a jigsaw-like pattern – which you can then move or remove, one piece at a time. We show you how it works on page 46.

Reflection creates a reflection of your picture, which you can customize so that it appears to be shining off a floor below your photo, a sheet of glass or even rippling water.

Shape Overlay Effect adds a semi-opaque shape (a heart, a starburst) over your photo.

The **Speed Effect** adds trails behind a person or object in a photo, making him or her appear to be zipping through the scene.

Speed Pan motion blurs the background of a photo to make it appear a person in the foreground is moving very quickly across the frame.

Zoom Burst Effect guides you through adding a zoom blur around the focus of your photo.

The Meme Maker Guided Edit

Memes are those little, usually funny photo and text graphics that people pass around on Facebook and other social media sites. With the templates in the **Meme Maker**, creating your own is fun and easy.

With the photo open in the **Guided Edits** workspace, select **Meme Maker** on the **Fun Edits** option panel.

1 Select a **Meme** template.

Click the **Create Meme Template** button. A generic border will appear around your photo. You can swap in a new one later in the edit.

2 Customize the text.

Click the **Type Tool** button. Select and overwrite each block of text. You can change the font, style and color of the selected text by selecting from the **Tool Options** along the bottom of the panel.

3 Position the photo.

Select the photo in your meme. Use the **Zoom** slider to enlarge or shrink the photo. Drag on the photo to tweak its position.

4 Select a new border.

If you'd like, click a **Border** button to select either a new border pattern or color for your meme.

5   Optionally add an effect.

Click the **Effects** button to add a color grade or effect to your photo. When you're satisfied with your creation, click **Next**.

6   Select how you'd like to proceed.

On the panel that opens, you'll find the options to save your photo as a PSD file, to continue editing in **Quick** or **Expert Editing** and to upload your image directly to **Flickr** or **Twitter**.

The Multi-Photo Text Guided Edit

The **Multi-Photo Text** effect places your selected photos into text shapes.

With the photo open in the **Guided Edits** workspace, select **Multi-Photo Text** on the **Fun Edits** option panel.

1   Select a **Type** template.

Click the **Type Tool** button and type text into the editor. You can change the font, style and color of the selected text by selecting from the **Tool Options** along the bottom of the panel.

2   Select **Fit** to size your text to fill the screen's width or **Fit to Fill** to stretch the text so that it fits horizontally and vertically.

3   Click the **Create Frames** button.

The tool will create a separate "drop zone" for each letter.

4   Add photos.

Browse your **Computer** or your **Photo Bin** (open photos) and select as many photos as you there are letters in your text. The program will automatically drop a photo into each letter shape. **Double-click** on each letter to resize and reposition the photo within the shape.

5   Choose a background.

Select a color for your background or make your background transparent.

6 Optionally select a **Bevel** to make your text look 3D.

Click **Next**.

7 Select how you'd like to proceed.

On panel that opens, you'll find the options to save your photo as a PSD file, to continue editing in **Quick** or **Expert Editing** and to upload your image directly to **Flickr** or **Twitter**.

The Double Exposure Guided Edit

The **Double Exposure** effect adds a mask around the outside of your selection will overlay the selected area with imagery from another photo.

1 With the photo open in the **Guided Edits** workspace, select **Double Exposure** on the **Fun Edits** option panel.

The **Panel Bin** will display the **Double Exposure Edits** options panel.

2   Crop your picture.

Click the **Crop Tool** button and crop your picture so the person or object you are selecting is centered.

3   Select your subject.

Using the **Smart** and **Quick** selection tools, draw a selection around the subject in your picture.

A new feature in Photoshop Elements 2019, the **Smart Selection** tool (see page 69) will automatically select a person or object in your photo based on a rough outline you draw around it.

Once you've made a basic selection, use the **Quick** selection tool to refine the selection, holding down the **Shift** key to add to it and the **Alt/Option** key to remove from it.

4   Add a **Background** overlay.

Select from the library of images provided by the tool (**Forest, City** or **Cloud**) or click **Import Background** and select a photo from your hard drive.

Once you've selected a **Background** image, it will be overlayed onto your selection. The area outside of your selection will be masked and will appear white.

To increase or decrease the opacity of your overlay, adjust the **Intensity** slider.

To reposition the overlay, click the **Move** tool button and drag over your image.

4   Add an effect.

Optionally, you can affect the look of your composite by clicking the **Effect** button and selecting one of the thumbnails. The Intensity of this effect can be adjusted by moving the slider.

When you're happy with the results, click **Next**.

5   Select how you'd like to proceed.

On the panel that opens, you'll find the options to save your photo as a PSD file, to continue editing in **Quick** or **Expert Editing** and to upload your image directly to **Flickr** or **Twitter**.

The Painterly Guided Edit effect

The **Painterly** effect creates an uneven edge for your photos, making your photo look almost as if it were painted onto canvas – or as if it were printed onto a background and its edges painted with a large brush.

1. With the photo open in the **Guided Edits** workspace, select **Painterly** on the **Fun Edits** option panel.

   The **Panel Bin** will display the **Painterly Guided Edits** options panel.

At the top of this panel is a photo showing an example of the finished effect. If you roll your mouse over it, you'll see the "before" picture that the **Painterly** effect sample was created from.

2. Click the **Paint Brush** button.

   Your photo will appear "onion-skinned", with a semi-opaque overlay. This overlay represents the areas of your photo that will be removed (technically, masked) by this edit.

   Select a brush from the **Preset** menu on the options panel. The options include a **Bold Strokes, Rough Bristles, Confetti** and **Round Rhythm** brush – all brushes which produce rough, scratchy patterns.

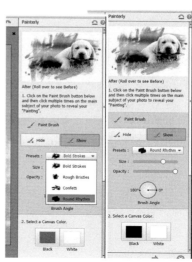

You can also set the **Size, Opacity** (transparency) and **Brush Angle** for your paint strokes.

Click and/or drag to paint from the center of your photo outward, leaving a rough, painterly-looking edge.

If you paint too much, you can set the brush from **Show** to **Hide**. The **Hide** brush can be used to "un-paint" an area you've painted.

3   When you're happy with the look of your painterly edge, select a **White** or **Black Canvas** for your picture's background.

When you select a canvas color, you'll see a preview of the finished photo. If you're not happy with the look, you can select **Paint Brush** again and repeat **Step 2**.

4   If you'd like, you can add a **Texture** for the "canvas" your photo has been painted onto.

When you're happy with the results, click **Next**.

5   Select how you'd like to proceed.

On the panel that opens, you'll find the options to save your photo as a PSD file, to continue editing in **Quick** or **Expert Editing** and to upload your image directly to **Flickr** or **Twitter**.

Your image will remain in the editing workspace as a layered file, the layers of effects and masks appearing as layers on the **Layers** panel. To revert to the original photo, delete all but the **Background** layer.

The "Out of Bounds" Guided Edit effect

Creating an **Out of Bounds Effect** involves basically two steps. The first is redefining the frame of your photo, which will be cropped down from its current size. The second is designating which elements in the photo will not be affected by this cropping.

For my example, I've chosen an action shot of a young girl doing a tae kwon do high kick. To make this shot more interesting, we'll crop the photo's frame around the girl so that her kick seems to be popping right out of the picture.

1   With the photo open in the **Guided Edits** workspace, select **Out of Bounds** on the option panel.

The **Panel Bin** will display the **Out of Bounds Effect Guided Edits** options panel.

Out Of Bounds

At the top of this panel is a photo showing an example of the finished effect. If you hover your mouse over it, you'll see the "before" picture that the **Out of Bounds** effect was created from.

2   Click the **Add a Frame** button.

A box will appear over your photo. Drag the corner handles of this box to define what will be your photo's newly cropped frame.

When this cropping box is in your desired position, lock it in place by clicking the green check mark or by pressing the **Enter** key on your keyboard.

1.   Add Frame

The photo will now appear with its new cropping displayed as a semi-opaque overlay, as illustrated at right.

3   Click the **Quick Selection Tool** button on the **Guided Edits** panel. (You may need to scroll down the panel to see this button.)

As we show you on page 71 of **Chapter 5, Get to Know the Photoshop Elements Toolbox**, the **Quick Selection Tool** works like a paintbrush, selecting areas as you "paint" over them.

2.   Selection Tool

Click and drag the tool over the elements in your photo you'd like to extend beyond the photo's newly cropped frame. In my case, this will be the girl and her foot.

As you drag the tool over your photo, your selected area will be displayed with a moving dotted line around it (commonly called "marching ants").

If it adds more than you'd like to your selection, you can always un-select these areas later.

In the **Tool Options Bin** below your photo, you'll find the settings for the **Quick Selection Tool**.

The **Brush** settings allow you to set the size of the tool's selection brush. (You can also quickly widen or narrow your brush's size by pressing the **[** and **]** keys on your keyboard.)

To add to your selection, select the **+** tool from the **Tool Options Bin** or hold down your **Shift** key as you continue to paint with the **Quick Selection Tool**.

To de-select a selected area, select the **−** tool in the **Tool Options Bin** or hold down the **Alt/Option** key on your keyboard as you paint with the **Quick Selection Tool**.

4   When you're satisfied with your selection, click the **Out of Bounds Effect** button on the **Panel Bin**.

The program will crop your photo per your settings, except for the areas you've selected.

When you're happy with the results, click **Next**.

5   Select how you'd like to proceed.

On the panel that opens, you'll find the options to save your photo as a PSD file, to continue editing in **Quick** or **Expert Editing** and to upload your image directly to **Flickr** or **Twitter**.

Click **Done** to leave this workspace.

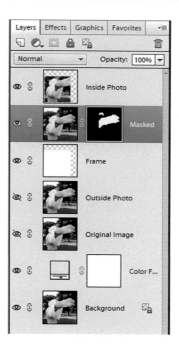

Your image will remain in the editing workspace as a layered file, the layers of effects and masks appearing as layers on the **Layers** panel. To revert to the original photo, delete all but the **Background** layer.

The Photo Stack Guided Edit turns your photo into a photo collage.

Create a Picture Stack

A fairly automatic effect, the **Picture Stack Guided Edit** breaks your photo into four, eight or twelve pieces, making it look as if it's assembled from a collage of several photos.

1 With the photo open in the **Guided Edits** workspace, select **Picture Stack** on the option panel.

   The **Panel Bin** will display the **Picture Stack Guided Edits** panel.

2 Customize your effect.

   Select the **Number of Pictures** you would like your photo broken into, the **Border Width** you'd like around each picture and the **Background Color** the photos will be stacked on.

   When you're happy with the results, click **Next**.

3 Select how you'd like to proceed.

   On the panel that opens, you'll find the options to save your photo as a PSD file, to continue editing in **Quick** or **Expert Editing** and to upload your image directly to **Flickr** or **Twitter**.

Create a Puzzle Effect

The **Puzzle Effect Guided Edit** walks you through the semi-automatic process of overlaying your photos with a jigsaw puzzle-like pattern – and then, for added effect, gives you the option of moving or removing the individual pieces!

1 With the photo open in the **Guided Edits** workspace, select **Puzzle Effect** on the option panel.

   The **Panel Bin** will display the **Puzzle Effect Guided Edits** panel.

2 Click to select your puzzle piece size.

   As illustrated on the following page, you have the option of creating a puzzle with small, medium or large pieces.

   The tool will overlay a jigsaw puzzle pattern over your photo.

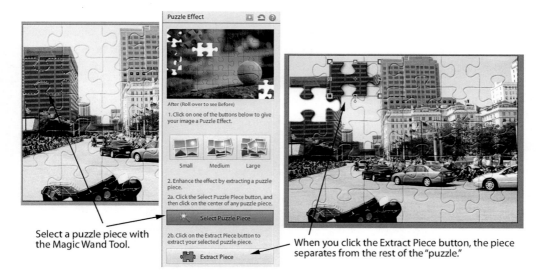

Select a puzzle piece with the Magic Wand Tool.

When you click the Extract Piece button, the piece separates from the rest of the "puzzle."

3   Select a puzzle piece.

Click on the **Select Puzzle Piece/Magic Wand** tool on the panel.

When you click on the photo with this **Magic Wand** tool, it will select a puzzle piece.

4   Extract a puzzle piece.

Click on the **Extract Puzzle Piece** button. The tool will separate the selected piece from the rest of the puzzle.

With the **Move Tool** you can then drag the piece to any location or, by dragging around its corner handles, rotate the piece.

Note that a drop shadow automatically applied to your photo gives the illusion that you're working with three-dimensional puzzle pieces. Continue to remove and reposition as many pieces as you'd like.

5   Clean up the extra lines.

If you remove two adjacent pieces from the photo, the outline between them remains in the empty space. Click to select the **Eraser Tool** and clean up any unwanted lines.

When you're happy with the results, click **Next**.

6   Select how you'd like to proceed.

On the panel that opens, you'll find the options to save your photo as a PSD file, to continue editing in **Quick** or **Expert Editing** and to upload your image directly to **Flickr** or **Twitter**.

Special Edits

Special Edits change the look of your photo in intriguing or surreal ways. As with all **Guided Edits**, the program walks you through the process of creating them, step-by-step. In addition, this workspace includes walk-throughs of some advanced photo correction and re-compositing tools, including the **Recompose** tool (discussed in detail on page 92).

Depth of Field sharpens the subject in your photo and blurs the background, giving your photo the illusion of being shot with a very short depth of field. We demonstrate this edit on page 49.

Frame Creator walks you through the process of turning any photo or image into a custom picture frame. This frame can then be permanently added to the Photoshop Elements **Frames** library (see page 32)!

The Orton Effect softens your photo to give it a gently blurred, dreamy look. You can increase or decrease the effect by custom-adjusting the blur, noise and brightness levels.

Perfect Portrait is a simple, all-purpose guided cleanup with step-by-step instructions for softening or sharpening your photo, adjusting contrast, healing blemishes, removing red-eyes and enhancing eyes and eyebrows.

Recompose is used to move people or elements in a photo closer together without changing their shapes. This tool is discussed in detail on page 92.

Replace Background, as you might expect, replaces the background behind a selected person or object with a pattern or background from another photo.

Restore Old Photo guides you through the process of repairing a worn photo.

The Tilt-Shift effect gives your scenic photos the exaggerated depth of field of photos of miniatures.

Scratches and Blemishes includes tools for softening flaws and erasing blemishes.

Text and Border Overlay adds stylish text and borders to your photo. We show you how it works on page 50.

Tilt-Shift, illustrated to the right, adds a blur to the top and bottom of a photo shot from an oblique angle, creating the illusion of exaggerated depth of field and making your photo look as if it were composed of miniatures.

Watercolor Effect walks you through the process of making your photo look like a watercolor painting.

The Depth of Field Guided Edit

The **Depth of Field Guided Edit** uses a blur and layer mask to create a focused center and blurred background for your photo.

To use the **Depth of Field Guided Edit**:

1   With the photo open in the **Guided Edits** workspace, select **Depth of Field** on the option panel.

2   On the **Depth of Field** panel, select either the **Simple** or **Custom** workspace.

A **Simple Depth of Field** effect will add a blur around the outside of your photo, leaving it unaffected in the center, as in the illustration to the right.

If you select the Simple option.

3   Click the **Add Blur** button, as illustrated below.

Your entire photo will blur.

4   Click the **Add Focus Area** button.

Click on the focal object in your photo, then drag.

The program will mask the effect on your focal object, removing the blur from it – creating a graduated blur around the rest of your photo, based on the area defined with your mouse drag.

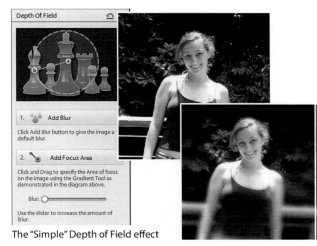

The "Simple" Depth of Field effect

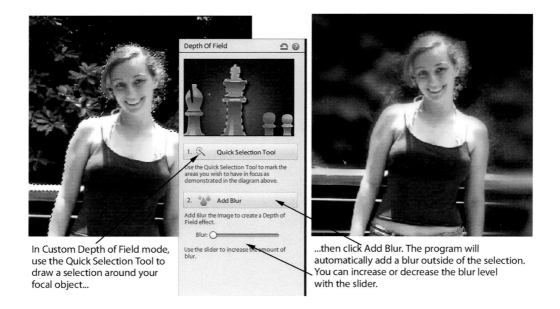

In Custom Depth of Field mode, use the Quick Selection Tool to draw a selection around your focal object...

...then click Add Blur. The program will automatically add a blur outside of the selection. You can increase or decrease the blur level with the slider.

In a **Custom Depth of Field** effect, you designate the area of your photo that the blur will not apply.

If you select the Custom option:

3   Click the **Quick Selection Tool** button.

Drag the tool over the subject of your photo, "painting" to select the area you want to keep in focus.

4   Click the **Add Blur** button.

The area outside of your selection will blur.

If you'd like, you can increase the level of blur around your focal point by dragging the slider at the bottom of the panel.

5   Select how you'd like to proceed.

On the panel that opens, you'll find the options to save your photo as a PSD file, to continue editing in **Quick** or **Expert Editing** and to upload your image directly to **Flickr** or **Twitter**.

The Text and Border Overlay Guided Edit

The **Text and Border Overlay Guided Edit** places custom text and a border design over your photo.

With the photo open in the **Guided Edits** workspace, select **Text and Border Overlay** from the **Special Edits**.

1   Select a border overlay.

Click the **Select a Border** button and choose a design for your picture's border.

Once your selected border appears over your photo, you can use the slider to adjust its size. Click the **Color** button to set the border's color.

2 Add a text overlay.

Click **Add Text Overlay**. A text box will be added in the upper left corner of the frame and the **Type Tool** will be activated.

3 Add your custom text.

Type your text in the text box.

You can change the font, style and color of the selected text by selecting from the **Tool Options** along the bottom of the panel.

If your text doesn't fit in the box or if it breaks into two lines when you want to keep it all on one, drag the side to resize the text box.

4 Position the text.

Click the position diagram to select where your text will overlay the border graphic.

5 Choose a **Text Style**.

Optionally choose a preset look for your text.

When you're happy with the results, click **Next**.

6 Select how you'd like to proceed.

On the panel that opens, you'll find the options to save your photo as a PSD file, to continue editing in **Quick** or **Expert Editing** and to upload your image directly to **Flickr** or **Twitter**.

Photomerge Guided Edits

Photomerge Guided Edits combine elements from two or more photos in order to either create an enhanced picture or to create a brand new photo composition.

Photomerge Compose is a tool for grabbing elements from one photo and placing them into another. We explore it in detail on page 52.

Photomerge Exposure is a tool for compositing the best-lit elements from two or more photos. We demonstrate it on page 54.

Photomerge Faces is a tool for creating a perfect portrait by combining the best elements from several photos of the same face.

Photomerge Group Shot is a tool for creating a composite shot in which a person or people who appear in one photo can be painted into another.

Photomerge Scene Cleaner combines elements from two photos of the same scene, borrowing the best elements from each shot, so that you can remove unwanted elements – or even unwanted *people* – from an otherwise perfect shot!

Photomerge Panorama arranges several photos of and around a scene to create a panoramic photo. We look at it in more detail on page 57.

Paste between photos with Photomerge Compose

Photomerge Compose makes an easy task of cutting people or other elements from one photo and pasting them into another.

To use **Photomerge Compose**, first ensure that you have at least two photos open in your Photoshop Elements Editor workspace.

1 With the photos you want to cut and paste between open in the Photoshop Elements Editor, select the **Guided** tab and select **Photomerge**, then **Photomerge Compose**. If you have more than one photo open in the Editor, you'll be prompted to select the two you want to **Compose**.

2 Following the prompt, drag the photo you want to cut people or elements from up into the **Compose** workspace, as illustrated above.

3 Follow the prompts in the panel to the right of the workspace to draw a selection around the people or elements you want to cut from your photo using the panel's **Quick**, **Outline** and **Refine** tools individually or in combination.

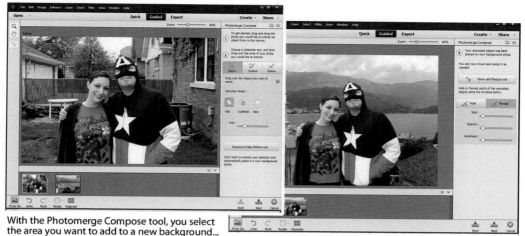

With the Photomerge Compose tool, you select the area you want to add to a new background...

...then, in the new background, you can refine your selection and tint the pasted imagergy to match the background.

The best workflow is to do most or your selection work using the **Quick Selection** tool (page 71). By painting along the edges of your selection with the **Outline** tool, you can further define it. Then, if further shaping of the selection is necessary, use the **Push** feature on the **Refine Selection Brush** tool (see page 73).

The size of your selection tool's brush can be controlled with the slider on the tool's panel or by using the bracket open **[** and bracket closed **]** buttons on your keyboard. The **Snap** level controls how automatically the selection tools follow color breaks in your picture.

If the **Mode** on the panel is set to **Add**, any selections you make will be added to the current selection. If the **Mode** is set to **Subtract**, the selection tools will remove from the current selection.

4   To refine your selection, click the **Advanced Edge Refinement** button on the panel.

In the **Advanced Edge Refinement** panel, you can **Set Background As Black**, **White**, **Transparent** or as your **Source** Image (the default). Setting your background to display as a different color can help you see more clearly if you've made a good, accurate selection.

With the background set to **Black, White** or **Transparent**, you can continue to use the panel's selection tools to refine your selection.

5   When you've got a good, accurate selection, click the **Refine Edge** button.

As discussed on page 73, the **Refine Edge** tool can be used to detect and select fine elements (like hair) as well as to create a slightly feathered, more natural edge so that your cut-and-pasted element won't look so cut-and-pasted.

When you're happy your selection, click the **Next** button at the bottom of the panel. Your cut image will be automatically pasted into your second photo.

But the beauty of the **Compose** tool is that, because the transparency behind your selection is created with a **Mask** (see page 140) rather than by actually deleting the old background, you can continue to refine your selection even after you've pasted it into its new background. You can even re-add things that you've deleted!

6   Click the **Move and Resize Tool** button to scale and position your pasted image onto its new background.

If necessary, you can further refine your selection by using the **Reveal Brush** and **Hide Brush**.

Paint over your selection with the **Reveal Brush** to add to your selected area. For instance, if in cutting and pasting from your original image you accidentally omitted your subject's ear, using the **Reveal Brush**, you can "paint" the ear back into your pasted area.

Paint over your selection with the **Hide Brush** to remove elements you inadvertently cut and pasted over.

Sliders under these brushes control the **Size, Opacity** (transparency) and **Hardness** (of the edge) of the elements you add or remove.

When you're happy with the results, click **Next**.

7   On the final panel for this tool, adjustments will be made to the color of your pasted element so that it is more naturally integrated into its new background.

When you click the **Auto Match Color Tone** button, the program will match the color tone of your pasted element to the background.

You may also manually tweak the **Luminance, Contrast, Color Intensity** and **Saturation** using the sliders.

When you're happy with the results, click the **Done** button.

Combine the best-lit elements from two photos with Photomerge Exposure

Another **Photomerge** tool is **Photomerge Exposure**, a tool for taking the best elements of two or more photos and combining them into one great-looking picture.

This is a terrific tool for combining the best parts of several shots taken with a flash at night or in which the subject is standing in front of a window or other brightly-lit background.

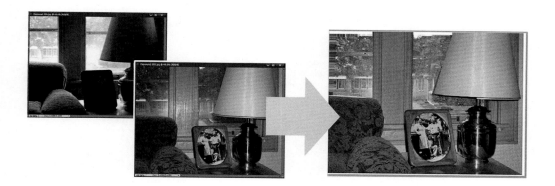

It works similarly to **Photomerge Faces** and **Photomerge Scene Cleaner** in that you select acceptable elements in each photo and the program combines them into a best-of composite photo.

Above are two photos. The first was shot with a flash – lighting the foreground but over-lighting the view out the windows. The second photo was shot with natural lighting, the result being that the background (the view through the windows) is perfectly exposed but the furniture in the foreground is too dark.

1   Open both photos in the Editor workspace.

    You need at least two photos to create a **Photomerge Exposure** – although you can potentially use several photos, combining the best elements from each to create your **Final** photo.

2   Select the Photoshop Elements **Guided** tab and select **Photomerge**, then **Photomerge Exposure**.

In **Automatic** mode, which the program opens into by default, **Photomerge** will automatically make its best guess at the ideal blending of the two photos. Sometimes **Automatic** mode will give you the results you need – although it may also benefit from some tweaking by moving the sliders in either **Simple Blending** or **Smart Blending Mode**.

I prefer to work in **Manual** mode. It gives me more control. So I clicked on the **Manual** tab on the **Photomerge Exposure** panel.

3   The program will use the first photo in the **Photo Bin** (below the Editor workspace) as my **Source**. The **Source** is the photo that **Photomerge** will draw its new elements from.

If you'd prefer to use another open photo as your source, drag it to the first position in the **Photo Bin**.

4   If necessary, drag the photo you want to use as your **Final** – the photo that my **Source's** elements will be added to – from the **Photo Bin** to the **Final** window.

It only took a couple of scribbles drawn through the window area to select these elements for Photomerging onto my Background photo. The second photo shows the results of the Photomerging of elements.

Photomerge automatically adjusted the positions of similar photos to line them up as closely as possible.

5   With the panel's **Pencil Tool**, indicate the elements on the **Source** photo that you'd like to add to your **Final**, as in the illustration on the facing page. (I designated that the **Source's** views out the windows be added to my **Final** photo).

You can adjust the **Pencil Tool's** size with the slider.

As illustrated, you don't need to completely cover the selected elements in the **Source** photo. Drawing over part of an area tells the program to grab all the similarly-colored elements around your drawing.

Use the **Eraser Tool** to de-select selected elements.

To make the combination of elements look more natural, you can select the **Edge Blending** option.

Manually align your photos for Photomerging

If the program does not automatically align your **Foreground** and **Background** photos, you can manually align them by selecting the **Alignment Tool** under the **Advanced Options** button on the **Photomerge** panel.

When the **Alignment Tool** is selected, three alignment points will appear on your **Background** photo. Place those three alignment points on key reference points in the photo. Then click to select the **Foreground** photo. When three similar alignment points appear on it, move them to the exact same reference points as you did on the **Background** photo and click **Align**.

The biggest challenge with the tool is, because the **Pencil Tool** selects elements in your photos based on pixel color similarity, you sometimes end up taking more from your **Source** photo to your **Final** photo than you'd like. In my example, for instance, when I used the photo with the over-exposed background as my **Final**, every time I selected the lamp shade, I also got the whited-out windows!

The solution for me was to swap the photos I was using as my **Source** and **Final**. Remember, just because you plan to use elements that are in the *background* of your photo doesn't necessarily mean that the photo with these elements won't make a better **Final** source image!

Combine photos with Photomerge Panorama

Sometimes a single photo doesn't capture the entirety of a scene or landscape. The Grand Canyon, the Golden Gate Bridge, Vatican Square – a single snapshot just can't tell the whole story.

Photoshop Elements' **Photomerge Panorama** tool combines several photos of a scene into one complete photo – producing, for instance, a panoramic image of a wide scene from three or four photos taken of adjacent areas of that scene.

The tool works amazingly well in most cases – even compensating for lens distortion and slight color differences between shots. About the only requirement is that there be a little bit of overlap in the photos' contents so the program can interpret the scene composition and calculate where to combine the images.

In my illustration on the following page, I gathered a number of photos I'd shot while watching a Harley-Davidson "birthday" parade in downtown Milwaukee.

1   With the photos you want to cut and paste open in the Photoshop Elements Editor, select the **Guided** tab, then select **Photomerge**, then **Photomerge Panorama**.

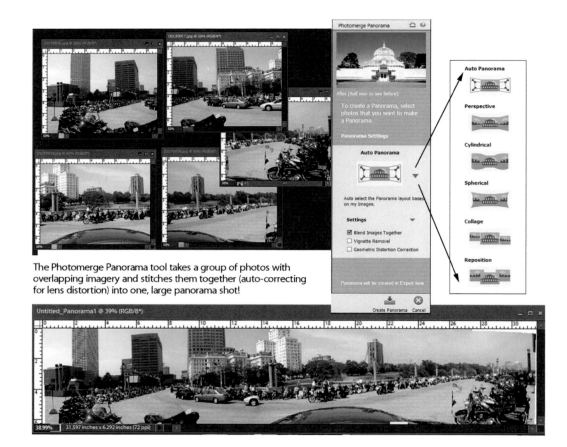

The Photomerge Panorama tool takes a group of photos with overlapping imagery and stitches them together (auto-correcting for lens distortion) into one, large panorama shot!

2 In the option screen that appears, browse to select the photo files or photo folder you'd like included in your **Panorama**.

(You can also indicate for the tool to use the photos that are currently open in the Editor workspace.)

3 In most cases, the **Auto Layout** setting produces very good results. However, should you need to tweak the composition, the **Interactive Layout** option opens a dialog box for manually repositioning your **Photomerge** elements.

As you can see in my example on the facing page, there is a small flaw.

In the center of the picture, you can see the front end of a car that appeared in one photo but not the photo adjacent to it. But, otherwise, the results are nearly perfect.

And, at 32 inches long, it might make a very nice poster!

The Actions panel

The **Actions** panel is a cool feature borrowed from the professional version of Photoshop.

The **Actions** panel offers a number of pre-recorded, multi-step tasks, tasks that can be applied to a photo open in your editor simply by selecting **Action** and then clicking the **Play** button on the top right of the panel.

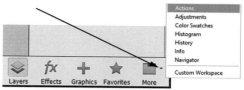

The **Actions** panel can be opened by selecting the option under the **More** button in the lower right of the Photoshop Elements interface or by selecting **Actions** under the program's **Window** menu.

There are four categories of **Actions** included with Photoshop Elements:

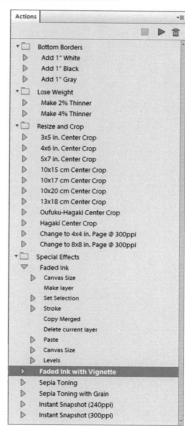

Bottom Borders adds a border below your photo onto which you can add text.

Lose Weight narrows your photos, distorting it slightly to make your subject look a little taller and thinner.

Resize and Crop automatically crops and resizes your photo to a specific shape and resolution.

Special Effects automatically give your photo the look of being printed with faded ink, add vignetting or a sepia tint, age your photo or make it look like a Polaroid snapshot by resizing it or adding a white border to it.

If you click on the arrow to the left of any **Action**, you can see the individual steps the program takes to complete the **Action**. You have the option of applying the entire **Action** to your photo or, by selecting a sub-task, just one of the main task's individual steps.

Part III
The Expert Photo Editing Workspace

Background/Foreground Colors

Move and View Tools

Selection Tools

Enhance Tools

Draw Tools

Modify Tools

Color Tools

Chapter 5

Get to Know the Photoshop Elements Toolbox
Your main photo editing toolkit

In Expert mode, the most visible tools in the Photoshop Elements Editor workspace are those gathered into the Toolbox, displayed as two columns of little icons along the left side of the Editor workspace.

Understanding these tools, how they work and how to customize them for your particular needs will take you a long way toward mastering this program.

| Quick | Guided | **Expert** |

The Toolbox

When Photoshop Elements is set to **Expert** editing mode, the full Photoshop Elements **Toolbox** will appear along the left side of the Editor workspace. The tools in the **Toolbox** are divided into six categories:

View Tools. Tools for zooming into, out of or changing the view of your image files.

Select Tools. Tools for selecting and isolating areas in your image files.

Enhance Tools. Tools for cleaning up and changing your image files. This category includes the tools for blurring, sharpening, dodging and burning, based on techniques long used by professional photographers.

Draw Tools. Tools for drawing, painting, coloring and erasing. Among the **Draw** tools are tools for adding text. Because working with text is a category all its own, we'll discuss these **Type** tools in depth in **Chapter 10, Create and Edit Text**.

Modify Tools. Tools for cropping, shaping and straightening your image files.

Color Tools. Tools for setting the colors of the elements you will add to your files.

The Tool Options

Tool Options

Sharing space with the **Photo Bin**, below the **Editor** workspace, the **Tool Options Bin** gives you access to the options for customizing how each tool works. (This space is toggled on by clicking the **Tool Options** button in the lower left of the interface.)

Some of these custom settings are so deep that one tool can actually work as several tools. And a few tools even allow you to *add* custom settings of your own!

Tool Options for some tools, for instance, include drop-down menus that list patterns, brushes or effects and sliders for setting specific brush sizes. We'll discuss specific **Tool Options** for each tool as we discuss each individual tool.

Access many tools under one button

Most buttons in the **Toolbox** will grant you access to more than one tool. When the **Blur** tool button is selected, for instance, buttons in the **Tool Options Bin** allow you to optionally select the **Blur, Sharpen** or **Sponge** tools. As we discuss the individual tools in this chapter, we'll indicate which sets of tools share a single **Toolbox** button.

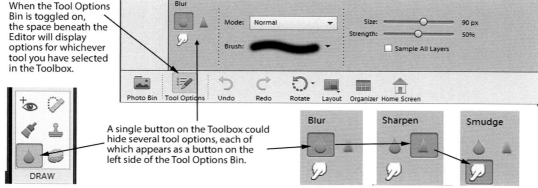

When the Tool Options Bin is toggled on, the space beneath the Editor will display options for whichever tool you have selected in the Toolbox.

A single button on the Toolbox could hide several tool options, each of which appears as a button on the left side of the Tool Options Bin.

Set Foreground and Background Colors

You'll likely refer often to this swatch icon, displayed at the very bottom of the **Toolbox**. The colors that are set here play a role in how a number of your tools function.

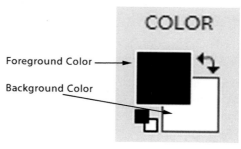

Foreground Color

Background Color

The **Foreground Color** will usually be the color in which new items you create will appear.

- When a paintbrush, drawing or shape tool is selected, for instance, the brush will paint this shape with the **Foreground Color**.

- When you use the **Typing Tool,** your text will also appear, by default, in the **Foreground Color**.

- When you use the **Eraser Tool**, the area you erase will be replaced by the **Background Color**. (At least when you're erasing from a background layer or flattened image file. When you erase from a layer [see **Chapter 9**], the area you erase will become transparent.)

- When you use **Fill** or add a **Stroke**, you will have the option of doing so with the **Foreground** or **Background Color**.

- When you use the **Gradient Tool**, the area will be painted, by default, with a gradation or blend of color from the **Foreground Color** to the **Background Color**.

The Color Picker

There are a number of ways to set which colors appear as your **Foreground** and **Background Colors**. The easiest way is to simply click on either the **Foreground** or **Background Color** swatch icon on the **Toolbox**.

This will launch the **Color Picker**.

The **Color Picker** displays a color sampling screen and a slider bar, representing **hue, saturation** and **brightness**. (Hue is your color's shade or tint; saturation is the amount of that hue in your color; brightness is the amount of lightness in your color.)

Your current color is displayed in the lower half of the box, located in the upper center of the **Color Picker**, as illustrated to the right.

Your new color will appear in the upper half of this box.

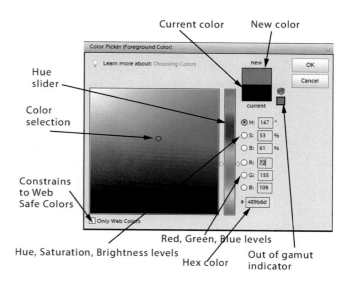

Current color   New color

Hue slider

Color selection

Constrains to Web Safe Colors

Hue, Saturation, Brightness levels

Red, Green, Blue levels

Hex color

Out of gamut indicator

To adjust the hue for your color, move the white triangles up or down on the **Hue slider** that runs down the center of the **Color Picker**. Then to pick your color, click in the big "picker" box, representing the saturation and brightness of that hue.

By checking the **Only Web Colors** box in the lower left corner of the **Color Picker**, you can restrict the available colors in the picker to only those colors that display consistently on Web pages.

Colors can also be set digitally in the **Color Picker** by typing in numbers for **Hue**, **Saturation** and **Brightness** or for the 256 levels of **Red**, **Green** and **Blue** in the color mix. The alpha-numeric **Hex** numbers for the color, in the lower right, can also be manually designated.

Once you've selected your color, click **OK**. Your selected color will become your new **Background** or **Foreground Color**.

The Eyedropper/Sampler Tool

Another way to set the **Foreground Color** is by sampling a color from an open photo or image with the **Eyedropper/Sampler** (located among the **Draw** tools) on the **Toolbox**.

To sample a color, select this tool from the **Toolbox** and then click on a color area in an open image file.

The **Tool Options** for this tool includes options for selecting an average color sample from a block of pixels and for selecting colors that appear on either the current layer or all layers of your image file.

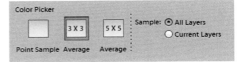

The Color Swatch panel

The **Color Swatch** panel can be opened by selecting it from the Photoshop Elements **Window** menu or by selecting the option from the **More** button in the lower right corner of the interface.

When you click on a swatch in the **Color Swatch** panel, it will become your **Foreground** Color.

The **Color Swatch** panel includes hundreds of color options, categorized in several swatch sets. These various swatch sets can be accessed from the drop-down menu at the top of the panel, as illustrated to the right.

You can even create custom colors for your swatch library.

To do so, set your **Foreground Color** using the **Color Picker**, then click the **New Swatch** icon in the lower right of the **Color Swatches** panel. The color will be permanently added to your swatch library.

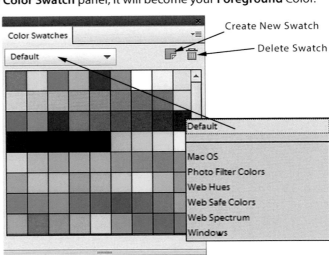

The Foreground and Background Colors can also be set by selecting a chip from the Color Swatches palette. The drop-down menu at the top of this panel offers options for displaying a number of additional color libraries.

The size and number of swatches displayed can be set by clicking the option switch on the upper right of the panel.

Additional Foreground/Background Color options

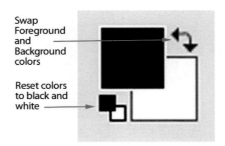

Swap Foreground and Background colors

Reset colors to black and white

Swap Foreground and Background Colors. You can quickly switch the **Foreground** and **Background Colors** by clicking on the double-headed arrow to the upper right of the **Foreground/Background Color** swatch icons, or by pressing the **X** key on your keyboard.

Quickly set Foreground/Background Colors to black and white. You can quickly reset the **Foreground** and **Background Colors** to black and white, respectively, by clicking on the black/white icon to the lower left of the **Foreground/Background Color** swatch icon on the **Toolbox**. A keyboard shortcut for setting the colors back to black and white is the **D** key.

Move and View Tools

Three tools in the **Toolbox** are for viewing and positioning your image file.

The Zoom Tool

One of two **View** tools, the **Zoom Tool** is represented by a magnifying glass. The tool is used, naturally, to zoom in and out of your image.

Select this tool and click on your image and you will zoom in. (Or you can use the keyboard shortcut **Ctrl++** on a PC or **⌘++** on a Mac.)

Hold down the **Alt/Option** key and click on your image and you will zoom out. (Or you can use the keyboard shortcut **Ctrl+−** on a PC or **⌘+−** on a Mac.)

The buttons and checkboxes on the tool's **Tool Options Bin** can be used to 'jump' your view to specific zoom levels.

The Hand Tool

Represented by a **Hand** icon, this **View** tool is useful if you're zoomed in so closely to an image that sections of your image are outside the file's window. When the **Hand Tool** is selected, you can click and drag the image's view around within the viewable area.

A keyboard shortcut for the **Hand Tool** is the **Spacebar** on your keyboard. No matter what tool you're working with, you can always reposition your view by holding down the **Spacebar,** then clicking and dragging your image around in the viewing area.

The Move Tool

The top left **Select** tool in the **Toolbox,** and more or less the default tool in Photoshop Elements, **the Move Tool** is used to move or drag the elements, selections, text or layers in your image files to new positions.

The settings in the **Tool Options** for this tool are useful for arranging the positions and order of objects in your image.

The selected area of your image file will appear surrounded by a moving dotted line, commonly called "marching ants."

Toggles in the Tool Options Bin for the Selection Tools set whether the tool adds to or subtracts from the selection.

New Selection

Add to Selection (or hold down Shift key)

Remove from Selection (or hold down Alt key)

Select Intersection of old and new selections

Selection Tools

The **Toolbox's Select** category tools are used to select areas of your image files.

A selected area can be cut, copied or pasted. But, more so, a selected area is *isolated*, so that any effects you add to your photo or image file will be applied *only* to the selection without affecting the rest of the image. Selecting and isolating is a very powerful function of Photoshop Elements, which is why we spend an entire chapter (**Chapter 6, Select and Isolate Areas in Your Photos**) discussing it in depth.

Your selected areas will be surrounded by little, moving dotted lines – which are traditionally referred to as "marching ants."

Add to and subtract from a selection

When selecting an area in a photo or image file, you don't have to get the selection exactly right the first time:

- Once you've selected an area, you can add to the selection by toggling **Add to Selection** in the **Tool Options Bin** (as illustrated above) or by holding down the **Shift** key as you continue to select.

- To deselect areas from your selected area, toggle **Subtract from Selection** in the **Tool Options Bin** or hold down the **Alt/Option** key as you drag over the area you want to deselect.

- To select only the area overlapped by your current and your new selection, toggle **Intersect with Selection** in the **Tool Options Bin**.

Using these tools to add to or subtract from your selection, you can hone your selection until it is precisely the area you want to work with.

- To turn off, or **deselect**, all of the selected areas for your image file, press **Ctrl+d** on a PC or ⌘+**d** on a Mac.

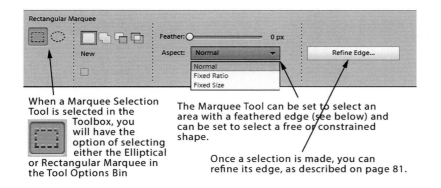

When a Marquee Selection Tool is selected in the Toolbox, you will have the option of selecting either the Elliptical or Rectangular Marquee in the Tool Options Bin

The Marquee Tool can be set to select an area with a feathered edge (see below) and can be set to select a free or constrained shape.

Once a selection is made, you can refine its edge, as described on page 81.

The Marquee Selection Tools

The **Rectangular Marquee Tool** and the **Elliptical Marquee Tool** are both available under the same **Toolbox** button. To switch between them, click on the button for whichever tool is displayed in the **Toolbox,** and then select one or the other tool in the **Tool Options Bin**, illustrated above.

To select an area on your image with either of these tools, click and drag across your image file. As long as that tool remains selected in the **Toolbox**, you can reposition the selected area by dragging it. To deselect the area press **Ctrl+d** on a PC or ⌘**+d** on a Mac.

Beyond the **Feathering** (discussed below), the **Tool Options** for this tool include a few functions which can also be activated with keyboard shortcuts.

> To constrain the tool to select a perfectly circular or square area, select the **Fixed Ratio** option from the **Aspect** drop-down in the **Tool Options Bin** – or hold down the **Shift** key as you drag to make your selection.

> When the **Aspect** is set to **Fixed Size**, you can designate the exact size of the area you will select.

Feathering

Most selection tools include an option to allow **Feathering**. This option is available in the **Tool Options Bin** for the **Marquee Selection Tools** as well as a refinement option under the program's **Select** menu.

Feathering means softening the edge of a selected area so rather than a sharp division between the selected and unselected areas, there is a soft gradation of selection.

A "feathered" selection has a softer edge so that, when the selection is removed or an effect is added to it, the distinction between the selected and unselected area of your image is a gradation rather than a solid line.

We look at this feature in more detail in the **Feathering** sidebar on page 99.

The Lasso Tool selects as you draw freehand.

The Polygonal Lasso Tool draws a selection from point to point as you click.

The Magnetic Lasso Tool follows the edge of a color break as you drag or click to create points.

Lasso Selection Tools

The three "lasso" tools share the same **Toolbox** button.

To switch between these tools, click the button for whichever tool is displayed in the **Toolbox**, then select the tool you'd like to use in the **Tool Options Bin**.

Lasso Selection Tools define a selected area by drawing a line around it (as if wrapping it in a lasso). There are three **Lasso Tools**, each functioning slightly differently.

The Lasso Tool is a freehand tool for selecting an area. To select an area with the **Lasso**, you just drag and draw. When you release your mouse button, the defined area will be selected.

The Polygonal Lasso Tool works similarly to the **Lasso Tool** except that, to designate an area to be selected, you click and release to create a series of points, which will be connected by straight lines. To close a **Polygonal Lasso Tool** selection, finish the selection by clicking onto your selection's starting point.

The Magnetic Lasso Tool is also a freehand tool for selecting an area. However, as you draw your selection with this tool, it will try to automate your selection by following the edge of an object, based on its color.

In other words, in the picture above, I dragged around the dog to select it in the photo. As I dragged my mouse around the dog's head, the **Magnetic Lasso** automatically made fine adjustments to my selection (based on the distinction in color between the dog and the background) to more precisely select the dog.

An important **Tool Option** setting for this tool is **Edge Contrast**. This setting defines the tool's tolerance for color contrast between the areas it does and the areas it does not select.

In other words, if the color of the subject you are drawing a selection around is a very different color than that of the background, you can use a high **Edge Contrast** percentage to ensure that the tool finds the edges.

If the subject is not so clearly distinguished from the background, you'll need a much lower **Edge Contrast** percentage. And you'll likely need to be more careful guiding the tool around the selection, or you may need to add to or subtract from the selection to refine it.

The Magic Wand Tool selects everything within a color range, based on the Tolerance level you've set.

The Selection Brush Tool draws a selection as you "paint" an area with its brush.

The Quick Selection Tool combines the the behaviors of both tools, selecting a similar color range as you "paint" across your image file.

Quick Selection Tools

The **Magic Wand, Quick Selection, Selection Brush, Refine Selection Brush** and **Smart Selection** tools share the same button in the **Toolbox**.

To switch between these tools, click the button for whichever tool is displayed in the **Toolbox**, then select the tool you'd like to use in the **Tool Options Bin**.

The Magic Wand Tool. One of the most useful tools in the **Toolbox**, the **Magic Wand Tool**, automatically selects an area on your image based on color similarities. (We put it to good use in **Chapter 12, Photoshop Elements Tricks**.)

When you click or drag on your photo with this tool, adjacent pixels of a similar color are automatically selected. By holding down the **Shift** key to add and the **Alt/Option** key to subtract, you can continue to select or de-select areas of your image file to build your desired selection.

The most important **Tool Options** setting for this tool is **Tolerance**. The lower the number, the narrower the range of colors the **Magic Wand** will consider similar. A higher **Tolerance** number widens the range of similar colors the **Magic Wand** will select as you click.

The Selection Brush Tool works just like it sounds like it would – as you "paint" with it, you create a selected area. **Tool Options** include settings for defining the size and hardness of the brush. You'll find more information on brush options in our discussion of **Brush settings and options** on page 82.

The Quick Selection Tool works like a combination of the **Magic Wand** and the **Selection Brush Tool**. As you drag it across your image, it "paints" a selection area, grabbing nearby areas of similar color along the way. This is a great tool for quickly paint-selecting a flat-colored background that you'd like to remove or replace. Its **Tool Options** include settings for the size, shape and hardness of the brush.

The Refine Selection Brush and Push tool

 Once you've created a basic selection using any of Photoshop Elements' **Selection** tools or brushes, the **Refine Selection Brush** can be used to adjust and tweak the selection. Once your selection is precisely defined, the **Edge Selector**, discussed in the sidebar on the facing page, can be used to select very fine details like fur or hair.

To use the **Refine Selection Brush** and **Push** tool:

1. Make a basic selection using one of the **Selection Brushes** or a **Lasso** or **Marquee Selection** tool.

2. Choose the **Refine Selection Brush** and the **Push** option on the **Tool Options** panel, as illustrated below.

    When you select the **Refine Selection Brush,** your cursor will appear over your photo as a gray dot inside a white circle.

3. Click and drag from inside and outside your selection to "nudge" the selection into the precise shape you'd like.

    When the gray dot is inside of your selection, dragging will "push" the selection edge out, adding to the selection from areas similar in color to the area under the white circle.

    When the gray dot is outside of your selection, dragging will "push" the selection edge in, subtracting the selection from areas similar in color to the area under the white circle.

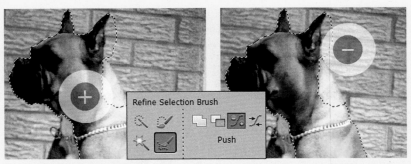

When the Refine Selection Brush/Push option is selected and the cursor is inside your selection, dragging will add to the selection. When the cursor is outside of your selection, dragging will subtract from your selection.

The size of the brush or gray dot can be set using the **Size** slider on the **Tool Options** panel or by using the bracket open **[** and bracket closed **]** buttons on your keyboard.

The **Snap Strength** setting controls the tolerance level for your automatic selection – in other words, how closely the automatically selected areas must match the colors of the areas you drag the gray dot over.

To see a demonstration of this tool, check out my free tutorial at Muvipix.com/pe14.php, under the **New Feature** demos.

The **Refine Selection Brush and Push tools** are discussed in the sidebar on the facing page.

The **Smart Selection** tool, a new feature of Photoshop Elements 2019, automatically makes a precise selection for you, based on your rough selection. Naturally, the tool is most effective when there is a clear difference in color or contrast between the object you want to select and its background – but it works remarkably well!

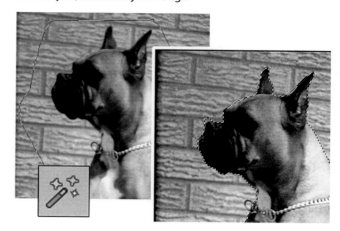

To create a **Smart Selection**, simply drag to draw an approximate selection around your person or object. The program will automatically detect the person or object within your rough outline and select it for you.

The Refine Selection Brush Edge Selector

By using the various Selection tools and the **Refine Selection Brush**, you can very precisely select objects and people in your photos. However, many of the objects and people you will draw a selection around won't have neat, clean edges. Hair and animal fur can be particularly challenging to precisely select. Fortunately, the **Edge Selector** feature makes this often challenging task much easier.

The **Edge Selector** is a feature of the **Refine Selection Brush** tool, discussed on the facing page. As discussed in that sidebar, when the **Refine Selection Brush** is set to **Push, it** will indicate a **+** sign when the cursor is inside a selection and a **–** sign when it is outside.

However, between the **+** and the **–** modes – when you hover your mouse along the edge of the object your are selecting – the cursor will indicate a black dot. This is the **Refine Selection Brush's Edge Selector** mode.

When in **Edge Selector** mode, hold down your mouse button and move slowly along your object's edge. When you release the mouse button, the tool will automatically create a very fine selection along the color breaks between your selected and unselected areas.

For a free demonstration of this tool, go to Muvipix.com and type "Refine Selection Tool" in the product search box.

Enhance Tools

Enhance Tools are used to change your image file – whether to clean up a photo or to change it or add a special effect. Some of these tools are simple and almost automatic. Others can do some pretty complex effects!

Eye Tools: The Red Eye Removal Tool

You know what this tool is for. It's for when you've taken a flash picture in dim lighting and you find that, in the final photo, your best friend or your dog has eyes that glow like those of some evil robot!

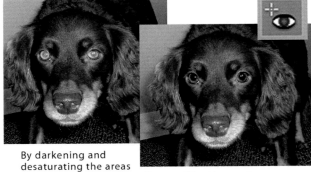

By darkening and desaturating the areas you click on, the Red Eye Removal Tool instantly tames demonic-looking subjects.

To use it, select the **Eye Tool** and then click on the subject's bright, red pupils. (The **Tool Options** panel includes an **Auto Correct** button, which can locate and fix red eyes automatically.) The tool essentially strips the color out of the pupil area and darkens it.

Tool Options for this tool allow you to set the **Pupil Size** and **Darken Amount.** You'll also find a checkbox option for fixing **Pet Eyes**, which can sometimes glow red, yellow and even gree**n!**

Open Closed Eyes

Ever take one of those photos that's nearly perfect –except that a key person in the photo has his or her eyes closed? Relatively new to Photoshop Elements is a tool to help you save the shot.

To open closed eyes.

1 Open the **Closed Eyes Corrector**

With your photo open in the Editor, select the **Eye Tool** button on the Toolkit. Then, on the **Tool Options** panel, click the **Open Closed Eyes** button. The workspace panel will open.

This panel can also be launched by selecting the **Open Closed Eyes** option under the program's **Enhance** menu.

The program gives you the option of either adding open eyes from a library of eyes (the effect of which can sometimes be kind of creepy!) or by "borrowing" eyes from another photo.

2 Find a set of eyes

Locate another photo (ideally of the same person) from your currently open photos (**Photo Bin**), **Computer** hard drive or from the **Organizer**'s catalog. The closer in composition and lighting to your original, the more effective the fix will be.

3 Click on the photo

When you select the photo's thumbnail, the eyes will automatically be swapped in for the closed eyes in your original photo.

The Spot Healing Brush Tool

 Sharing a button with the **Healing Brush Tool**, this tool is great for getting rid of unwanted moles, blemishes or other such flaws in your photos, as illustrated at the top of the next page.

When you click an area or "paint" with it, the tool blends the selected area with color information from the surrounding pixels. **Tool Options** include settings for the brush's size and hardness (For more information on brushes, see **Brush settings and options** on page 82) as well as the option to remove objects using **Content Aware Fill** (see the sidebar on page 76).

What is Anti-Aliasing?

Anti-Aliasing is a method of smoothing or slightly feathering the edges of an object or text so that it looks more natural. When **Anti-Aliasing** is turned off, the object or text will have very sharp edges, usually resulting in a very blocky, unnatural look.

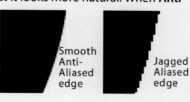

Smooth Anti-Aliased edge

Jagged Aliased edge

The Healing Brush Tools

Similar to the **Clone Stamp Tool** (discussed on page 74), this tool borrows color and texture information from one area of your photo (which you've defined by **Alt-clicking** on it) and uses it to paint over another area.

The difference between this tool and the **Clone Stamp** is that the **Healing Brush Tool** then blends this borrowed imagery with the colors of the existing pixels to form a natural "healing patch" over the area.

As with the **Spot Healing Brush Tool**, the **Tool Options Bin** includes settings for the brush's size and hardness.

You can see the **Healing Brush** at work in our **Photo Editing Tricks** on page 173.

The Healing Brush uses a Content Aware Fill system to replace blemishes, telephone lines and other unwanted elements in your photos with imagery from the surrounding area!

Using a Content Aware Fill system, the Spot Healing Brush uses nearby imagery to replace blemishes and other flaws in your photos virtually invisibly!

Content Aware Fill

A very exciting enhancement to the **Spot Healing Brush Tool** in Photoshop Elements is something Adobe calls **Content Aware Fill**.

In past versions of the **Healing Brushes**, the tool filled areas that you designated by averaging the colors of the surrounding pixels to create a smooth patch. This was very effective for removing blemishes and small marks in a photo – but it was less so at patching larger areas.

Content Aware Fill essentially looks at the entire area around what you're trying to hide or remove, and it smoothly fills the area you designate with similar, very natural-looking imagery.

This makes it especially effective at removing telephone wires from an otherwise perfect picture of a sunset – or even painting former friends completely out of a scene!

The Content Aware Fill feature in the Healing Brush Tools makes it easy to remove even large objects from many scenes.

The Smart Brush Tools

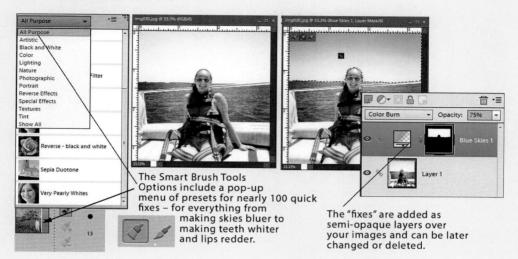

The Smart Brush Tools Options include a pop-up menu of presets for nearly 100 quick fixes – for everything from making skies bluer to making teeth whiter and lips redder.

The "fixes" are added as semi-opaque layers over your images and can be later changed or deleted.

The **Smart Brush Tool** and the **Details Smart Brush Tool** are part of a great **Quick Fix** tool set built into Photoshop Elements. (To toggle between these two tools, select the button on the **Toolbox** representing the currently active tool and then select one of the two **Smart Brushes** in the **Tool Options Bin**.)

Both tools work similarly, the main distinction being that the **Details Smart Brush Tool** affects only the area you "paint" with the brush (like the **Selection Brush** described on page 71), while the **Smart Brush Tool** expands the selected areas of your picture, based on their similarities to the areas you paint (like the **Quick Selection Tool** also described on page 71).

The **Smart Brush Tools** enhance your photos automatically, using presets available under the pop-up menu on the **Tool Options Bin**. These presets will make grass greener, skies bluer, teeth whiter, lipstick redder, etc. – or they can add color or texture effects to your photos.

To apply a **Smart Brush** fix, select the appropriate preset from the **Tool Options Bin's** drop-down menu, as illustrated above, and then paint over the area in your image file that you'd like to add effects to.

When you finish selecting the area of your photo and release your mouse button, the program will make the adjustments to your picture, as in the illustration above.

Using the **+** and **–** brush icons that appear on your image as you work, you can paint to add to or remove from the selected area (or hold down the **Shift** key to add and the **Alt/Option** key to subtract). The program will update the effect automatically.

The true beauty of these adjustments is that they don't permanently change the image itself! If you look at the **Layers** panel, you'll see that these adjustments are actually just masks added as what are called **Adjustment Layers**, as illustrated above. By clicking on these **Adjustment Layers**, you can reactivate the **Smart Brush Tools** and make further adjustments, or even delete the **Adjustment Layers** completely. The original image remains unmolested! At least until you flatten the layers or save the file as something other than a PSD file.

A favorite tool for "stunt photo work," the Clone Tool lets you paint over portions of your image file – removing objects or even people – with imagery from another area of your image file (defined by Alt+clicking).

The Clone Stamp Tool

This amazing tool takes imagery from one area of your photo file (an area indicated with an **Alt-click**) and paints it onto another.

The tool is popular for doing special effects, like "erasing" somebody or something from a scene (see pages 174).

In addition to settings for the brush size and hardness, the **Tool Options Bin** includes an **Opacity** setting. Opacity (the opposite of transparency) controls whether the area you paint over is replaced entirely with the new image or whether the new image is blended in semi-transparently with the old to some degree.

The Pattern Stamp Tool

Rather than painting an area in your photo with imagery from another area in your image, the **Pattern Stamp Tool** paints over your image with a pattern, as selected from the pop-up menu in the **Tool Options Bin**.

There are many pages of patterns available for this effect, by the way. And you can see the other categories of patterns by clicking on the flyout menu button in the upper right corner of the option box that appears when you click on the "pattern" drop-down.

An **Impressionist** option turns the pattern into a liquid swirl of paint that intensifies as you hold down on your mouse button.

The Pattern Stamp tool paints over your image with any of dozens of patterns.

The Blur Tool blurs
the area you drag across

The Smudge Tool
smears your image as
you drag acrosss it

The Sharpen Tool
increases pixel contrast
in the areas you drag across

Blur, Smudge and Sharpen

These three tools, which share the same button in the **Toolbox**, treat your image file a bit like liquid, allowing you to blur, smear or sharpen it.

To switch between these tools, click the button for whichever tool is displayed in the **Toolbox**, then select the tool you'd like to use in the **Tool Options Bin**.

The three tools share similar settings on the **Tool Options Bin** – Brush size, hardness and **Strength** (amount) of the blur, smudge or sharpening. (For information on brush settings, see **Brush settings and options** on page 82.)

The Blur Tool

Dragging this tool across your image softens the pixel edges of the area you drag across, blurring your picture.

The Smudge Tool

This tool treats your image as if it were wet paint. When you drag across it, you smear it!

The Sharpen Tool

The Sharpen Tool increases the contrast between pixels, giving your image a crisper look as you drag across it.

Unlike the general **Unsharp Mask** (discussed in **Chapter 8, Correct Color and Lighting**) which sharpens your entire photo, the **Sharpen Tool** sharpens only the areas of your picture that you drag across.

The Sponge Tool desaturates, or removes color from, an area

The Dodge Tool lightens the area you drag across

The Burn Tool darkens the area you drag across

The Sponge, Dodge and Burn Tools

These three tools are sometimes referred to as the "darkroom tools" because they're based on techniques photographers used to use in the darkroom to enhance their prints.

To switch between these tools, click the button for whichever tool is displayed in the **Toolbox**, then select the tool you'd like to use from the **Tool Options Bin**.

The three tools share similar **Tool Options** for setting brush hardness and size.

The Sponge Tool

The Sponge Tool desaturates, or removes color from, an area of your image as you drag over it. (The **Tool Options Bin** includes an option for reversing the process, or increasing color saturation.)

The **Flow** setting on the **Tool Options Bin** determines how much color is removed.

The Dodge Tool

The Dodge Tool lightens the area you drag over, as if it were a photographic print which received less exposure in the darkroom. The **Tool Options Bin's Exposure** settings control how intensely the area is dodged.

The Burn Tool

The Burn Tool darkens the area you drag over, as if it were a photographic print which received more exposure in the darkroom. The **Tool Options Bin's Exposure** settings control how intensely the area is darkened.

Draw Tools

The Brush Tools

The three **Brush Tools** share the same button on the **Toolbox**.

To switch between these tools, click the button for whichever tool is displayed in the **Toolbox**, then select the tool you'd like to use in the **Tool Options Bin**.

The Paint Brush

This tool is your basic paintbrush – similar to the **Pencil Tool** as a line drawing tool, except that the **Brush Tool** includes options for painting soft-edged or even textured lines.

The **Tool Options** for this tool include settings not only for the size and hardness of the brush and the opacity of the paint but also for switching the brush to **Airbrush** mode – which, as you'd expect, paints a stroke that grows more intense the longer you "spray" it on one spot.

In addition, if you click on the **paintbrush icon** in the **Tool Options Bin**, you'll find an option panel for creating your own brush. (For information on brush settings, see **Brush settings and options** on page 82.)

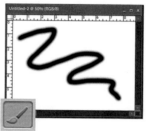

The Brush Tool paints a soft or textured freehand line.

The Impressionist Brush

The **Impressionist Brush** is a pretty cool special effects tool.

When you click and hold, or paint, with this brush, it "liquefies" and swirls the colors in your image so it resembles an impressionist painting.

The Color Replacement Brush

The **Color Replacement Brush** replaces the color of an area you "paint" over in your image file with the **Foreground Color** (although, in **Tool Options**, you can also set it to replace only the hue, saturation or luminosity of your picture).

Because of the way this brush senses the differences in color ranges within your image, it can, amazingly enough, paint the leaves on a tree but leave the sky behind them unchanged or even, as illustrated on the right, tint the darker leaves of a tree in the background while leaving the brighter leaves of the tree in the foreground unchanged!

The **Tolerance** level you have set in the **Tool Options Bin** determines how much distinction there must be between the areas to be re-colored and those left intact.

The Impressionist Brush swirls your image.

The Color Replacement Brush overlays color, but only over the range of colors you designate.

Brush settings and options

Many tools behave like brushes. The tool's effects or colors are essentially painted on.

In fact, the size and softness settings in the **Tool Options Bin** for many tools are nearly identical to those of the **Paint Brush Tool**.

There are two basic brush settings: the **Size** of the brush (measured in pixels) and its **Hardness**.

Brush sub-categories, textures and sizes on the Tool Options panel.

Hardness determines sharpness of the edge of the stroke that the brush paints. The softer the edge, the more feathered the area between the brushed area and the unbrushed area. When using the **Clone Tool**, for instance, a softer edged brush may show a more natural, less abrupt line between your old and newly-added image areas.

Some brushes, called **Scatter** brushes, create an effect like painting with steel wool. Their effect is scratchy and hard.

Brushes can also have shapes. These oblong shapes (included among the **Calligraphy** presets) will paint a wider line when you are painting one direction than they will another, as when you are writing with a calligraphy pen.

Brushes can even be set to paint **patterns**. When a pattern is selected for a brush, the pattern's image will appear again and again as you paint. This can be used, for instance, to paint several stars across a sky in a single brush stroke or to paint a trail of footprints.

In addition to the over 300 preset brushes you'll find in Photoshop Elements, you can also save your own personal brush settings. To do this, once you've set your brush to the shape and size you want, click on the 📋 menu on the upper right of the brush preset drop-down menu and select the option to **Save Brush**.

The **Paint Brush** tool also has some cool advanced brush tool settings in the **Tool Options Bin**, which we discuss on page 84.

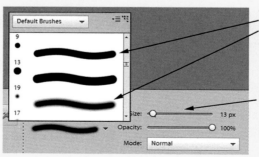

Brushes can have soft or hard edges or can even be set to paint patterns

Brush sizes are measured in pixels and can be selected from the presets or set using the slider

The Eraser Tool removes what you drag across, replacing it with your Background Color or, if a layer, transparency.

The Background Eraser erases up to color breaks, based on the Tolerance level you've set in the Tool Options.

The Magic Eraser instantly removes an area you click on, based on its color range and the Tolerance level you've set.

Eraser Tools

Simply put, the **Eraser Tools** remove imagery from your file as you drag across it.

The three **Eraser Tools** share the same button on the **Toolbox**. To switch between these tools, click the button for whichever tool is displayed in the **Toolbox**, then select the tool you'd like in the **Tool Options Bin**.

The Eraser

- If you're erasing from a flattened image or a background layer, what you erase will be replaced with your **Background Color** (see page 65).

- Erasing from a layer creates transparency through that layer.

Tool Options for this tool include settings for brush size, hardness and opacity (transparency level).

The Background Eraser Tool

The **Background Eraser** erases one color or color range and ignores dissimilarly colored areas in your image file.

For example, this tool can be used to erase the background from the photo of a person and yet not erase the person!

The tool determines the color you want erased based on the pixels that are in the tool's crosshairs as you "paint" with it. So, as you erase, if you keep the crosshairs off of what you don't want removed, the tool will erase along the edge of the color break, as in the illustration above, in which it erased the wall but not the dog.

Tool Options include settings for brush size and hardness as well as **Tolerance** – how much distinction must exist between the area you're erasing and the area you're not in order for the tool to recognize the difference.

The Magic Eraser Tool

Like the **Magic Wand Tool,** this tool selects and then erases areas in your image file that fall within a range of colors, based on the pixel you click on or the pixels you drag across.

For example, using this tool, you could easily remove a consistently green background from an image in a single click or simple click and drag.

The **Tolerance** setting, in the **Tool Options Bin**, designates how wide a range of color is considered similar to your selected pixels, and thus is erased. (The higher the number, the more "tolerant" the tool is of variations in the background color.) The **Opacity** level determines if the image is erased completely or simply softened or made semi-transparent.

Advanced brush tool settings

Adobe has included a couple of **Tool Options** in Photoshop Elements that make working with the brush tools even more intuitive. When the **Paint Brush** is selected, these tools appear on the far right of the **Tool Options Bin**.

Brush Settings

Brush Settings allow you to create a brush with whatever characteristics you'd like, including **Fade** (How much the opacity of the paint changes along your brush stroke), **Hue Jitter** (How much the stroke wavers between your selected **Foreground** and **Background Colors** as

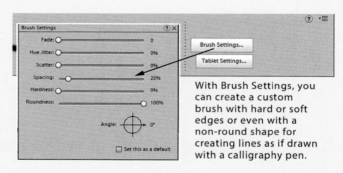

With Brush Settings, you can create a custom brush with hard or soft edges or even with a non-round shape for creating lines as if drawn with a calligraphy pen.

you paint), **Scatter** (How much the stroke appears as speckles rather than a solid line), **Spacing** (How much the stroke appears as a series of dots rather than a solid line), **Hardness** (How soft the edges of the stroke are) and **Roundness** (the shape of the brush; an oval brush can be used to make the brush draw variable-width strokes, as if drawn with a calligraphy pen).

Tablet Settings

Drawing tablets, such as those made by Wacom, enable you to draw and paint in Photoshop Elements using a very intuitive pad and stylus. The **Tablet Settings** enable you to use your tablet to create custom brushes.

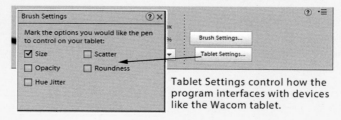

Tablet Settings control how the program interfaces with devices like the Wacom tablet.

The Paint Bucket (Fill) Tool

When you drag the **Paint Bucket** to your canvas, it paints your image file with the current **Foreground Color**. It does this in one big, even flow of paint.

If you have a **Selected** area on your canvas or on your image file, the **Paint Bucket Tool** will fill only the selection.

There are two keyboard shortcuts that also fill with color, by the way:

Alt+Backspace will fill a selected area with your **Foreground Color.**

Ctrl+Backspace (⌘+Backspace on a Mac) will fill a selected area with your **Background Color.**

In the **Tool Options** for the **Paint Bucket**, the tool can be set to fill an area with a selected pattern rather than a color.

The Paint Bucket fills your canvas or your selected area.

The Gradient Tool

The **Gradient Tool** paints your image or selected area with a gradation or blend of one color to another. By default, this gradation will begin with your **Foreground Color** and blend to your **Background Color.**

Tool Options include a number of patterns for your gradients, from linear gradients to radial gradients to pattern gradients. The gradient they create will be a blend of your **Foreground** and **Background Colors.**

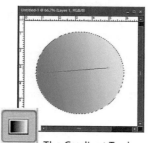

The Gradient Editor also includes presets for color blends other than the default. You can access them by clicking the **Edit** button in the **Tool Options Bin.**

The Gradient Tool fills your canvas or selected area with (by default) a gradation from the Foreground to the Background Colors.

Tool Options also include a setting for **Opacity,** so you can set whether the gradient covers your image file completely or blends semi-transparently to some degree with the existing image.

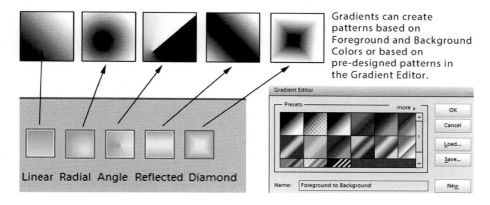

Gradients can create patterns based on Foreground and Background Colors or based on pre-designed patterns in the Gradient Editor.

Linear Radial Angle Reflected Diamond

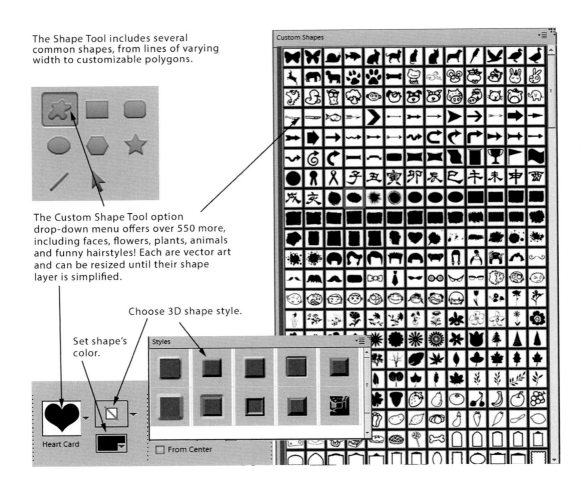

The Shape Tool includes several common shapes, from lines of varying width to customizable polygons.

The Custom Shape Tool option drop-down menu offers over 550 more, including faces, flowers, plants, animals and funny hairstyles! Each are vector art and can be resized until their shape layer is simplified.

Choose 3D shape style.

Set shape's color.

Heart Card

From Center

Custom Shapes

Styles

The Shape Tools

The **Shape Tools** draw shapes as you drag across your image file. These shapes appear as a new layer on your file, and remain editable until you simplify the layer or flatten your image. (See **Simplify or flatten layers** on page 138 of **Chapter 9, Work with Photoshop Elements Layers**.)

There are about half a dozen common shapes available under the **Shape Tool** button. To switch between them, click the button for whichever tool is displayed in the **Toolbox**, then select the tool you'd like in the **Tool Options Bin**.

If you select the **Custom Shape Tool** option, you will have access to hundreds of more shapes. These custom shapes are available on the pop-up option panel in the **Tool Options Bin**, and include everything from basic snowflakes and arrows to cartoon talk bubbles, animals, flowers, faces and ornaments. (To access more than the default shapes on this pop-up panel, click on the drop-down menu at the top of the option box and select a category or **All Elements Shapes**.)

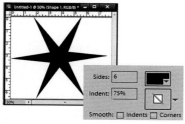 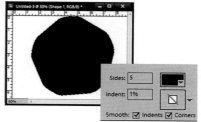 

Using custom settings on the Tool Options panel, the same tool can be used to create many different shapes.

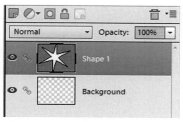

Because shapes are composed of paths rather than pixels, they can be resized and reshaped without concern for their resolution.

When **Add to Shape Area** is selected on the **Tool Options Bin**, you can even combine several shapes to create just about any shape!

Shapes possess some unique characteristics. As you can see, if you look at your **Layers** panel after you've added a shape to your image file, shapes aren't simple raster objects, but are, rather, "masks" with color added to them.

The designers at Adobe have decided to treat shapes this way so that they behave like vector art. In other words, once you've added a shape to your image file, you can resize it and reposition it without any concern for its resolution or pixel depth. You can also re-color a shape just by double-clicking on the shape in the **Layers** panel and then changing its color on the **Color Picker** that pops open.

Some **Shape Tools** have interesting customization settings available in their **Tool Options**. For instance:

The Rectangle Tool, Ellipse Tool and Rounded Rectangle Tool
These tools include options for constraining their shapes to a perfect square or a circle. Additionally, the **Rounded Rectangle Tool** has an option for setting how round its corners are.

The Polygon Tool
The Polygon Tool (illustrated at the top of this page) has options for setting the number of sides on the polygon you will create, how round its corners are and if the sides make it a flat-sided polygon or a starburst-like shape.

The Line Tool
The Line Tool Options panel includes options for setting the line's width and if it includes arrowheads on its start and/or end points.

Typing Tools

Because working with text is a subject unto itself, we've dedicated an entire chapter to it and the **Typing Tools**. For more information, see **Chapter 10, Create and Edit Text**.

The Pencil Tool

As the name implies, this is a freehand line drawing tool. (Unlike the **Paint Brush**, the **Pencil** always draws lines with a hard edge.)

Tool Options for this tool include settings for the size of the pencil and the opacity of the line. The **Auto-Erase** option allows you to toggle the **Pencil Tool** (with a click of the mouse) between working as a drawing tool and working as an erasing tool.

The Pencil Tool draws a hard-edged freehand line.

Modify Tools

Cropping Tools

The **Crop Tool,** the **Cookie Cutter** and the new **Perspective Crop Tool** share the same button in the **Toolbox**. With these tools you can cut or reshape your photos and image files.

To switch between these tools, click the button for whichever tool is displayed in the **Toolbox**, then select the tool you'd like to use in the **Tool Options Bin**.

The Crop Tool resizes your canvas based on your selected area. Once selected, the area can be resized, repositioned or canceled. To finalize your crop, click the green check mark or press Enter on your keyboard.

A dotted line overlay indicates the Rule of Thirds "power alleys" for your photo's composition.

The Crop Tool

The **Crop Tool** is the tool used for cutting both the image and canvas. In other words, this tool changes the canvas size of the actual image file. To use it, click to select the tool, then drag to create a box on your image file.

Crop pre-selections

When the **Crop Tool** is selected, it will automatically offer you four **Suggestions** or "pre-selections" for your crop. These suggestions are based on the program's analysis of your photo's content – in particular, the faces it identifies in the photo.

To preview each crop suggestion, hover your mouse over the thumbnails on the lower right of the **Tool Options** panel, as illustrated to the right.

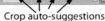
Crop auto-suggestions

You can modify the size and position of a suggested crop by dragging on the corner handles or by dragging directly across the suggested crop. To finalize and crop your photo, click on the green checkmark or press **Enter** on your keyboard.

To turn this feature off so you can freely select your own croppings, go to the program's **Preferences** (under the **Edit** menu on a PC) and, on the **General** page, uncheck the option **Enable Crop Pre-Selection**.

Constrain crop dimensions   Hover over for crop auto-suggestions   Overlay guides   Constrain Resolution

Crop Tool size/shape presets

The size/shape pop-up menu in the **Crop Tool's Tool Options** (illustrated below) gives you options for constraining the area that you've cropped to specific shapes, sizes or resolutions. When you have a preset selected from this drop-down menu or you have manually typed in a set Width, Height and Resolution, the shape of your crop will be constrained. In other words, although it can be resized, it will remain locked to a specific shape. (To allow you to freely set the size and shape of your crop, set the preset menu to **No Restriction**.)

When **Width, Height** and **Resolution** are set, either by selecting a preset or by manually typing in the measurements, cropping will automatically size your finished photo to these exact specs.

A photo composed with its subject on one of the picture's "thirds" (off-centered) is much more interesting and dynamic than one in which the subject is merely centered (above).

MODIFY

Crop Tool composition overlays

In the lower right of the **Tool Options Bin** for the **Crop Tool**, you will find overlay options for the **Crop Tool**:

None

When you've selected the **None** option for your **Crop** overlay, the program will display no overlay on your potential crop.

The Rule of Thirds overlay

When you've selected the **Rule of Thirds** overlay, your potential crop will be overlayed with guides that divide your photo into three vertical and three horizontal panels, as illustrated on page 88.

Unless you're trying for a certain effect, centering a subject in your photo can make for a fairly boring picture. As many photographers and graphic artists know, pictures are much more dynamic if the focus of the photo is slightly off-center, as illustrated above.

Grid overlay

When you've selected the **Grid** option for your Crop overlay, the program will overlay your potential crop with a grid to help you crop an evenly composed photo.

The Cookie Cutter Tool

The **Cookie Cutter Tool** will crop your picture into any of hundreds of custom shapes, from starbursts to butterflies to ragged-edged photos.

(The shaped image will have alpha, or transparency, around it so, if you save your image file as a PSD, the shaped image will appear with no square background when the file is used in Premiere Elements.)

The Cookie Cutter Tool cuts your image into any of over 550 shapes

The Cookie Cutter Tool Options Bin

Once you've selected the tool, select a shape from the **Cookie Cutter** pop-up menu in the **Tool Options Bin** and then drag to draw the shape onto your image file. Once you click on the green checkmark or press **Enter** on your keyboard, your image file will be cut to that shape.

There are many pages of options for shapes, by the way. And you can access them by clicking on the drop-down menu at the top of the panel that appears when you click on the **Tool Options Bin's Cookie Cutter** pop-up menu, as illustrated above.

The Perspective Crop Tool

Relatively new to Photoshop Elements, the **Perspective Crop Tool** not only crops to resize your photo but also includes tools for reshaping the photo in order to correct for any distortion that occurs when a photo is taken at a low, high or side angle.

In other words, if you have a photo of a building taken from an angle that makes the nearer side of the building appear larger than the far, you can use **Perspective Crop** to shape the photo to even these elements out.

The low angle shot makes the house look wider at the bottom. When Perspective Crop is applied, this distortion can be corrected by dragging in the top corners of the Crop overlay.

When the Crop is applied, the photo is reshaped, correcting the distorted shape of the house.

MODIFY

With the Recompose Tool, you can make a photo of people sitting too far apart look much cozier.

The Recompose Tool

The cool and powerful **Recompose Tool** gives you the ability to reshape a photo – re-positioning people or other elements in it nearer together – without distorting these elements in any way.

What's most amazing about this tool is that it does most of what it does automatically (although there are also manual ways to "protect" certain elements in the photo).

When you **Recompose** a photo, you squeeze it, either from top to bottom or from side to side, compressing the elements of the photo so that they become closer together – *but without changing the shapes of any of the key elements in the picture!*

In many cases, when you're using this tool, the **Recompose Tool** will automatically recognize people in your photo and it will protect them as much as possible from distorting as you resize your photo. It will also try to keep certain major elements in the background of the photo – trees or cars – from distorting. It merely makes these key elements look closer together.

In our experience, however, the program can often use a little help identifying which elements in the photo you want to preserve. Fortunately, this is very simple to do.

1   With your photo file open, click to select the **Recompose Tool**. (The tool will launch a help screen that explains how to use the tool. You

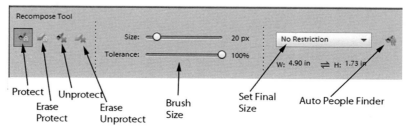

can elect not to see this screen again by checking the box in its lower left corner.)

In **Recompose** mode, you'll see handles on each corner and in the middle of each side of your photo file. Dragging on these corner handles will resize your photo.

2   Drag one side of your photo in to squeeze your photo. In most cases, people and other major elements in the photo will move closer together – though they may very soon begin to distort.

3   To "protect" the elements you don't want to distort, select the green paint brush from the **Recompose Tool Options Bin** and paint over the elements you want to preserve. As with any brush-based tool, you can enlarge or reduce the size of the brush by setting its size on the **Tool Options Bin** or pressing the **[** (open bracket) or **]** (closed bracket) keys on your keyboard.

In my illustration below, I've painted "protection" over the three people and their chairs.

To remove protection from an area, switch to the green eraser tool and drag across a "painted" area.

To designate an object or person as something you *want* to see distorted or removed, paint it with the red "unprotect" brush. To remove this indicator, use the red erase brush.

There is also a green "people finder" tool that can often automatically find and protect the people in your photo. It tends to work best when the photo was shot in ideal lighting conditions.

4   With your designated elements protected, drag the handle on the side of your photo in to compress the photo. As you do, the elements and people you've protected will move closer to each other and yet will not change shape.

With key elements in your photo designated as protected, these elements move closer together, undistorted, as you resize the photo by dragging on its side handle.

(There is, of course, a saturation point at which even protected elements will distort.)

You can also change the dimensions of the photo numerically by typing a width or height in the **Tool Options Bin**.

When you are happy with your new composition, click the green check mark or simply press **Enter**. Photoshop Elements will process and re-render your photo.

Note that, because of the way this tool works, your new photo will be layered. In order to save it as something other than a PSD or layered TIF, you will need to flatten the layers by selecting **Flatten Image** under the program's **Layer** menu.

The Content Aware Move Tool

The **Content Aware Move Tool** expands on concepts put to use in the **Content Aware Fill** aspects of the **Healing Brushes** (see page 76). The **Content Aware Move Tool** fills the area of a moved object with background from the area around it and then blends the moved selection into its new location.

When an object in your photo is selected with the Content Aware Move tool and then dragged to a new location, the program will fill the old space with background and blend the object into its new location.

To use this tool, select the **Content Aware Move Tool** in the **Toolbox** and drag to draw a selection around an object or area in your photo – then drag this selection to another area of your photo.

The program will both fill in the space left behind with "content aware" background and blend your selected object into its new location's background. (The **Extend** option will duplicate your selected object and blend the duplicate naturally into its second location.)

Obviously, this tool works more effectively on some photo compositions, with smaller selections and with less defined backgrounds, than it does others. But, when it does work well, the results are really pretty cool!

The Straighten Tool

I love this tool! It's great for straightening a photo whose subject is a bit crooked.

To use it, just select the tool and then drag to draw a line along an element in your image (a rooftop, a mantle, somebody's shoulders) that you would like to appear perfectly horizontal.

As below, when you release your mouse button, the image will instantly rotate and straighten!

On the **Tool Options** panel for the **Straighten Tool**, you'll find the option to apply **Content Aware Fill** (see page 76) to your straightened photo. **Content Aware Fill** will fill any blank areas around your photo's edges – blank areas created by straightening the photo – with natural background, based on the surrounding imagery.

With the Straighten Tool selected, drag a line to define an object you would like to appear perfectly horizontal. The tool will automatically rotate and straighten your photo accordingly.

Making Selections

Refining Selections

Effects and Selections

Cutting & Pasting Selections

Stroking & Filling Selections

Chapter 6

Select and Isolate Areas in Your Photos
Working with selections

A key function in Photoshop Elements – and one which a number of tools support – is object or area selection.

Selecting means isolating areas of your image file so effects can be applied to those areas only, without affecting the rest of the image, or so those areas can be cut or removed completely.

Selections can have hard edges or soft. They can be changed and refined and even saved.

Selecting and isolating make many of this program's most powerful effects possible.

When an area of your image file is selected (surrounded by a moving dotted line), effects and tools applied will only affect the selected area, leaving the rest of your image unchanged.

Why select and isolate?

There are three main reasons for selecting an area of your image file:

To apply an effect or adjust the color or lighting of one area of your image file without affecting the rest of the image;

To protect areas of your image file so that, for instance, you can paint or erase one area without affecting another area of your image;

To cut an area of your image file – cutting a person from a photo, for instance – so you can either paste him or her into another image file or remove him or her completely.

In **Chapter 5, Get to Know the Photoshop Elements Toolbox**, we discuss a number of tools that can be used to select and isolate areas of your image file.

The Marquee Tools, which include the **Rectangular Marquee** and **Elliptical Marquee Tools,** allow you to select a circular or rectangular area of your image file.

The **Lasso Tools**, which include the **Magnetic Lasso, Polygonal Lasso** and freehand **Lasso Tool**, allow you to draw any shape as a selected area.

The **Magic Wand Tool** automatically selects an area of your image that shares a similar color range, based on the tolerance level you've set.

The **Quick Selection Tool** allows you to select an area by "painting" across it, selecting adjacent pixels of similar color as you paint.

A complicated selection may require several passes with several tools to get it exactly right – using the Add to Selection and Subtract from Selection controls to refine the selected area.

As you select an area, it will appear with a moving, dotted line surrounding it – commonly referred to as "marching ants." As we discuss in the individual descriptions of each tool in **Chapter 5**, the selection tools can be used in combination with each other – while selecting the **Add to Selection** and **Subtract from Selection** options (see page 68) – to create or refine your selection into any shape you'd like.

Feathering

Selection tools usually include an option to "**feather**" your selection. **Feathering** means softening the edges of the selection.

For instance, if you were to use the **Elliptical Marquee Tool** to select an area of your image file, this selection would be, by default, a perfect oval or circle, with a clearly defined, hard edge.

But in a number of situations, you'd like that edge softer.

A "feathered" selection has a softer edge so that, when the selection is removed or an effect is added to it, the distinction between the selected and unselected area of your image is a gradation rather than a solid line.

If you're applying an effect to a selected area in a photograph, for instance, you might like the boundary between the affected area and the non-affected area to be softly defined. This can make the effect seem more natural than a hard, abrupt edge might.

Also, when you're cutting a subject from one photo in order to paste him or her into another, a slight feathering around the edge can help blend the pasted image so it fits more naturally into the new background.

Feathering is measured in pixels. This means that, when working with a low-resolution image, you'll need fewer pixels in your feathering than you will in a higher-resolution image to achieve a similar softened edge effect.

Feathering also plays a role in the **Refine Edge** tool, as discussed on page 101.

The Tool Options for each Selection Tool include settings for adding to or subtracting from your selected areas.

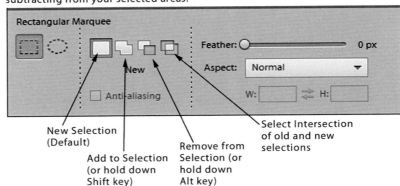

New Selection (Default)

Add to Selection (or hold down Shift key)

Remove from Selection (or hold down Alt key)

Select Intersection of old and new selections

You can add to an already selected area by clicking on the **Add to Selection** button in the **Tool Options Bin,** or by holding down the **Shift** key as you continue to select.

You can remove an area from your selection by clicking the **Subtract from Selection** button in the **Tool Options Bin** or by holding down the **Alt/Option** key as you select.

You can refine your selection so it includes only the area overlapped by your current and new selections by clicking the **Intersect with Selection** button in the **Tool Options Bin.**

As you build your selected area, two other keyboard shortcuts are worth noting:

To go back a step at any point in the program – even deselecting the most recent area you've selected or removed from your selection – press **Ctrl+z** (⌘+z on a Mac) or click the **Undo** button in the upper right of the interface.

To deselect an area completely, press **Ctrl+d** on a PC or ⌘+d on a Mac.

The Select menu

Once you've selected an area of your image file, the Photoshop Elements **Select** menu (illustrated on the facing page) offers a number of options for refining and changing your selected area.

Select All (Ctrl+a on a PC or ⌘+**a** on a Mac) selects your entire displayed image. If you are working on a layered file, you will select only the image that appears on the active layer. (For more information, see **Chapter 9, Work with Layers.**)

Deselect (Ctrl+d or ⌘+**d)** deselects all of your selections.

Reselect (Ctrl+Shift+d or ⌘+**Shift+d)** re-selects all that you've just deselected – in case you suddenly change your mind.

Inverse (Ctrl+Shift+i or ⌘+**Shift+i)** switches your selection so the areas you currently have unselected become your selected areas and vice versa.

All **Layers** and **Selected Layers** expand your current selection to other layers in your image file, if you are working on a layered file.

Grow expands your selected area to similarly colored adjacent pixels in your image file, based on your current selection.

Similar selects all similarly colored pixels throughout your image file, whether they are adjacent to your current selection or not.

Feather (Ctrl+Alt+d or ⌘+Option+d) allows you to apply feathering to soften the edge, after the fact, of your currently selected area.

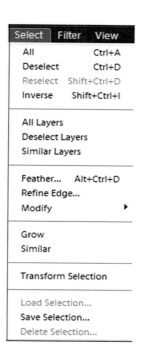

Refine the edge of your selection

Once you've selected an area in your image file, you can refine the edge of the selection by using the **Refine Edge** tool, accessed under the **Select** menu or by clicking the **Refine Edge** button in the **Tool Options Bin**. Adobe has made some great improvements to this tool, borrowing some amazing features from the professional version of Photoshop.

Edge Detection

The amazing **Edge Detection/Smart Detection** feature in the **Refine Edge** panel can help you find the edges of a selection that includes very fine details, such as fur or strands of hair. (This is truly an amazing feature!)

Note that you'll get the best results if your subject's background is a smooth color and is distinct in color from the hair, fur or detailed edge of your subject.

1   Using the **Magic Wand, Selection Brush** and/or the **Quick Selection Tool**, select your subject as accurately as possible.

2   Open the **Refine Edge** panel by selecting the option under the **Select** menu or clicking the button in the **Tool Options Bin**.

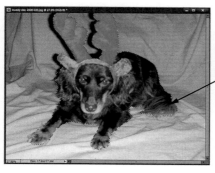

Selecting fine details along the edge of your selection, like fur or strands of hair, can be very challenging.

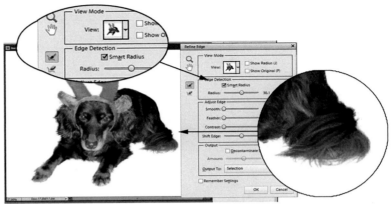

The Smart Radius Edge Detection feature makes selecting even fine details like strands of hair possible!

The **View Mode** pop-up menu at the top of the **Refine Edge** panel allows you to see your selected area in a variety of modes. **On White** is a good mode for this process, since it makes everything outside your selected area appear as white, as seen above.

3 Check the **Smart Detection** box and set **Radius** to about 30 px. (You can adjust it later if you need to.)

4 Select the **Edge Detection Brush** to the left of **Edge Detection/Radius** and drag to "paint" the area of your selection's edge that includes details or stray hair, trying to keep the crosshairs on the brush over the background as much as possible. When you release your mouse, your new selection will be visible, as illustrated above, with some very fine details selected!

You can correct any over-selection with the **Selection Eraser Tool**, below the **Edge Detection Brush**.

Refine Edge Adjustments

Other ways to make adjustments and refine the edge of your selection include:

Radius is how detailed any refinements you make in this panel are. The smaller the radius, the finer the adjustments.

Smooth determines how detailed your selection is. The higher you set **Smooth**, the more the fine details in the edge of your selected area will be rounded out.

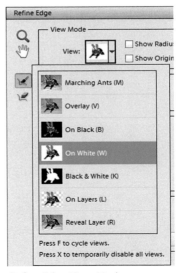

Refine Edge View Modes

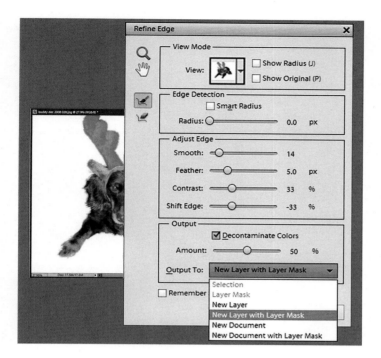

Feather. As discussed on page 95, feathering softens the boundary between your selected and unselected areas, giving a more natural, less abrupt edge to your selection.

Contrast controls how soft or sharp the edge is between your selected and unselected areas.

Shift Edge removes or adds a few extra pixels from around the edge of your selection. This can be helpful if, for instance, you're cutting a person from a background and, in your current selection, some of the background is still showing around the edges. **Shift Edge** and **Feather** are often used in combination to create a very clean, natural edge.

Decontaminate Color replaces any fringe colors that you've selected with colors from surrounding pixels. In other words, if you've selected brown hair and some green background has crept into your selected area, **Decontaminate Color** will tint this green "fringe" brown to match the hair so you don't have any stray color in your selection.

Output gives you options for automatically cutting your selected area into a new layer on your image file, masking your selection on its current layer or copying to a new document.

Checking the **Remember Settings** box will make your current settings your default **Refine Edge** panel settings.

By drawing a selection around the dog, I can isolate him – applying, for instance, color correction to him only, not affecting the background

When I reverse the selection (by selecting Inverse from the Select menu) – my selection becomes everything in the image file *except* the dog. I am now able to apply effects or use brushes – I can even paint a new background with the Clone Tool – affecting everything in the photo *except* the unselected dog!

Use a selection to protect an area

A key reason to select an area of a photo is so that an effect can be applied to the area you've isolated without affecting the rest of your image file.

In the example above, for instance, the dog in the original picture was too yellow for my tastes. However, I preferred that any color corrections I made affect the dog only, and left the rest of the picture as is.

Using a combination of tools – adding to and subtracting from my selection and then refining the edges – I isolated the dog as a selection. I was then able to make color changes to the dog only, without changing the color values of any other part of my image file.

I then inversed the selection (choosing **Inverse** from the **Select** menu) so that the background was selected and the dog was not. Using the **Clone Stamp Tool** (see page 78), I painted in more foliage behind the dog. Because the background was selected and the dog was not, the **Clone Stamp Tool** added these trees and leaves right *around* the dog, as if he were on a whole other layer!

Cut and paste a selection into another photo

As you work with Photoshop Elements, you will likely be doing a lot of cutting and pasting. This is, for instance, a simple way to take a person photographed in front of one background and place him or her in front of another.

Because she was shot against a green screen, the young woman is easily selected by selecting the background with the Magic Wand Tool and then inversing the selection. Once she was selected, I could cut her from one photo and paste her into another.

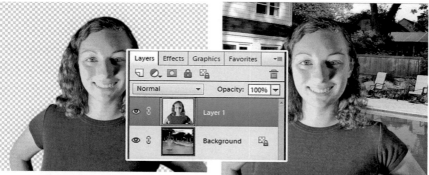

Because pasting places her on a layer, her image can be refined separately – the edges can be softened and she can be tinted to match the background more naturally.

To cut your subject from a background, draw a selection around him or her by using a combinations of tools – adding to and subtracting from your selection as needed. (If your subject is well defined from the background, you may be able to do most of this with the **Magic Wand Tool**, using the other selection tools and the **Add to Selection** or **Subtract from Selection** options.)

Then, to ensure your selection has a slightly softened, natural edge, use **Refine Edge** to **Shift Edge** and **Feather** it. For detailed edges, you can use the **Edge Detection** tool described on page 97.

To cut your subject from his or her current background, press **Ctrl+c** on a PC or ⌘+**c** on a Mac.

To paste your subject into a new file or onto a new background, press **Ctrl+v** on a PC or ⌘+**v** on a Mac.

Whenever you paste an image into another image file, it will appear as a new layer in that file, as seen in the illustration above. (In fact, even if you paste the image into the *same* image file you cut it from, it will become a new layer.)

This is to your advantage for a number of reasons:

1   If you need to, you can continue to refine the edge of your pasted-in image so it fits more naturally with its new background (even using the **Eraser Tool**, if you'd like, to remove more of the image). A very effective feature for adding a more natural edge to your pasted image is the **Defringe Layer** tool, which we discuss on page 119 of **Chapter 8, Correct Color and Lighting**;

2   While it remains a layer, you can resize the pasted-in image separate from the rest of the image file.

Resizing a layer is very easy in Photoshop Elements.

When a layer is selected (by clicking on it to activate it in the **Layers** panel), it appears in your image file outlined by a rectangle, defined on each side and on the corners with a "corner handle." (If your layer image is larger than your current image file, these corner handles may appear outside of the image file, and you may need to **Ctrl+‒** on a PC or **⌘+‒** on a Mac to see these handles.)

To resize the image on your selected layer, click and drag on these corner handles, as illustrated at the bottom of this page.

As you drag the corner handles, you may notice that the **Tool Options Bin** displays a number of **Transform** options. Using these transform options, you can resize or rotate your layer's image precisely by typing numbers into the spaces in the **Tool Options Bin**.

If **Constrain Proportions** is checked, your image will resize its height and width proportionately – which is usually what you'll prefer. If you uncheck **Constrain Proportions**, you will resize the layer's height and width separately, resulting in a squeezed or disproportionate picture.

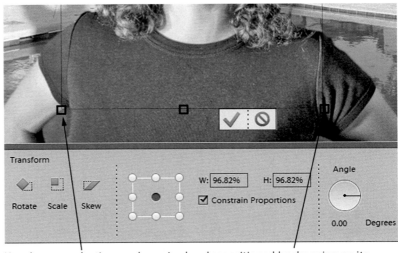

Your layer or selection can be resized and repositioned by dragging on its corner handles or by setting the Transform options in the Tool Options panel.

To finish the resizing, click the green checkmark on your image file or press the **Enter** key.

(While you're in resizing image mode, no other functions in Photoshop Elements will work. So, if you find after resizing your image that no other tool will activate, press **Enter** or click on the green checkmark to complete the resizing.)

If you're enlarging your layer's image by dragging the corner handles, keep in mind the golden rule of raster art: *You can't add details or pixels where they don't exist.*

You can expand the size of your image only so far before the pixels will begin to break up and your image will appear fuzzy or pixelated. For this reason, it's best to cut and paste between image files that are of similar size and resolution.

Your layer will remain a layer until you flatten your layers or save your file as a file format other than a Photoshop (**PSD**) file. (For information on flattening a layered image see page 138 of **Chapter 9, Work with Photoshop Elements Layers**.)

Fill or stroke a selection

Any area that's selected can also be filled or stroked. In fact, even a selected area on an otherwise blank layer can be filled or stroked.

Filling means painting the selected area with color or a pattern.

A selected area can be filled in any one of a number of ways:

1   Drag the **Paint Bucket Tool** onto the selected area. The selection will then be filled with the **Foreground Color**.

2   Select the **Gradient Tool** and drag a line across the selection. The selection will be filled with a gradation of the **Foreground** to **Background Color** (or however you've defined your gradient), colored from the beginning to the end of the line you've drawn.

3   Press **Alt/Option+Backspace**. The selection will be filled with the **Foreground Color**.

4   Press **Ctrl+Backspace** (or ⌘+**Backspace** on a Mac). The selection will be filled with the **Background Color**.

5   Select the **Fill Selection** option from the **Edit** drop-down on the Menu Bar.

The **Fill** option panel offers a number of possible ways for filling your selection, including: with the **Foreground Color, Background Color** or a custom color; black, white or gray; or a **Custom Pattern** from the dozens of patterns available in the pattern library.

The Paint Bucket fills your canvas or your selected area.

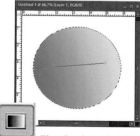

The Gradient Tool fills your canvas or selected area with (by default) a gradation from the Foreground to the Background Colors.

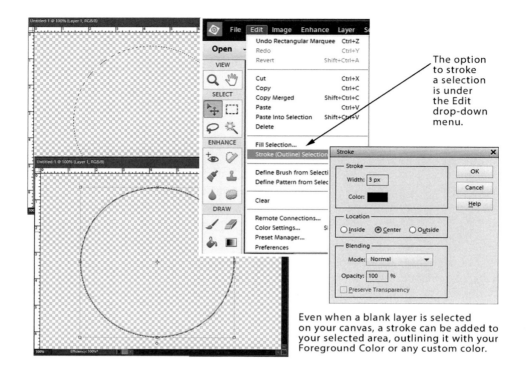

The option to stroke a selection is under the Edit drop-down menu.

Even when a blank layer is selected on your canvas, a stroke can be added to your selected area, outlining it with your Foreground Color or any custom color.

Stroking means outlining a selected area.

A selected area can be stroked by selecting **Stroke (Outline) Selection** from the **Edit** menu.

By default, the stroke color will be the current **Foreground Color**. However, by clicking on the color swatch square on the **Stroke** option panel, you can launch the **Color Picker** (See page 65 of **Chapter 5**), from which you can select any color for your stroke.

The width of the stroke is measured in pixels, by default. And you may set the stroke to appear just outside your selected area (**Outside**), on your selection line (**Center**) or just inside the selection line (**Inside**).

Chapter 7
Resize Your Images
Image and canvas sizes

Resizing can mean a number of different
things in Photoshop Elements.

- You may want to enlarge or reduce the
  overall size of your image file.

- You may want to enlarge or reduce the
  canvas your image appears on.

- You may want to trim the edges off your
  image by cropping.

Each of these functions has methods and
challenges for getting the best results.

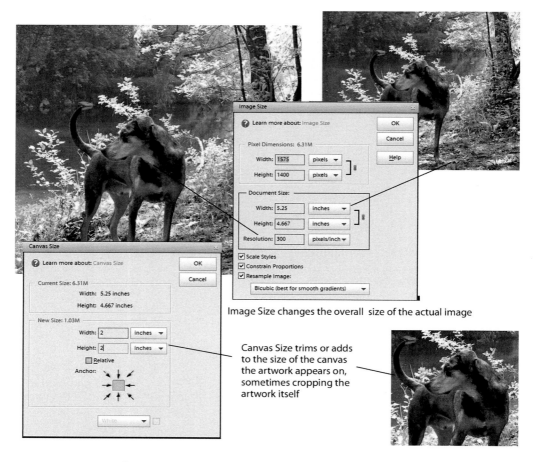

Image Size changes the overall size of the actual image

Canvas Size trims or adds to the size of the canvas the artwork appears on, sometimes cropping the artwork itself

Image Size vs. Canvas Size

As we discussed in **Chapter 1, Things You Need to Know,** there is a key difference between **Image Size** and **Canvas Size**.

Image Size (page 112) is the overall size of your image file. Changing the **Image Size** changes the size of the entire image file without removing or adding to its basic content. In other words, in changing the **Image Size** of your photograph of a city skyline, the content of the picture will remain essentially the same. The entire skyline image will remain. Only the size and/or resolution of the image file will change.

Canvas Size (page 114) refers to the size of the *canvas*, or background, your image appears on. Changing the **Canvas Size** changes the *content* of the image file, either adding to or subtracting from (essentially cropping) the image itself. Reducing the **Canvas Size** of the photograph of the city skyline, for instance, will *chop off* the edges of the image itself without changing the resolution of the image file.

Cropping is a form of changing the **Canvas Size**. When you crop an image, you don't change the size or resolution of the content. You merely trim the canvas. (For more information on cropping, see the **Crop Tool** on page 88 of **Chapter 5, The Photoshop Elements Toolbox**.)

Both **Image Size** and **Canvas Size** are available under the program's **Image** menu, under the **Resize** sub-menu.

You can't create pixels!

This is a principle we repeat several times in this book.

Your image file is made up of pixels – thousands or even millions of little boxes of color. You can't create pixels where none exist. You can't add more resolution to a low-resolution image.

Well, *sometimes* you can. But mostly you can't. And it's usually not a good idea to try.

When you add to the **Image Size** of a file – increasing a 640x480 pixel image to 800x600 pixels, for instance – you're essentially telling the program to create more pixels for that image. Photoshop Elements will do its best to oblige – but it can't work miracles. So what the program does is create new pixels by duplicating existing pixels.

This works to a certain extent. (A rule of thumb is that it will work somewhat effectively for up to about a 10% increase in size.) But, since the result will simply be made of *duplicated* pixels, your image will be larger – but you won't get any more detail.

In fact, if you increase your image's size too much, your image will eventually just look fuzzy and pixelated. (Officially, "over-rezzed.")

Remember that those little blocks of color can only get so big before they start to show. And, if you've ever downloaded a photo or a logo from a web site and then tried to enlarge it and print it, you know exactly what I mean. There's no magic way to increase detail where none exists.

However, there may well be times when you need to *cheat* your image resolution just a bit. Force it up in size – maybe 10%. Going from 640x480 to 700x525 pixels, for instance. And when you do, Photoshop Elements allows you to set *how* it creates these new pixels for the best possible results. This process is called **Resample Image**, and we discuss it in **Image Resizing**, on the following page.

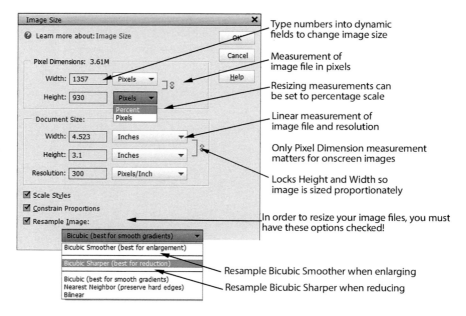

Type numbers into dynamic fields to change image size

Measurement of image file in pixels

Resizing measurements can be set to percentage scale

Linear measurement of image file and resolution

Only Pixel Dimension measurement matters for onscreen images

Locks Height and Width so image is sized proportionately

In order to resize your image files, you must have these options checked!

Resample Bicubic Smoother when enlarging
Resample Bicubic Sharper when reducing

Image Resizing

The option panel for resizing an image is launched by selecting **Image Size** under the program's **Image** menu, on the **Resize** sub-menu.

Resizing an image means increasing or reducing the size or resolution of the image file itself, usually without substantially changing the photographic content of that image.

In other words, resizing a photograph of a scene from 2048x1536 pixels (the size of an image from a 3-megapixel camera) to 640x480 pixels (the size, in square pixels, of a standard definition video frame) reduces the file size, details and resolution of the photo, but it does not change the essential scene in the photograph itself.

The **Image Size** option screen displays the size of your image file in pixels as well as in linear measurements (inches, centimeters, etc.). It also includes a resolution setting, listed in **Pixels per Inch** (or centimeters, etc.). (For more information on picture resolution, see **Resolution** on page 5 of **Chapter 1**.)

The information listed on the **Image Size** option panel includes:

Pixel Dimensions, a measurement of your image file's size, an actual count of the number of pixels (**Width** and **Height**) that make up your image file.

As we discussed in **Chapter 1, Things You Need to Know**, if you're working on photos or graphics for video or for the Web, these **Pixel Dimensions** are the *only* measurements that you really need to be concerned with. Linear measurements, including resolution, are meaningless in the onscreen image world.

Document Size, a linear measurement of your image file in inches, centimeters, points, picas, etc. (the drop-down menu next to each number allows you to change the measurement method), as well as resolution.

If you are producing photos and graphics for print, these three measurements are very important, since stretching, or "over-rezzing," an image beyond its actual size can produce a poor quality or fuzzy picture. All three numbers are important in the print world because, to produce a relatively clean print image, your photo or graphic will need at least 150-200 pixels per inch and 300 or more p.p.i. for a very high-quality print.

Changing the Image Size changes the size of the photo itself without affecting the content.

These measurements are all dynamic fields, and you can change the size of your image by typing new numbers into the boxes. (The **Pixel Dimensions** fields, in fact, can be changed from **pixel** measurements to **percentages** so you can accurately re-scale your image.)

Note that, as indicated in the illustration on the facing page, **in order to change the size or resolution of your photo or image file, you must have the Scale Styles, Constrain Proportions and Resample Image options checked.**

>   **Scale Styles.** This checkbox applies to any styles or effects you've added to your image file. (**Drop Shadows**, for instance.) When this box is checked, the size of the **effect** is changed, proportionately, as your image file is resized.

>   **Constrain Proportions.** When checked, this feature automatically calculates the **Width** to match whatever **Height** you type in (or vice versa) in order to keep your image file proportionate.

>   **Resample Image.** Resampling is a vital function of resizing. Resampling is how Photoshop Elements creates new pixels when you enlarge an image, and how it averages pixel information when you reduce an image's size.

>   If this box is unchecked, with the **Nearest Neighbor** option set, you will not be able to dynamically change your **Pixel Dimensions**.

The **Resample Image** drop-down menu offers a number of options for resampling your image's pixels when you resize a file. Only two are really of value for the vast majority of your work.

>   **Bicubic Sharper.** When you are **reducing** an image file's size, select this resampling method. This creates the cleanest-looking reduced image.

>   **Bicubic Smoother.** When **enlarging** an image file, select this resampling method. As we've said, there are limits to how much you can increase the size of any image file – but the **Bicubic Smoother** will create the smoothest and most natural blends of color among the new pixels it creates.

Photoshop Elements also includes a function for batch-resizing a number of photos or image files at once. For more information on batching processes, see **Process Multiple Files** on page 186 of **Chapter 13, Advanced Photoshop Elements Tools**.

When the Canvas Size is changed, the image file itself will either be cropped or it will have its background area extended.

Canvas Resizing

The option panel for resizing your image's canvas is launched by selecting **Canvas Size** under the **Image** menu, on the **Resize** sub-menu.

The "canvas" is the image file itself, the canvas on which your imagery exists. When you reduce or enlarge the canvas for a photo, you are adding more to the sides or cropping from the size of the image file.

This tool is particularly effective for changing the shape (aspect ratio) of your image file.

The **Canvas Size** option panel displays the dimensions of your image file.

The **New Size** area of this panel contains two dynamic measurement listings, which you can write over. Using the drop-downs, you can set the measurements for these dimensions to any of the standards available in Photoshop Elements. For video, web or other onscreen graphic or photo, you will want to set these measurement standards to **Pixels**.

Though the most common way to resize your canvas is to designate what you want its new **Height** or **Width** to be, you can also simply designate how much you want to be removed instead. Checking the **Relative** option allows you to designate precisely the amount of your canvas that will be added or removed when it is resized. In other words, if you check **Relative** and set the **Width** to -20 (minus 20) pixels, 20 pixels will be cropped from the width of your canvas.

The **Anchor** area of this panel displays a square with arrows that point up, down, right, left and from each corner of the square. This **Anchor** setting represents how and from where your image canvas will be added to or subtracted from when you resize it – as indicated by the directions its arrows point.

Each of these arrows determines which area of your canvas will be affected by the changes to the **Height** or **Width**.

In other words, if you were to set the **Anchor** so that the arrows point down and to the right and then *decrease* the size of your canvas, your image would be resized by cropping from the *top left* of your image file. (Think of it as cropping toward the bottom right).

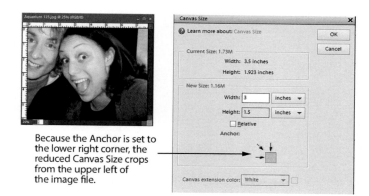

Because the Anchor is set to the lower right corner, the reduced Canvas Size crops from the upper left of the image file.

Likewise, if you were to set the **Anchor** so that the arrows point up and to the right, increasing the size of the canvas would add space *above and to the right* of your current image, as illustrated below.

If no arrow is selected, the tool will crop from or add to your canvas equally, around all sides.

By default, any canvas added to your image file will appear in the **Background Color**. However, the **Canvas Extension Color** drop-down menu at the bottom of this option panel allows you to set the added canvas to appear in the **Foreground Color**, black, white, gray or any other custom color.

Foreground and **Background Colors** are set using the tools described on page 65.

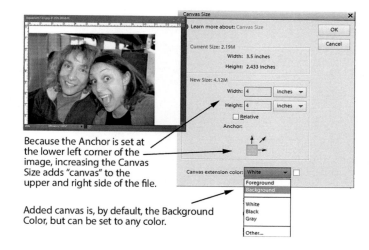

Because the Anchor is set at the lower left corner of the image, increasing the Canvas Size adds "canvas" to the upper and right side of the file.

Added canvas is, by default, the Background Color, but can be set to any color.

Auto Fixing Your Photos

Adjusting Color

Adjusting Brightness & Contrast

Adjusting Facial Features

Adjusting Sharpness

Removing Shake and Haze

Adjustment Layers

Chapter 8

Correct Color and Lighting

Adjust and clean up your images

Under the Enhance drop-down menu, Photoshop Elements includes a number of tools for cleaning up, correcting color and adjusting the lighting of your image files.

Many of these tools are based on advanced tools in the professional version of Photoshop. Others are more simplified "quick fixes."

Whether your goal is to clean up your photos or to change the colors in your image files to produce a special effect, there's likely an adjustment tool for your general or specific need.

Auto Fixes

Under the **Enhance** drop-down on the Menu Bar, there are nine automatic fixes for your image files. In many cases, an automatic fix may be the easiest way to correct your photo's lighting and color.

But remember that automatic fixes are just math, not magic. Automatic fixes merely look at the lightest spot in your image file and assume it should be pure white, then look at the darkest spot in your image file and assume it should be pure black – and then they calculate the rest of the image's color and light values as a range between them.

So, although in many cases, auto fixes can be very effective – they're still just a best guess. And, depending on the results, you may want to move on to manual adjustments from there or even **Ctrl+z** (⌘**+z** on a Mac) to undo the fix and do it entirely manually.

Photoshop Elements includes a number of "auto" fixes under the Enhance menu.

Virtually every auto fix has a manual adjustment alternative.

The nine automatic fixes are:

Auto Smart Fix. A good, general automatic fix, correcting for poor exposure, contrast problems, color balance and color saturation in a single sweep. (There's also an **Adjust Smart Fix** tool a little further down the Enhance menu list which allows you to control the overall intensity of these adjustments.)

Auto Smart Tone. We discuss this cool, relatively new addition to Photoshop Elements' "Auto" set in detail on page 120.

Auto Levels considers the luminance values of red, green and blue in calculating its best color and lighting adjustments.

Auto Contrast considers only the brightness and contrast levels in calculating its best guess settings, without regard to the image file's colors.

Auto Haze Removal automatically enriches the color in your photos to remove the effects of fog and haze. See also the **Haze Removal** tool on page 126.

Auto Color Correction focuses on the mid-tones in the image, correcting the image file's color by presuming the middle range of colors as gray and balancing the other colors based on that. Unlike **Auto Levels**, **Auto Color Correction** does not look at the individual color channels but judges the colors of the image file as an overall mix.

Auto Shake Removal sharpens your photo to remove some of the blur from photos shot with a shaky hand. See also **Shake Reduction** on page 129.

Auto Sharpen increases the contrast between pixels, which can make a photo appear clearer, sharper or more focused. See also the **Unsharp Mask** on page 127.

Auto Red Eye Fix uses its best guess to locate "red eyes" on the people in your photos and then darken and desaturate (un-color) them.

Control what gets changed

When an area of your image file is selected (defined by "marching ants"), any changes made to color or lightness will affect *only* the area within the selection.

The color and lighting adjustments you make to your image files may be applied to the entire file or to isolated areas of your file. You may, for instance, want to brighten or adjust the color of a person in the foreground of a photo but not change the color or lighting settings for the background. Or you may want to make the sky bluer in a picture but keep the grass a rich green.

There are three ways to control how and where your effects are applied to your image files:

1 **Selection**. As we discuss in **Chapter 6, Select and Isolate Areas in Your Photos**, when you select an area in your image file, only that area will be changed by any added effects or adjustments. This is far and away the most common way to control which areas of your image files are affected.

2 **Brush Tools**. As we discuss in **Chapter 5, The Photoshop Elements Toolbox**, the **Smart Brush** tools are designed for applying effects only to certain areas of your image file. With **Smart Brushes**, you "paint" the effect onto only certain, specific areas of your image file.

Additionally, the **Red Eye Removal Tool** darkens and desaturates only the area you brush – removing the bright red reflections from your subject's eyes. And the **Dodge** and **Burn Tools** allow you to lighten or darken specific spots of your image file.

Brushes, as we explained in **Chapter 5,** can be large and wide or very small and fine, and may have hard edges or soft, feathered edges.

3 **Layers**. As we discuss in **Chapter 9, Work With Photoshop Elements Layers**, unless you specifically direct Photoshop Elements to affect several layers at once, any changes you make to an active layer in a layered image file will apply *only* to that layer. As we demonstrate in **Cut and paste a selection** on page 104, this is a very useful function as you work to match a person who has been cut and pasted from another document onto a new background.

Auto Smart Tone

Auto Smart Tone is one of the most advanced of the "Auto" tools in the Photoshop Elements toolkit. This is not only because of its unique interface for adjusting the levels of blacks, whites and midtones in your photos. **Auto Smart Tone** is also a tool which can be set to "learn" from your adjustments.

This means that, as you make adjustments with the **Auto Smart Tone** tool, the tool will essentially record the settings you make and the levels of tone you prefer and, when you next use it to adjust a photo, it will automatically adjust the tool to favor your preferences.

Auto Smart Tone allows you to adjust your photo's tone levels by dragging around a control dot in a very intuitive interface.

Optionally, the tool will remember your usual settings.

The **Auto Smart Tone** tool is very easy to use.

1. Select **Auto Smart Tone** from the program's **Enhance** menu.

   The **Smart Tone** workspace will open.

   A grid with a control dot in the center will appear over your photo. On each of the four corners of the panel will appear thumbnails representing your photo with various levels of blacks, whites and midtones. (Tone is similar to brightness and contrast, but is somewhat more sophisticated, usually based on the range of individual red, green and blue levels in your photo.)

2. Adjust your photo's tone.

   To adjust your photo's tone, simply drag the control dot toward the corner thumbnail that best represents the tone you'd like your photo to have.

   To reset your tone back to center, click the **Reset** button along the bottom right of the workspace. To accept your adjustment click **OK**.

In the lower left of this workspace panel is a little menu icon (as seen in the illustration above). Clicking on this icon will give you the option to set the tool to **Learn From This Correction**.

If you elect for the tool to remember your tone adjustment settings, the next time you apply **Auto Smart Tone**, its default setting will be based on the tone levels you've set in the past.

To erase the "learning" history for this tool, go to the program's **Preferences** (under the **Edit** menu on a PC) and, on the **General** page, click the button labeled **Reset Auto Smart Tone Learning**.

Preview changes

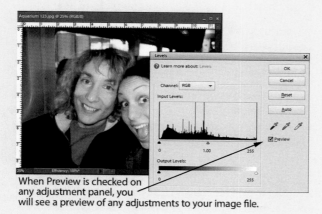

When Preview is checked on any adjustment panel, you will see a preview of any adjustments to your image file.

When you launch an option screen for any adjustment or effect, you may notice a checkbox labeled **Preview** on the screen. **Previewing** allows you to see, in real time, how your adjustments will affect your final image.

When this function is enabled, your image file will temporarily display any changes or adjustments you make.

Additionally, by checking and unchecking the **Preview** option as you make your adjustments, you can do a before-and-after comparison of your changes.

If you click **OK**, these changes will be permanently applied to your image file. If you click **Cancel**, your changes will not be applied.

Adjust Color

As every photographer knows, there's almost no such thing as perfect lighting. Natural sunlight tends toward blue while indoor lighting tends toward yellow, and even the best cameras can have a problem adjusting their white balance for every situation. Fortunately, Photoshop Elements offers a number of tools for adjusting and correcting color.

These tools are available under the **Enhance** menu, on the **Adjust Color** sub-menu.

Remove Color Cast

This tool is a smart fix that bases its color correction calculations on a single point that you define. To use it, click on the eyedropper on the panel and then click on a spot on your image file that you'd like to appear as either pure white, pure black or pure gray. The tool will then automatically adjust all the other colors in the image based on that definition.

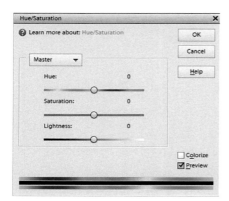

Adjust Hue/Saturation

Hue is the *tint* of a color (essentially the color itself), its level based on the 360 degrees of a color wheel.

Saturation is the *amount* of color. (The opposite of saturation is no color, or black & white.)

Lightness is how *dark or light* the color is.

Adjust Hue/Saturation is probably less effective as a color correction tool than it is as a color *changing* tool. But it does serve as an alternative to adjusting your image's colors based on red, green and blue values.

Remove Color

Remove Color desaturates your image file, leaving it as pure grayscale (black & white). But it's probably not the best way to get a quality grayscale image from a color photo.

A better, more powerful alternative for creating a grayscale image from a color photo is **Convert to Black and White**, discussed on page 126.

Replace Color

Replace Color uses the same color adjustment tools as **Adjust Hue/Saturation**, but it applies these changes to a defined area of your image file only.

To define the area of your photo to be changed, create a **Selection** using the eyedropper in the option panel (as well as the add to/subtract from eyedroppers). Your selected areas will appear as levels of white in the preview window. Once you've defined your selection, the mixture of **Hue, Saturation** and **Lightness** you create in this panel will replace the colors in your selected areas.

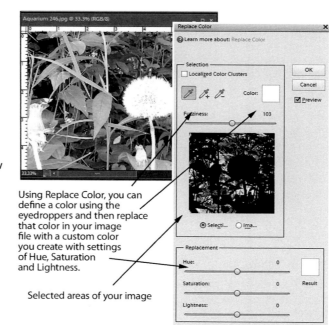

Using Replace Color, you can define a color using the eyedroppers and then replace that color in your image file with a custom color you create with settings of Hue, Saturation and Lightness.

Selected areas of your image

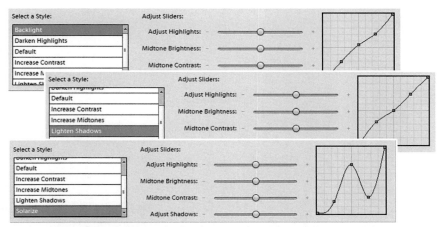

Curves adjusts the color for your image files from five separate levels of brightness. The styles listed under Select a Style offer preset curves for making some general adjustments.

Adjust Color Curves

Adjust Color Curves is a very high-level correction tool that allows you to not only adjust the levels of the darkest and lightest areas in your image file but also, by adjusting the points in the curve or by moving the sliders, adjust the intensity for several color level points in your image, as illustrated above.

The **Select a Style** window allows you to select some color curve presets. Once selected, these settings can be further tweaked by moving the sliders.

Adjust Color for Skin Tone

Skin tones are often the single most challenging element in a photo to color correct. With this tool, you focus on skin tones only, assuming the rest of your photo will follow suit. To use it, click to select a sample of skin tone in your photo, then adjust the **Tan**, **Blush** and color **Temperature** sliders until the skin colors look right.

Defringe Layer

Defringe Layer is designed to work with layered image files. It's particularly effective when you're pasting a person or other subject from one image file into another (which automatically places the pasted image on a new layer, as we demonstrate in **Cut and paste a selection** on page 104 of **Chapter 6, Use a selection to protect an area**). Based on the number of pixels you designate, **Defringe Layer** blends the outline of the pasted layer so that it fits more naturally with its new background.

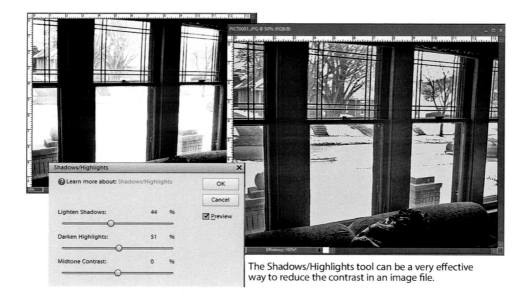

The Shadows/Highlights tool can be a very effective way to reduce the contrast in an image file.

Adjust Lighting

Certainly the most basic adjustments you'll make to your photos will be adjustments made to their brightness and contrast. As with all adjustments you can make in Photoshop Elements, there are simplified and complex tools for making these adjustments. The more complicated the adjustment, the more control you will have over the results.

These functions are located under the program's **Enhance** menu, on the **Adjust Lighting** sub-menu.

Brightness/Contrast

As basic an adjustment as you'll find in Photoshop Elements, **Brightness** lightens or darkens your photo while **Contrast** determines the difference between the blackest blacks and whitest whites in your image file.

Shadows/Highlights

A personal favorite, this great tool has saved many photos for me. Basically, it decreases the contrast in your image file by enhancing the midtones, as illustrated above. This is helpful if, for instance, you have a photo of a bird in flight, which appears as just a dark silhouette against the bright sky. The tool reduces the contrast between bird and sky and brings out details in the bird that would otherwise be indiscernible. It's great for bringing out details in an image shot on a very sunny or snowy day, or any photo with such high contrast that its lights are too light and its darks are too dark.

The Levels histogram displays a count of all of the pixels in your image file, graphed by level. It can be set to display the color mix or only the red, green or blue channel.

Darkest point

Midtone center

Whitest point

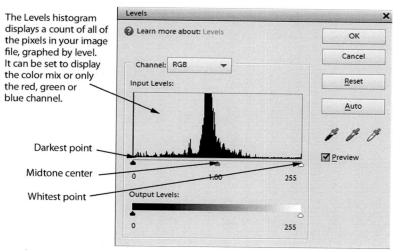

Levels

In my opinion, **Levels** really is more of a *color* adjustment than a lighting adjustment. In fact, it's my favorite go-to tool for color correcting an image file.

The histogram on the **Levels** option screen (illustrated above) maps the pixels in your image from darkest to lightest.

By moving the arrows on either end of the histogram in or out, you define the darkest dark and lightest light points in your image file. The middle arrow defines the center midtone. The **Output Levels** widen the distance between dark and light. In essence this is a more precise way to set your brightness and contrast.

But you can go even deeper in your adjustments on this **Levels** screen. If you drop down the **Channel** menu at the top of the panel, you'll see that you can set these levels for each individual color also. It makes this tool one way to, say, lower the amount of red in a photo or increase the amount of blue.

I show you how to use the **Levels** tool to color correct your photos in the sidebar on page 131.

Quick Fixes and Guided Fixes

Quick Fixes are semi-automatic fixes to color and lighting that Photoshop Elements applies to your image file. These include "red eye" fixes, fixes for enriching the color of the sky or whitening teeth and many simplified and automatic fixes for correcting color and light. We discuss them and how to use them in greater detail in **Chapter 3, Quick Fixes**.

Guided Fixes, as the name implies, are adjustments that are automatically applied to your image file as you work through a list of options. We discuss them and how to use them in greater detail in **Chapter 4, Guided Edits**

Convert to Black and White

As the name implies, this tool desaturates – or removes the color from – your image file, rendering it as grayscale. But, unlike the simplified **Remove Color** tool discussed earlier in this chapter, **Convert to Black and White** includes options for enhancing the grayscale in your image so your final black & white image is as vivid as the original color image.

Under **Select a Style**, you'll find half a dozen presets for improving your image. In most cases, one of these presets alone will give you a strong, vivid grayscale. But if you'd prefer, by adjusting the sliders, you can further tweak the image to give you the strongest possible results.

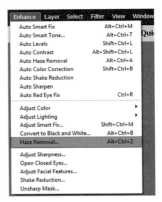

With the proper adjustments (or preset adjustments), a black & white photo can look as vivid as the original color photo.

Haze Removal

The **Haze Removal** tool enriches the color and contrast in your photos to reduce the effects of haze and fog in your photos. (The **Enhance** menu also includes an **Auto Haze Removal** tool, as discussed on page 118.)

The **Haze Removal** tool offers options for controlling the amount of **Haze Reduction** as well as the **Sensitivity** (or tolerance level) to the fog or haze.

Naturally, there's a limit to how much haze or fog this tool can remove before things just get ugly – but, in most situations, it's very effective!

Adjust Sharpness

A somewhat simplified version of the **Unsharp Mask**, **Adjust Sharpness** uses pixel contrast levels to correct for a certain amount of fuzziness in your photos.

It can't make an out-of-focus picture suddenly look crisp and focused, of course. But, when a photo is just a bit soft or blurred, **Adjust Sharpness** can make it appear crisper and clearer.

As with the **Unsharp Mask**, you can only add so much sharpness to an image before it becomes counter-productive. Too much sharpness can make your photo appear grainy and overly-sharp, its individual pixels too highly contrasted. So remember, the goal with either of these tools is sharpness, not crystal clarity.

Unsharp Mask

Traditionally, the last adjustment made to any photo is the application of an **Unsharp Mask.**

Although the results for **Unsharp Mask** and **Adjust Sharpness** are similar, **Unsharp Mask** is usually considered the more "professional" of the two. **Unsharp Mask** increases the contrast in your pixels (dark pixels become darker, light pixels become lighter), the result being a cleaner, sharper image.

As a general rule, **Amount** should not be set to more than 80%, **Radius** is usually set to 1.0 pixels and **Threshold** is set to 0 levels. Although the best settings will vary depending on the needs and resolution of your photo, too much **Unsharp Mask** can result in an overly sharpened, grainy image.

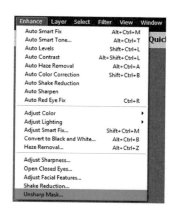

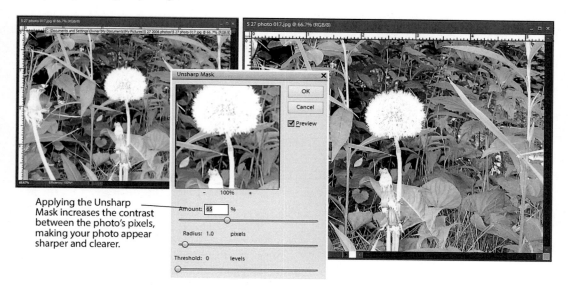

Applying the Unsharp Mask increases the contrast between the photo's pixels, making your photo appear sharper and clearer.

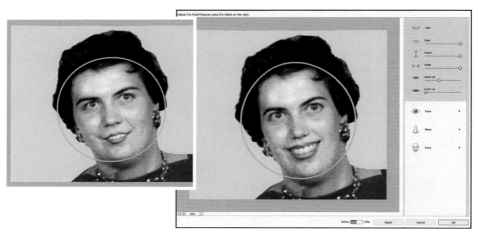

Adjust Facial Features

Relatively new to the program is a very cool tool for working some magic on a less than perfect photograph. **Adjust Facial Features** gives you the ability to add or reduce a smile, narrow or widen a face and even enlarge or reduce the size of someone's eyes! It's actually pretty amazing how effectively it allows you to manipulate someone's looks.

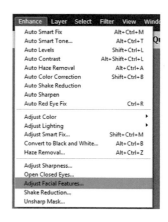

When you select the option under the **Enhance** menu, your photo will open in the **Adjust Facial Features** workspace. The tool will automatically identify the face or faces in your picture. (The program is designed to work exclusively with straight-on headshots. Profile shots and pictures of people not looking directly at the camera won't be identified.) If more than one face has been identified in your picture, click to select the circle around the face you'd like to adjust.

The workspace provides tools for enhancing four features:

> **Lips**, including the size of the smile, the width and height of the mouth and the width and height of the lips.
>
> **Eyes**, including the width, height, size, tilt and distance between.
>
> **Nose**, including the width and height.
>
> **Face**, including the overall width, forehead and chin height and the jawbone shape.

As you can see from the before-and-after image above, this tool gives you the ability to make some pretty drastic changes to a person's looks!

In addition to a tool for adjusting facial features, Photoshop Elements also includes a tool that will **Open Closed Eyes**. For information on this cool tool, see page 74.

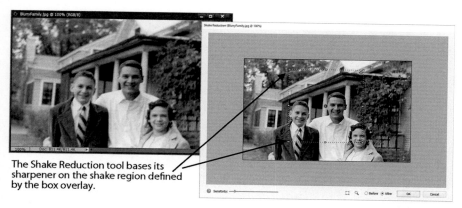

The Shake Reduction tool bases its sharpener on the shake region defined by the box overlay.

Shake Reduction

The **Shake Reduction** tool can take some of the blur out of a photo with a bit too much jiggle.

Basically, the tool is just a variation of the **Unsharp Mask** – though the **Shake Reduction** tool is designed specifically to reduce the blur in a photo shot with a shaky hand.

Work with Adjustment Layers

When working with most adjustment tools in Photoshop Elements, any changes you make to your image file are permanent. The image itself is changed – the pixels are lightened or darkened or colors are shifted. The only way to remove an adjustment is to undo it (by pressing **Ctrl+z** on a PC or ⌘+z on a Mac or by using the **Undo** button or the **Undo History** panel) – and then you're also undoing whatever other work you've done since that adjustment.

However, Photoshop Elements also provides a way to keep these changes separate from the original image file. The effect is the same – your adjustments show as changes in the edited image file. But the changes are not permanent until you save the file as something other than a Photoshop (**PSD**) file or you flatten the image.

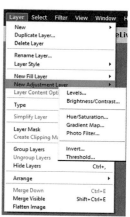

To launch an **Adjustment Layer** for your image file, go to the program's **Layer** menu and select **New Adjustment Layer** and then, from the sub-menu, whatever adjustment (**Levels**, **Brightness/Contrast**, **Hue/Saturation**, etc.) you'd like to make. (An **Adjustment Layer** can also be created by clicking on the **Create Fill or Adjustment Layer** button at the top of the **Layers** panel, as illustrated on page 136.)

As when you make direct adjustments to your image file, your changes will be displayed on your image file if the **Preview** option is checked.

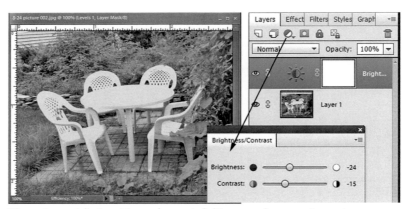

When using an Adjustment Layer, changes to lightness or color appear in your image –
but these changes are actually a separate layer and your original image remains unchanged.

The difference is that, when you **OK** your changes, the changes are not applied
to the original image. Rather, your adjustments show up as a separate layer – an
Adjustment Layer – in the **Layers** panel.

There are a number of advantages to using **Adjustment Layers** rather than changing
the actual image file:

1   **Your changes do not affect the original file.** Remember, once you change
    your native file and save it, there's no going back. Once you've closed and
    re-opened your image file, you can't even undo your changes. When you use
    Adjustment Layers, your original, native file remains in its original, unadjusted
    form.

2   **Adjustment Layers can be turned off and on.** As illustrated at the top of the
    following page, by clicking on the eyeball icon to the left of each layer in the
    Layers panel, you can turn that layer on or off. This is also true of **Adjustment
    Layers**. By turning your **Adjustment Layers** off and on, you can do a before-
    and-after comparison of your adjustments.

3   **You can create several alternative versions.** There's no limit to the number of
    Adjustment Layers you can add to an image file and, by turning these layers
    off and on, you can try to compare several different adjustments (**Levels** vs.
    Brightness/Contrast for instance) to see which gives you the best results.

4   **Adjustment Layers can be re-adjusted.** By double-clicking on the adjustment
    icon on any **Adjustment Layer** on the **Layers** panel, you can re-launch your
    adjustment screen for that layer, allowing you to further tweak your settings.

When none of your changes are permanent, you're freer to experiment, to try
a variety of changes and even make a few easily-undoable mistakes. And, with
Adjustments Layers, you're also able to compare your options.

Whenever possible – particularly if you're creating proofs for a client – I recommend
using **Adjustment Layers** to create your variations. The ability to turn any changes
off or on, or remove them completely, helps prevent you from making changes to the
original photo file that are impossible to undo.

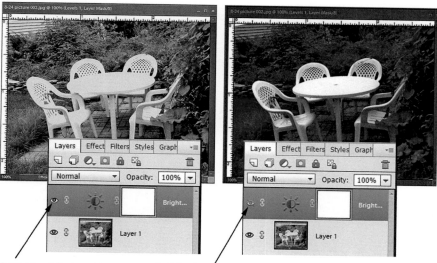

By turning Adjustment Layers on and off (by clicking the eyeball icon), you can do a before-and-after comparision for your adjustments or even compare several adjustments on several Adjustment Layers!

Use Levels to color correct a photo

Here's a professional trick that I often use to correct color in a photo using this **Levels** panel.

The three eyedroppers to the right of the histogram can be used to define the black, white and midtone points in your image file.

To correct the colors in a photo, click on the first (**Black Point**) eyedropper, then use that eyedropper to click, or "sample," the blackest spot in your photo (as illustrated below).

Then click on the third eyedropper (**White Point**) and sample the whitest spot in your photo.

If you want to further correct color, you can use the center eyedropper (**Gray Point**) to define a spot on your image file you'd like to appear as central gray.

By defining the blackest and whitest areas of your photo, you can usually neutralize any color hues and set a clear contrast level.

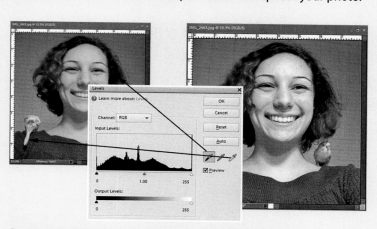

By using the eyedroppers to define the areas of your image you'd like to appear as pure white and pure black, you can very effectively color correct your photo.

The Layers Panel

Simplifying Vector Layers

The Layer Mask

Copying Layers from One File Another

Creating Non-Square Graphics

Chapter 9

Work With Photoshop Elements Layers

Stacks of images

If you're new to Photoshop Elements, layers may seem a bit intimidating – and maybe even a bit superfluous. But, as you work with them, you'll begin to see how powerful a feature they truly are.

It's not uncommon for an advanced Photoshop user to have a dozen or more layers stacked up in his or her image file at once.

Layers also play an important role in the creation and editing of DVD and BluRay templates for Premiere Elements.

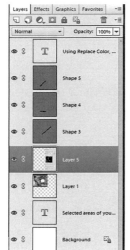
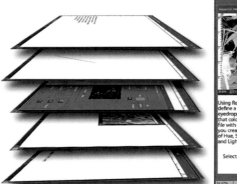
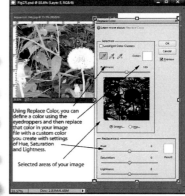

Layers are like a stack of images, with shapes and text on upper layers revealing lower layers through transparent areas.

How layers work

The simplest way to understand how layers work is to imagine them as a stack. The top layer in the stack is completely visible. And, if the top layer is text or does not cover the entire canvas or if there are transparent areas in it, the layers below show around or through it.

One advantage of having elements of your image file on separate layers rather than merged into a single layer is that each layer remains editable, separate from the rest of the image file.

Some other functions of layers include:

- As discussed in **Cut and paste a selection** on page 104 of **Chapter 6, Select and Isolate Areas in Your Photos**, when you cut and paste elements from one image file to another (or even cut from and paste into the same image file) the pasted elements will appear as a new layer. This function allows you to further manipulate and adjust the pasted layer so it better blends with the background.

- When you add text to an image file (as we discuss in **Chapter 10, Create and Edit Text**) it will appear as a separate layer. The text on this layer remains editable until the layer is simplified or flattened.

- When you create a shape for your image file, it also appears as its own layer (as we discuss on page 86 of **Chapter 5, Get to Know the Photoshop Elements Toolbox**). Like text, shapes remain editable until you simplify or flatten the layer. (See **Simplify or Flatten a Layer** on page 138.)

- As we discuss on page 129 of **Chapter 8, Correct Color and Lighting**, an **Adjustment Layer** allows you to make adjustments to the lighting and color of your image file without actually changing your image file. (The adjustments appear as a separate layer.)

The **Smart Brush Tool** (discussed on page 77 of **Chapter 5, Get to Know the Photoshop Elements Toolbox**) works similarly. The **Smart Brush Tool's** color and lighting adjustments remain separate from the image itself. These adjustments can then be further tweaked – or even removed altogether – without making any permanent changes to your original image file or photo.

Layers can also be grouped into **Layer Groups,** sometimes called **Layer Sets,** in the **Layers** panel. As we discuss on page 137, a **Layer Group** can be disabled or enabled as a group, allowing you to store several versions of your Photoshop Elements project in the same PSD file.

Additionally, there are a couple of other functions of layers worth mentioning.

You can duplicate your layers, making several versions of the same layer, each with unique effects or adjustments applied to it. In this way, you can create several versions of your image, comparing them to each other by simply turning the layers on and off.

The easiest way to duplicate a layer is to drag the layer, in the **Layers** panel, up onto the **Make New Layer** icon at the top left of the panel (as illustrated on the following page).

Layers are the key to creating non-square graphics! Non-square graphics include logos, shapes and text-only graphics files.

By removing the background, using layers and saving your files to the proper format, you can create and export graphics in any shape you want, without the constraints of that pesky rectangular background (as we'll demonstrate in **Create non-square graphics** on page 141).

Select a layer to edit

To select the layer you want to work on, click on it in the **Layers** panel. The selected layer will then be highlighted.

In Photoshop Elements, you can also select a layer simply by clicking on the graphic or text in your image file in the **Editor** workspace. (The layer that the graphic is on will automatically be selected in the **Layers** panel.)

This makes repositioning the layered elements in your image file fairly intuitive.

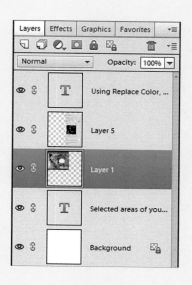

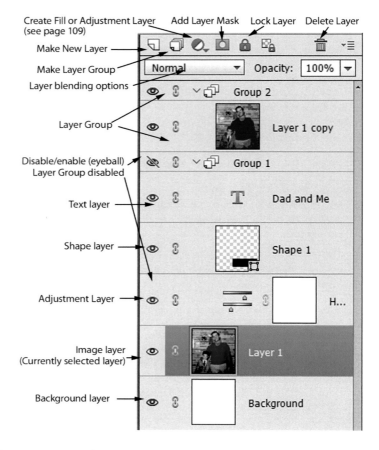

Create Fill or Adjustment Layer (see page 109)
Add Layer Mask
Lock Layer
Delete Layer
Make New Layer
Make Layer Group
Layer blending options
Layer Group
Disable/enable (eyeball)
Layer Group disabled
Text layer
Shape layer
Adjustment Layer
Image layer (Currently selected layer)
Background layer

The Layers panel

The layers of your image file will appear stacked in the **Layers** panel. Your image file will usually include, at the bottom of this stack, a **Background** layer (unless you've manually removed it).

With the exception of Photoshop (PSD) files (and some rare TIFs), graphic formats (JPEGs, GIFs, PNGs) are flat. When you open them in Photoshop Elements, the only layer that will appear in the **Layers** panel will be a **Background** layer. (This layer is locked by default, indicated by a padlock icon on it. However, it can be unlocked and turned into a layer simply by double-clicking on it.)

As can be seen in the illustration above, the **Layers** panel includes a number of tools for working with and managing your layers:

New layers can be created by clicking on the **Make New Layer** or **Create Fill or Adjustment Layer** buttons at the top left of the panel, as illustrated above. As mentioned earlier, some functions – such as cutting and pasting, creating shapes and adding text – automatically create new layers.

Layers can be re-ordered or re-stacked simply by dragging them around in the panel. For instance, if you'd like a shape on one layer to appear *over* rather than *under* the image in another, you can just drag it above the other in the stack on the **Layers** panel.

Layers can be deleted – singularly or several at once – by selecting them (or **Shift-clicking** to select several) and pressing the **Delete** or **Backspace** key on your keyboard or clicking on the trash can icon.

Layers can be linked. When you select two or more layers at once (by **Ctrl-clicking or ⌘-clicking** or **Shift-clicking** to select more than one), any transformation or positioning changes applied to one will apply to *all selected layers*. You can "permanently" link two or more layers by selecting them and then selecting the **Link Layers** option from the pop-up menu in the upper right corner of the panel.

Layers can be locked. Locking a layer (clicking on the padlock button at the top of the panel) prevents that layer from being edited or moved.

Layers can also be temporarily disabled (made invisible) by clicking on the eyeball icon to the left of each layer. When the eyeball icon is toggled off, your layer will be invisible. Clicking on the eyeball icon again will re-enable the layer.

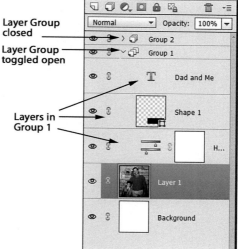

Layer Group closed

Layer Group toggled open

Layers in Group 1

Layer Groups, also known as **Layer Sets,** are essentially folders on the **Layers** panel that can contain groups of layers. Like layers, **Layer Groups** can be enabled or disabled (affecting all of the layers in the **Group**) or dragged to a new order on the panel either as a group or as individual layers.

On the **Layers** panel, **Layer Groups** can be displayed opened or closed, as illustrated to the right. When a **Layer Group** is toggled open, the layers inside it will be displayed slightly indented, as in the illustration.

Layer Groups also play a role in Premiere Elements **Movie Menu** templates, as discussed in **Create Premiere Elements Movie Menu Templates** on page 187.

Additionally, **Blending** options are available through the drop-down menu that appears at the top left of the panel, as illustrated on the facing page. By default it reads **Normal** – and it is not available for use with the **Background** layer.

Blending affects how a selected layer reacts with the layers below it. It's a pretty high-level tool, but it can also create some pretty interesting effects. When the **Overlay** blend option is selected, for instance, you can paint on one layer and it will "colorize" the image on the layer below it!

More advanced uses for this feature are beyond the scope of this book, but are worth experimenting with.

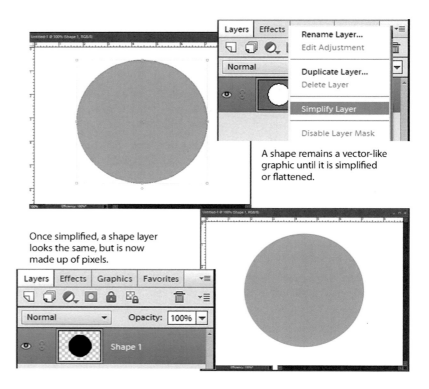

A shape remains a vector-like graphic until it is simplified or flattened.

Once simplified, a shape layer looks the same, but is now made up of pixels.

Simplify or Flatten a Layer

For the most part, the image layers you'll be working on in Photoshop Elements will be raster art. They'll be made up of pixels and, on some layers, may include transparent areas.

Two types of layers, however, are more vector than pixel-based, and include some unique abilities and liabilities.

> **Shape Layers** (as discussed on page 86 of **Chapter 5, Get to Know the Photoshop Elements Toolbox**) are in reality shapes created using something called "masks." (See page 140.) In other words, although a shape may look like a circle, it is actually a colored layer with all the area *except* the circle masked – or made transparent. (You can see this if you look at their representation in the **Layers** panel, as in the illustration above.) This gives shapes some unique characteristics – namely that you can manipulate them like vector art, resizing and reshaping them without regard for resolution.

> **Text**, likewise, is not rasterized, or pixel-based, art. It is a font, which behaves like vector art. In fact, if you click on a block of text with the **Selection Tool**, you can even resize the text block by dragging on its corner handles, just as if it were a shape! Text also remains editable as long as it remains a separate text layer.

These two types of Photoshop Elements objects float as layers over your other layers until one of two things happens:

The layer is simplified. To simplify a text or shape layer, **right-click** on it in the **Layers** panel and select the **Simplify Layer** option, as illustrated on the facing page. Although the shape or text may not appear different, it has now become raster art. It is now made up of pixels and can no longer be edited as vector art.

The file is flattened or layers are merged. You can flatten all of the layers in your image file onto your background, or you can just merge two layers together. The result is the same: The separate layers become one single collection of pixels.

Layers can be merged onto one another or flattened completely.

To merge one layer onto the layer below it, **right-click** on the layer in the **Layers** panel and select **Merge Down** (or press **Ctrl+e** on a PC or ⌘**+e** on a Mac).

To flatten all of the layers in your image file, **right-click** on the **Layers** panel or select from the program's **Layers** menu the option to **Flatten Image**. All of your layers will flatten into a single, rasterized **Background** layer.

Although TIFs can also be forced to maintain layers, only PSDs maintain all of your layers in an editable format. All other formats are flat. That's why, as you work on an image file, it's best to maintain a native, working PSD of your work file in addition to the JPEGs, TIFs or whatever else you are using for your output.

Although other file formats don't maintain layers, certain graphics formats can save transparency information in the form of something called an "alpha channel." That's an important function we'll explain in **Create non-square graphics**, on page 137.

Copy layers from one image file to another

Layers and **Layer Groups** can be easily copied from one image file to another.

Although you could certainly use **Copy and Paste** to move elements from one image file to another, you can more easily copy layers, layer sets, shapes and text by simply *dragging* the layers from the **Layers** panel of one image file onto another open image file.

By **Shift-clicking** to select several layers or groups at once, you can drag all of them from one image file to another at once!

This function becomes very useful when you **Create Premiere Elements Movie Menu templates in Photoshop Elements,** as discussed on page 187 of **Chapter 13, Advanced Photoshop Elements Tools.**

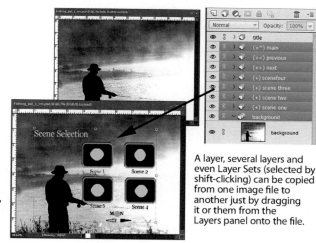

A layer, several layers and even Layer Sets (selected by shift-clicking) can be copied from one image file to another just by dragging it or them from the Layers panel onto the file.

Add transparency with Layer Masks

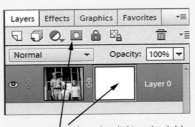

A high-level feature in Photoshop Elements is the ability to add **Layer Masks** to your image file layers – a feature previously available only in the professional version of the software.

Layer Masks create transparent and semi-transparent areas in your image layers. But, because they do so by *masking* rather than actually removing pixels, they don't actually change or remove any image data from the image itself. The areas are merely hidden or *masked*.

Add a mask to a layer by clicking the Add Layer Mask button. The Layer Mask appears as a white box, linked to the side of the layer in the palette.

1 To create a **Layer Mask**, select a layer in one of your graphics files.

   (If you are working with a flat graphic or photo, you can make the **Background** a layer by **double-clicking** on it in the **Layers** panel.

2 Click the **Add Layer Mask** button at the top of the **Layers** panel.

   A white box will be added to your selected image's layer, as seen above.

   This white box is that layer's **Layer Mask**.

   When you paint black on a **Layer Mask**, the corresponding area on the layer will be masked (made transparent). Shades of gray are read as levels of transparency.

3 Click to select this white box on the **Layers** panel, then select a brush from the Photoshop Elements **Toolbox**. Set the **Foreground Color** to black (by pressing **D** on your keyboard) and paint across your image in the **Editor** workspace. (You are actually painting on the **Layer Mask**.)

The areas of the **Layer Mask** that you paint black will mask, or make transparent, the corresponding areas of that layer's image. If you are using a soft-edged brush, the feathered edges of your brush strokes will appear semi-opaque.

In my example, I took a 640x480 pixel photo and, using a 104 px, rough-edged brush from the **Thick Heavy** brush collection, I painted a ragged black frame around the sides of my **Layer Mask**. The result, as you can see, is a photo with a ragged, grungy edge. However, this ragged edge is only a mask. The actual image has not been changed in any way. And, since this is only a mask, it can be easily revised or even removed completely without affecting the original photo.

Create non-square graphics

Most commonly-used graphics formats (JPEGs and TIFs, for instance) are rectangular. They are a certain number of pixels wide and a certain number of pixels tall, and they have four sides and four corners.

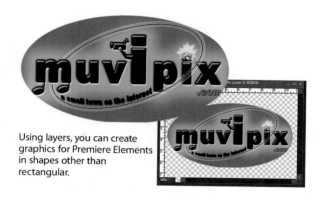

However, your graphics (logos, titles, etc.) are often not. And when you have a non-square graphic, you'll want to bring it into Premiere Elements in the shape of the graphic itself. Not square, not rectangular. And with any blank area around it – and even some blank areas through it – transparent.

Using layers, you can create graphics for Premiere Elements in shapes other than rectangular.

This is accomplished by utilizing something called an **alpha channel**.

Because of the way graphic files carry their visual data, transparency has to be communicated from program to program with a separate channel of visual information – the same way that the colors red, green and blue are communicated as individual channels. Transparency, then, is essentially a fourth color – commonly referred to as "alpha." Only a few graphics formats have the ability to carry transparency as an alpha channel.

Use graphics that include alpha channels

Not all graphics formats can carry alpha data. JPEGs and BMP files cannot. TIFs and PDFs can, but they aren't typically used for partially transparent graphics. There are five commonly-used graphic formats that can include transparency, and all five will work in Premiere Elements. They are:

Graphic formats that include alpha channel information are transparent around the layered graphic or text.

PSDs. This is the native Photoshop and Photoshop Elements format. It's far and away the most common way to deliver a non-square graphic to Premiere Elements. This is because, not only do PSDs communicate alpha information between the programs, but the original files also remain easily re-editable (even the text) in Photoshop Elements.

GIFs and PNGs. GIFs (pronounced "jiffs", according to their inventors) are the graphics you see all over the Internet. They're the ones that include animation (like those annoying, flashing Web banner ads). PNGs (pronounced "pings") were designed to replace GIFs, and they do display color much better. Outputting either of them with their alpha channels intact involves a similar process, which we demonstrate later in this chapter.

EPSs and AIs. These are vector-based file formats created by programs like Adobe Illustrator. Though they technically don't carry alpha as a separate color channel, vector art is created by connecting corner points rather than assembling pixels. Because of this, they have no background layers and therefore often include transparent areas.

Create a backgroundless graphic in Photoshop Elements

To create a partially transparent graphic in Photoshop Elements, you need to remove the background layer from the **Layers** panel.

When you first open a PSD or other graphics or photo file in Photoshop Elements, it will likely consist of one layer, labeled "**Background**" on the **Layers** panel. Even if the file does include layers, there may be a **Background** layer at the bottom of the layers stack.

Double-click on the **Background** layer in the **Layers** panel. The **Background** layer will become a layer.

Layered files behave very differently once they have no **Background**. Layers with no background have transparency behind them.

For instance, if you erase or cut an area on a **Background** layer, that area will be replaced by your **Background Color.** However, if you erase or cut an area from a layer, you will cut *through* the layer. What you remove will become transparent!

If you have converted your **Background** into a layer by double-clicking on it, you can remove areas of it by using the **Eraser Tool** or by selecting non-essential areas of the graphic (selecting the white around your logo, for instance, using the **Magic Wand** or the **Quick Selection Tool**) and pressing your **Delete** key.

That light gray checkerboard you see around your graphic (illustrated below) represents alpha. That means there is nothing there. No background. No canvas. Just transparency.

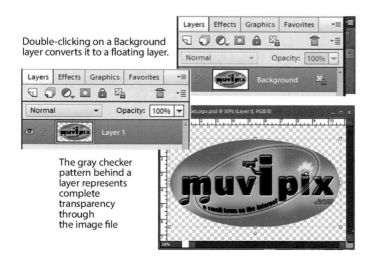

Double-clicking on a Background layer converts it to a floating layer.

The gray checker pattern behind a layer represents complete transparency through the image file

If you'd like to start with a clean slate, you can even remove everything on the layer (press **Ctrl+a** on a PC or ⌘+a on a Mac to select all and then press the **Delete** key).

Once you've removed the background, whatever you draw, write or place on a layer – a graphic, a shape, text, a photo of a person with the background cut from behind him – if it does not cover your entire canvas, there will be transparency around it.

And, if you were to save this file without flattening it in a format that supports alpha (ideally a **PSD**), that unused area would remain transparent when you imported the file into another Adobe program – such as Premiere Elements.

If you place a graphics file containing transparency on the upper track of a Premiere Elements video project, those transparent areas will also be transparent over your video. Only the graphic itself will show – your video on a lower track will be visible behind and around it.

File formats that support alpha

Although **PSDs** are the ideal (and easiest) format for sending non-square graphics to a Premiere Elements project, there are two other file formats you can export from Photoshop Elements that will include alpha. These are the formats you will use if you are creating non-square graphics for the Web or for a non-Adobe program that doesn't support PSD files.

GIFs were invented by Compuserve (remember them?) in the early days of the Internet, and they remain, along with JPEGs, one of the most common file formats used on the web.

But GIFs don't handle color very efficiently. **PNGs** were invented to unite the color qualities of a JPEG with the alpha channel abilities of a GIF.

To export a graphic as a GIF or PNG and maintain transparency around the graphic, go to the Photoshop Elements **File** menu and select **Save for Web**. This will open a workspace for resizing, compressing and optimizing your graphics for export as a JPEG, GIF or PNG (as in the illustration on the right).

Select **GIF** or **PNG-24** from the **Preset** drop-down menu.

Once you've done that, a checkbox will appear offering the option of **Transparency**.

Check this option and your graphic will be exported as a flat graphic, but with the same transparency as your original **PSD** file.

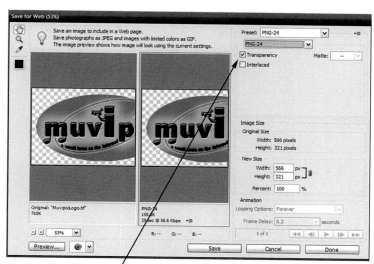

The option to preserve transparency on the Save for Web screen.

The Type Tools

Type Tools Options

Re-Editing Text

Shaping and Distorting Text

Typing on a Path, Selection or Shape

Chapter 10

Create and Edit Text

Typing, sizing, coloring and shaping

The text tools in Photoshop Elements run surprisingly deep.

Not only does the program allow you to work with such basic text attributes as font, style and color, but it also includes a variety of tools for shaping and warping text.

Text sizes and shapes can be edited using the text editor, or a block of text can be sized and shaped as if it were an object – all while remaining editable type.

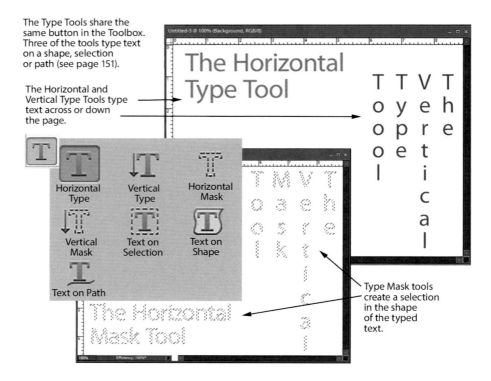

The Type Tools share the same button in the Toolbox. Three of the tools type text on a shape, selection or path (see page 151).

The Horizontal and Vertical Type Tools type text across or down the page.

Horizontal Type

Vertical Type

Horizontal Mask

Vertical Mask

Text on Selection

Text on Shape

Text on Path

Type Mask tools create a selection in the shape of the typed text.

The Type Tools

The seven **Type Tools** are accessed by clicking the **"T"** button in the **Toolbox** along the left side of the **Editor** workspace, and then selecting the specific **Type Tool** from the **Tool Options Bin**.

Two of these tools add text to your image file as you type.

> **The Horizontal Type Tool**, as the name implies, types your text from left to right, by default in the **Foreground Color** (see page 65).

> **The Vertical Type Tool** types your text from top to bottom, by default in the **Foreground Color**. When you press **Enter** as you type, a new column of text is created *to the left* of the first.

 Horizontal text on your image file can be turned into vertical text, and vice versa, by selecting the text and then clicking the **Change the Text Orientation** button in the **Tool Options Bin**.

Two other **Type Tools** create a "mask" or selection in the shape of the text typed.

> **The Horizontal Type Mask Tool** creates a text-shaped selection mask from left to right as you type.

> **The Vertical Type Mask Tool** creates a text-shaped selection mask from top to bottom as you type.

Though called **Masks**, these type tools actually create **selections**. (**Layer Masks,** discussed on page 140, are very different and have a very different function in the program.)

As you type with a **Type Mask Tool**, your image file will be temporarily covered by a semi-opaque, red mask. Your text will appear to be cut out of this mask. When you click off of your text or select another tool, your typed text area will become a **selection** (surrounded by "marching ants"). (For more information on making and working with selections, see **Chapter 6, Select and Isolate Areas in Your Photos**.)

The selection created by your **Type Mask Tools** can be manipulated in a number of ways:

- A **selection can be deleted** by pressing the **Delete** key, removing the area you've selected from the layer you've selected it on. Or you can select **Inverse** from the program's **Select** menu and, by pressing the **Delete** key, remove all *except* the text-shaped area.

- A **selection can be cut and pasted** into another image file or onto a new layer in the current file.

- If you switch to the **Move Tool, your selection can be resized or reshaped** by dragging its corner handles.

- A **selection can be colored** using **Stroke** or **Fill**.

- A **selection's lighting and color can be adjusted**, and your adjustments will affect only the selected area.

For the most part, **selections** made using the **Type Mask Tools** are no different than any other **selections** – except that their shape is defined by the shape of the text you type.

Re-edit a text layer

Your text will remain editable as long as it remains a separate text layer in a PSD file. You'll easily recognize a text layer in the **Layers** panel because the layer will appear as a big, gray "**T**", followed by the layer's name (which, by default, will be the text you typed).

Double-clicking the "T" on a text layer makes the text re-editable.

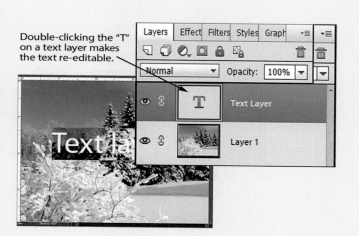

To re-edit a text layer, double-click on the big, gray "**T**" representing the layer on the **Layers** panel. The text layer will be activated and the **Type Tool** will automatically be selected.

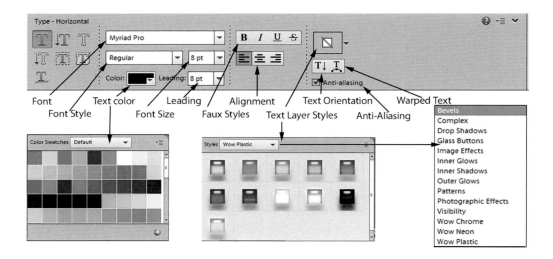

The Type Tool Options Bin

All of the **Type Tools**, whether text tools or mask tools, use a similar **Tool Options Bin**, which runs along the bottom of the **Editor** workspace.

The **Type Tool Options** are primarily used for setting basic fonts, text styles, colors and sizes.

In most cases, the default settings for the **Type Tools** options will be the *last settings you used*. In other words, if you used 8 pt. Myriad Pro Regular the last time you added text to your image file, the next time you select a **Type Tool**, it will be set to 8 pt. Myriad Pro Regular.

Font. The **Font** drop-down menu lists pretty much every font available on your system. These fonts will vary from computer to computer. Windows includes around 20 basic fonts. Other programs you've installed, including Premiere Elements and Photoshop Elements, may have added a few more.

The symbol to the left of each font in its listing indicates if it is a True Type (**TT**) or an Open Type (**O**) font. Without getting into too deep a discussion of font systems, True Type is the most basic font system. Open Type is the more advanced font system, sometimes including dozens of styles and options within the font. (An Open Type font, for instance, may include the option to use *ligatures* to make an adjacent "f" and "i" into one, combined character with no dot over the "i", as in the word "find.")

A quick way to "call up" a font is to type its name into the **Font** box on the **Tool Options Bin** (without opening the drop-down menu). As you type the name of the font, Photoshop Elements will automatically search and load the font for your **Type Tool**.

Font Style. Most fonts include specific text styles such as **Bold** and **Italic**. Because these styles are designed as part of the font itself, setting them in the **Font Style** drop-down menu is preferred to applying the **Faux Styles** to the right.

Font Size. Measured in points, font sizes are relative to the pixel density in your image files. In other words, a 14 point font on a low-resolution image will appear much larger than a 14 point font than on a high-resolution image. In addition to setting font sizes numerically, you can size your text as a block, as described in **Shape and Resize Your Text** on page 150.

Leading is the space between lines of text. In most cases, the **Auto** setting will give you the best results. However, for aesthetic reasons, you can manually set your leading tighter or looser. The numerical settings correspond to the font's size.

Text Color. By default, your text will be the **Foreground Color** (see page 61) that was set when you selected the **Type Tool.** You can manually change the **Text Color** by selecting it from this drop-down menu or by clicking on a swatch displayed in the **Color Swatches** panel (available under the program's **Window** menu).

Faux Styles are ways to add styling (bold, italic, etc.) to fonts. They're called "faux styles" because they aren't part of the font's original design, but rather the program's *simulation* of the style. In other words, faux bold merely thickens the font, faux italic slants it to one side, etc.

Paragraph Alignment aligns your text to the left, right or center. **Paragraph Alignment** is important if you plan to create Premiere Elements Movie Menu templates (see **Chapter 13, Advanced Photoshop Elements Tools**) because it will determine the direction your custom text will flow when you type in the names of your scenes or chapters.

Anti-Aliasing. Aliasing has to do with how sharp the edges of a font are. With **Anti-Aliasing** turned off, text can look unnaturally sharp and jagged. You'll probably want to keep the **Anti-Aliasing** checkbox checked. (For an illustration, see **What is Anti-Aliasing?** on page 75 of **Chapter 5, Get to Know the Photoshop Elements Toolbox.**)

Text Layer Styles. There are dozens of styles which can be applied to your text layer, from bevels to drop-shadows to glows to patterns. Click on the **Text Layer Styles** button, as illustrated on the facing page, to open the option panel. To see the various pages of available styles, click on the pop-up menu at the top of this **Layer Styles** panel.

Warped Text. You can choose a **Warp** style before, after or while you are typing your text. The various warps include arcs, bulges, fish-eyes, waves and twists. And, as you select each, your text will preview the warp for you. Also, once you've selected a warp, you can customize it by adjusting the **Bend, Horizontal Distortion** and **Vertical Distortion** to create pretty much any look you want.

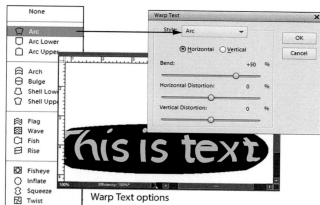

Warp Text options

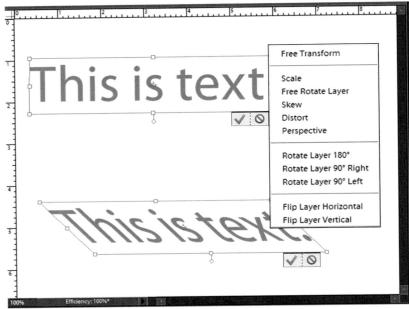

When the Move Tool is selected, text can be resized as if it were vector art by dragging on the corner handles. The right-click (Ctrl-click) option to Skew allows you to angle your text block.

Shape and resize your text

You can resize and reshape a text layer just as you can any other image or shape layer. Because it behaves like vector art, you can enlarge or stretch your text layer without regard to resolution.

 To resize a text layer, select the **Move Tool** in the **Toolbox** and then select the text layer by either clicking directly on it in your image file or clicking in the layer on the **Layers** panel.

Press **Ctrl+t** on a PC or ⌘+t on a Mac to put the Editor into **Transform** mode.

The text block will appear with handles on each corner and on the sides. Drag on these corner handles to resize and reposition your text. As long as the **Constrain Proportions** option is selected in the **Tool Options Bin**, the text block will resize proportionately.

Other reshaping options are available by **right-clicking** on the text block. These options are:

Free Transform (default). This option allows for both resizing and rotating of the text block.

Scale. You have the option of resizing the block, but rotation is locked out.

Free Rotate Layer. You will be able to rotate the block, but scaling is locked out.

Skew. By dragging the corner handles, you will slant the text block, as in the illustration above.

Lock in any changes by clicking the green checkmark or by pressing **Enter**. Cancel any changes by clicking the red cancel icon or pressing **ESC**.

Other transform options

The **Distort** and **Perspective** transform options are grayed-out of the text block's **right-click** menu. These options are only available for raster art, but can be applied to text if the text layer has been simplified (converted to pixels).

To simplify a text or shape layer, **right-click** on the text layer in the **Layers** panel and select the **Simplify Layer** option. (Simplifying text turns it into pixels, so it will no longer be editable.)

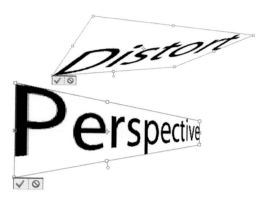

Distort. By dragging the corner handles of your layer, you will be able to shape it into any four-sided shape you'd like.

Perspective. Dragging the corner handles stretches two sides at once – allowing you to stretch and shape your layer so that it appears to have perspective.

For more information on simplifying layers, see **Simplify or Flatten a Layer** on page 134 of **Chapter 9, Work with Photoshop Elements Layers**.

Type on a Selection, Shape or Path

In addition to standard typing tools, Photoshop Elements includes options for typing your text around the outline of a selection or shape or on a path. To select a **Text On** tool, click on the **Type** button on the Premiere Elements **Toolbox** and then select the tool you want from the **Tool Options Bin** below the **Editor** workspace.

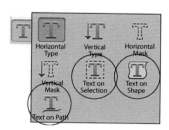

Type Text on a Selection

When **Text on Selection** is selected, your cursor will become a **Quick Selection Tool** (as described on page 67).

1   Drag over your photo to make a **Quick Selection**.

As you drag, the program will select adjacent areas of similar color. When you are satisfied with your selection, click the green checkmark or press **Enter**.

To Type on a Selection, first use the Quick Selection Tool to create a selected area. Click the checkmark to finalize it.

2   Hover your mouse over the selection path until your cursor indicates you are on the type path.

Select your font and text characteristics, then click and type. The text will flow around the outside of the selection, beginning at the point on the selection's outline at which you initially clicked.

Hover your mouse over the path created until your cursor displays as the type icon. Click and type.

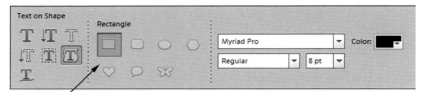

Tool Options for the Text on Shape Tool include a number of shape options as well as options for setting the color, size, font and style of your text.

Type Text on a Shape

You can create a shape to type along by selecting a shape from the **Tool Options Bin** or by using the **Shape Tool** (see page 82). (The shapes in the **Tool Options Bin** will create a type path only and not an actual shape.)

1 Create a shape.

To create a shape using the **Text on Shape Tool**, select one of the shape options in the **Tool Options Bin** (as above), then drag to draw the shape on your photo.

2 Hover your mouse over the outline of the shape until your cursor indicates you are on the type path.

Select your font and text characteristics, then click and type. The text will flow around the outside of the shape, beginning at the point on the selection's outline at which you initially clicked.

When you use the Text on Shape Tool, your type will flow around whatever shape you provide for it.

Type Text on a Custom Path

The **Text on Custom Path Tool** will align text along any path you create.

1 Create a path.

When you select the **Text on Custom Path Tool**, your cursor will become a pencil. Draw the path you would like your text to follow over your photo.

2 Hover your mouse over the path until your cursor indicates you are on the type path.

Select your font and text characteristics, then click and type. The text will flow around the outside of the selection, beginning at the point on the selection's outline at which you initially clicked.

With the Text on Custom Path Tool, your text will follow any path you draw.

Adjustment Filters

The Filter Gallery

The Effects Panel

Effects Filters

Effects Styles

Photo Effects

Chapter 11

Add Photo Effects and Filters
Use Photoshop Elements' special effects

Photoshop Elements includes hundreds of customizable effects and filters that can be applied to your image files.

Filters can add new elements to your image file or they can make your photo look like an artist's sketch or painting.

Effects can be used to add drop shadows and glows around your layers.

Additional effects can make your new photographs look like they were taken a hundred years ago!

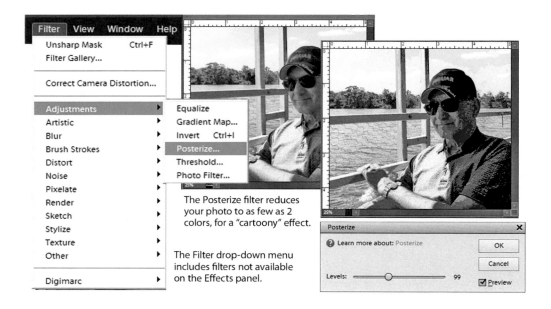

The Posterize filter reduces your photo to as few as 2 colors, for a "cartoony" effect.

The Filter drop-down menu includes filters not available on the Effects panel.

Effects and filters can be used to stylize or create interesting, new looks for your photographs and other image files. You can also just use them to have fun – to make your photo look like a watercolor painting, for instance, or to make a modern photo look like a worn, old snapshot.

Many of Photoshop Elements' filters can be found under the program's **Filter** menu. Except for those listed below, virtually all of these filters can also be found, displayed as intuitive thumbnails, in the **Effects** panel, located by default in the **Panel Bin** to the right of the **Editor** workspace. (If, for some reason, the **Effects** panel has been closed, you can open it by selecting the option under the program's **Window** menu.)

The Filter/Adjustments menu

We'll discuss the bulk of the program's **Filters** in our discussion of the **Filters** panel, beginning on page 159.

But there are six filters under the **Filter** menu that are *not* included in the **Filters** panel set. These are the **Adjustment** filters, and they include:

Equalize. This filter interprets the darkest area of your image file as black and your lightest area as white and then it evenly distributes the levels of colors between. The process often softens the contrast in a photo.

Gradient Map. This filter turns your photo into a grayscale image and then it replaces that grayscale with any set of colors, based on the selections you make by clicking on the pop-up menu (as displayed when you click the grayscale area on the option screen).

Invert. Creates a negative of your image file.

Posterize. This filter reduces the number of colors displayed in your image file, based on your settings.

Threshold. Converts your image file into a high-contrast, black & white image, based on the level you set.

Photo Filter. This filter applies one of 20 **photographic filters** to your image file, as if your camera shot your photo through a tinted lens. It can also be used to "warm" or "cool" the colors in a photograph.

Additionally, the **Filter** menu gives you access to an amazing tool for correcting some distortions caused by certain lenses (or, if you're of the mind to, creating some).

Correct Camera Distortion is a filter which reshapes your photo to compensate for rounding or keystoning – unnatural distortion to a photo which can occur because of the use of a wide-angle lens or because it was shot from an unusual angle. Launching the **Correct Camera Distortion** filter opens a workspace in which you can "un-round" or "round" your photo or even reshape it so that it widens at the top, bottom or side, as in the illustration below. This filter works automatically when you combine several shots in a **Photomerge Panorama**, as discussed beginning on page 57 of **Chapter 4, Guided Edits**.

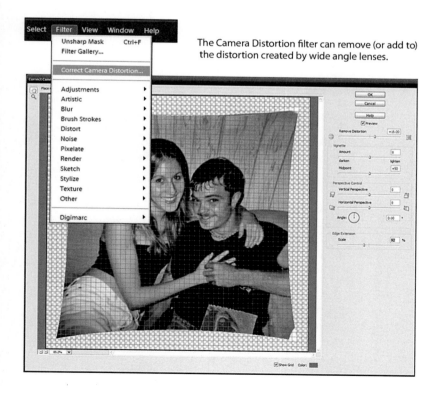

The Camera Distortion filter can remove (or add to) the distortion created by wide angle lenses.

The Filter Gallery is a workspace for test-driving and multiplying filters applied to an image file.

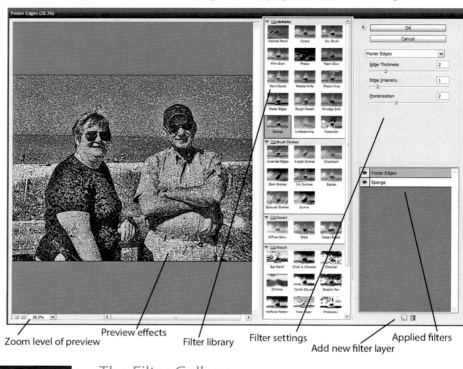

Zoom level of preview   Preview effects   Filter library   Filter settings   Add new filter layer   Applied filters

The Filter Gallery

Opened by selecting the option under the **Filter** menu, the **Filter Gallery** is a workspace for applying one or more filters to your image file, setting the filter levels and previewing the results.

It is also a means of quickly browsing a large portion of the **Filter** library, displayed as thumbnails down the center of the panel.

The **Filter Gallery** displays as four panels or work areas.

To the left is the **Preview** window. This window displays your image file as it will appear when the selected filter is applied to it. To the lower left of this display you will find controls for zooming in or out of your image.

The center column of the **Filter Gallery** contains a large portion of Photoshop Elements' library of **Filters**, each displayed as a thumbnail representing its effect. These filters are arranged in six categories, which you can open and close by clicking on the little triangles to left of each category's name.

As you click on each filter, a preview of its effect on your image file will be displayed in the **Preview** window. When you select a new filter, the old will automatically be removed when the new is applied.

156

The **levels** for each filter are set in the upper right of the **Filter Gallery.** (The drop-down menu above these settings is yet another way to switch from filter to filter.)

In the lower right of the **Filter Gallery** is a **properties** panel, which displays a listing of the filters you have applied to your image.

- You can combine and apply as many filters as you'd like to your image file. To add another filter, click on the **New Effect Layer** button at the bottom of this properties listing space.

- Your filters can be turned off and on in this area by clicking the eyeball icon to the left of each effect listing. And filters can be removed completely from this listing by selecting the filter from the list and clicking on the trashcan icon.

The Effects, Filters and Styles panels

There are nearly 300 effects available in the **Effects, Filters** and **Styles** panels which reside, by default, in the **Panel Bin** to the right of the Photoshop Elements Editor workspace. Each panel can be accessed by clicking on its button in the lower right of the program in **Basic** panel view, or by clicking on its tab at the top of **Panel Bin** in **Custom** view. (To switch between **Basic** and **Custom** panel view, click the little arrow to the right of the **More** button in the lower right of the interface.)

These effects and filters are available in different sub-categories, which can be accessed by clicking on the drop-down menu at the top of the panel, as illustrated to the right.

The Effects, Filters and Styles buttons in Basic View.

The Effects, Filters and Styles panel tabs in Custom View.

You can get a general idea of how each filter or effect will change your image file by looking at the thumbnails displayed in the panel.

The size of these thumbnails can be adjusted by selecting one of the **Thumbnail Views** available under the pop-out menu in the upper right of the panel, as illustrated.

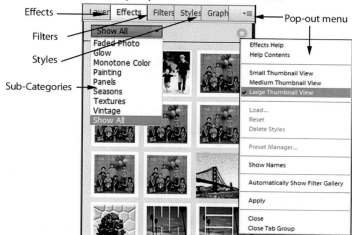

These panels, like all of the panels in the **Panel Bin**, can be undocked, if you'd prefer, and placed anywhere on your computer's desktop. To undock a panel, drag on its tab at the top of the panel.

Once you remove it from the bin, it becomes a "floating" panel and you can position it wherever you'd like in your workspace.

To re-dock the panel, just drag it by its tab back into the **Panel Bin** and release your mouse button. The panel will pop back into the bin.

To return the **Panel Bin** to its original array of panels, go to the **Window** menu and select **Reset Panels**.

The Effects panel

Effects are visual effects which can be applied to make your photographs look aged or to divide your photo into separate panels.

All but a few of these **Effects** work by creating a duplicate of the **Background** layer and then applying color or texture effects to it. Because of this, the effects they apply don't change the original artwork. The original photo remains in its unaffected state, hidden behind the layer to which effects have been applied.

The original and the layers to which effects have been applied remain separate as long as you save your file as a layered PSD (Photoshop) file and you do not flatten the layers or save your image file as a format that does not support layers (such as a JPEG or a non-layered TIF).

The layer to which the effect has been applied can then be accepted and kept or deleted (by opening the **Layers** panel, selecting the layer and clicking on the trashcan icon).

Photo Effects can make bright, new photos look old and worn.

Panels effects divide
your photo into panels
or sections.

Photoshop Elements includes a number of new categories and very cool
photo effects.

The **Effects** include:

Faded Photo creates an old photo effect by fading areas of your photo
from color to black & white.

Glow adds a glossy, foggy effect to the lighter areas of your photo.

Monotone Color reduces your color photo to tints of monochrome or a
single color.

Painting makes your photo look like a fluorescent, oil or watercolor
painting.

Panels divides your photo into four to nine separate panels.

Seasons add snow, rain or a summery or a wintery look to your photos.

Textures give your photo the look of lizard skin or a rubber stamp.

Vintage effects make your photo look like a faded, tinted photograph or
a pencil sketch.

The Filters panel

Photoshop Elements divides its over 90 **Filters** into 11 general
categories.

Artistic. These filters give your photo a "painterly" look, as if
they were created by an artist's brush or sketch pencil. It
includes **Plastic Wrap**, an effect which makes the elements
in your photo look as if they were sealed in Saran Wrap!

Blur. These filters soften or blur an image file or selected
area. Among the blurs are a **Radial Blur**, which gives your
photo a spinning effect, and a **Motion Blur**, which can
make your image file or selected area appear to be zipping
by your camera.

Render Filters, a close-up

The **Render** set of **Filters** deserves a more detailed discussion, because these filters often don't so much change your image file as add new elements to it. They include:

Clouds. When applied to an image file, layer or selection, this filter draws clouds. These clouds will be a combination of the **Foreground Color** and **Background Color** you currently have set (see page 65).

The Difference Clouds filter applies color values to your photo that are based on complements of your selected Foreground and Background colors.

Difference Clouds. This filter recolors your photos, basing the color values on hues that are complements of your selected **Foreground** and **Background Colors**.

Fibers. This filter draws a fibrous pattern, based on the settings you provide and the **Foreground Color** and **Background Color** you currently have selected. The option panel that opens when you apply this filter allows you to set the **Variance** and **Strength** of the fibers.

Lens Flare. A popular effect, this filter creates the effect of a bright light or sunlight shining back at the camera.

The Lens Flare filter adds a bright sparkle.

On the **Advanced Option** screen, you can set both the brightness and type of light and, by dragging the crosshairs, set where in the photo you'd like the flare to appear.

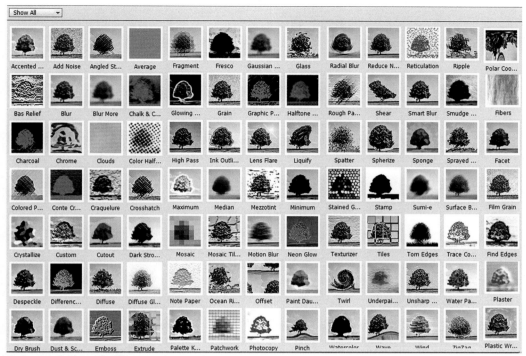

Options available on the Filters panel.

Brush Strokes. These filters make your photo look as if it were painted with artistic brushes or drawn with ink.

Distort. This category includes 3D filters for distorting and reshaping your image files. The **Liquify** filter makes your image file behave as if it were made of smearable paint.

Noise. Filters for softening scratches or flaws in a photo – or creating noise as an effect!

Other. A miscellaneous category of filters, like **High-Pass** and **Offset**, for creating customizable image effects.

Pixelate. Filters which clump pixels, creating mosaic-like versions of your images.

Render. We discuss this unique category of effects in detail in the sidebar on the facing page.

Sharpen. The **Unsharp Mask** in this category increases the contrast between pixels to sharpen the look of a photo.

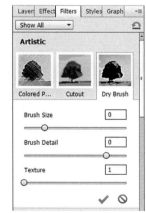

When you apply a Filter, an option screen for that Filter is displayed right on the panel!

Sketch. These filters give your photos a hand-drawn look, with some filters even simulating the look of various drawing papers. **Photocopy** makes your photo look as if it were run through a Xerox machine. **Chrome** makes it look as if it were formed out of metal.

Stylize. These filters create an impressionistic effect, or they create very unnatural special effects. **Emboss** makes your image file look as it if were pressed into a piece of paper. **Wind** makes the color look as if it was smeared by a blast of air.

Texture. **Texture** filters add a 3D texture to the image, as if it was printed onto a texturized paper. The **Stained Glass** filter adds a mosaic look, which makes your photo look like a stained glass window!

The Styles panel

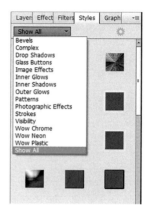

Styles are displayed in this panel as thumbnails representing their effect. Photoshop Elements includes over 175 **Layer Styles** effects in 15 categories.

Styles can be applied to text layers and shape layers as well as image layers. They can even be applied to layered image files with no **Background** layer.

A **Style** is applied by selecting a layer in the **Layers** panel and then either double-clicking on the style or dragging the style onto the layer.

Many **Styles** can be customized on the **Style Settings** screen. To open **Style Settings**, click the cog icon on the top right of the **Effects** panel, or double-click on the "***fx***" indicator on a layer to which **Styles** have been applied, as in the illustration on the facing page.

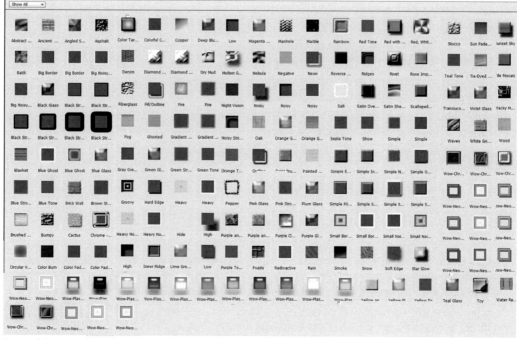

Some of the more than 175 options available on the Styles panel

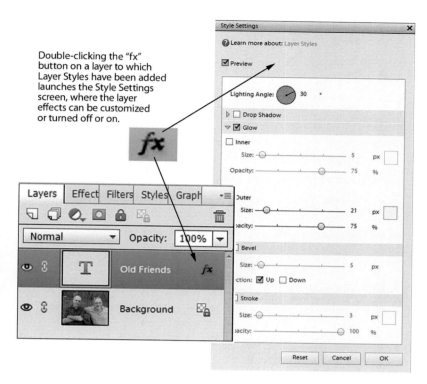

Double-clicking the "fx" button on a layer to which Layer Styles have been added launches the Style Settings screen, where the layer effects can be customized or turned off or on.

Style Settings for the **Bevel** effect, for instance, include settings for the depth of the bevel and a toggle for setting whether a selected layer bevels up or down. **Glow** settings affect the size, color and opacity of the glow.

Additionally, by checking or unchecking the styles listed on the **Style Settings** screen, you can toggle your **Styles** off and on.

To undo the effect, either click the **Undo** button or press **Ctrl+z** on a PC or ⌘+z on a Mac. To remove all effects from a layer, click the **Style Settings** panel's Reset button.

The 15 categories of **Styles** are:

Bevels. Bevels create a 3D effect by making your layer look as if it or its frame bulges out of your image file or is impressed into it.

Complex styles combine **Bevel**, **Pattern**, **Texture** and/or **Drop-Shadow** effects to your selected layer.

Styles can be added to text layers as well as shape and image layers – and more than one style may be applied to a single layer.

Drop-Shadow styles cast a shadow from the layer onto lower layers or the **Background**. To change the angle or other characteristics of a **Drop Shadow** once it has been applied, open **Style Settings** by double-clicking on the "*fx*" button on the layer in the **Layers** panel, as illustrated on page 163.

Glass Buttons styles turn your selected layer into a beveled, glass-like button.

Image Effects add effects like snow, rain, a jigsaw puzzle texture or a night vision look to your layer.

Inner Glows add a glow color inward from the edge of the layer.

Inner Shadows add a drop shadow inward from the edge of the layer, as if the layer were sunken into the image file.

Outer Glows add a glow outward from the edges of your layer.

Patterns replace your layer with a texture like a brick wall, blanket, stone, etc.

Photographic Effects add a tint to your layer or give it a sepia tone.

Strokes create a frame for your layer in a number of line weights and colors.

Visibility makes your layer semi-opaque, showing the other layers or the **Background** through it.

Wow Chrome replaces your layer with a 3D chrome texture.

Wow Neon replaces your layer with a bright, 3D glowing texture.

Wow Plastic replaces your layer with a shiny, 3D plastic texture.

Graphics

In addition to Styles, Filters and Effects, the **Panel Bin** includes a collection more than 1,000 **Graphics**.

Arranged in a number of categories, these graphics can be used as backgrounds, frames, shades, clip art and text styles.

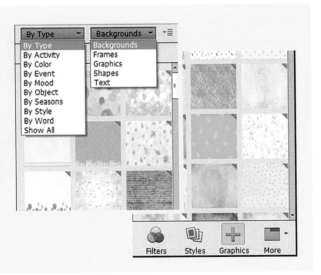

Part IV
Advanced Photo Editing

Swapping Out a Face

Swapping Out a Background

Healing Blemishes

Removing Things from Photos

Adding Things to Photos

Chapter 12

Photoshop Elements Tricks

Have fun with your photos

Stunt photography – or trick photography –
is the fun side of Photoshop Elements.

It's about swapping out elements in your
photos – or adding new things or removing
things you don't want.

It's about creating situations that didn't
really exist.

But there's a "legitimate side" to Photoshop
Elements tricks too. They can be very helpful
for cleaning up little photo problems.

Stunt photography can be a lot of fun. Swapping a friend's face for the Mona Lisa's, for instance. Or making your child look like she's walking on the Moon. It's fun – and surprisingly easy, using just a few basic tools.

But, of course, these tricks can also be functional. Occasionally you've shot a perfect photo – except for a stray wire hanging in the background or an untimely blemish. And sometimes, for a variety of reasons, you just want to place someone in a location other than where he or she was actually photographed.

It's all good. And it's all based on a couple of simple tricks and the basic Photoshop tools described earlier in this book.

Swap out a face

It's about more than just swapping faces, of course. It can be about placing someone into a scene – or even creating a composite of elements from a couple of photos.

I was challenged once with touching up the photo of a person who had a muscle weakness in one eye that caused his left eye to drift. In the photo I had of him, his eyes seemed to be looking in two different directions. By copying his left eye from another photo, I was able to seamlessly replace the drifting eye with one more in line with the right, creating a much more flattering picture.

The process of swapping in an element from one photo to another is best accomplished when you use two key principles:

- Ensuring that the two photo sources have similar resolution, lighting and color; and
- Blending the edges as smoothly as possible between the two photos

In my illustration below, I've gathered two classic Grisetti photos. The first is of me, at age 8, all fully equipped for a day of playing army with my friends. The second, from about 10 years later, is a real-life photo of me from my army days.

So what would happen if I grafted my somewhat adult face onto my childhood picture?

Well, the resolutions and textures aren't quite the same, and I'm facing a slightly different direction in each photo – but this is just for fun, so let's see how it goes.

1   Dragging the **Elliptical Marquee Selection Tool** over my Basic Training picture, I selected my head (and a little beyond).

   The **Elliptical Selection Tool** is one of the two **Marquee Selection Tools**. If the **Elliptical Tool** doesn't show in your Photoshop Elements **Toolbox**, select the **Rectangular Selection tool** and then switch to the **Elliptical Selection Tool** in the **Tool Options Bin**, as described on page 69.

2   Then, using the **Move Tool**, I (literally) dragged the selected area from my Basic Training photo onto my childhood picture, as illustrated above.

   Although I also could have done this with a cut-and-paste command, dragging from one file to another is the easiest way to copy elements (and even layers) between image files. Because my childhood picture is a black & white photo and my army photo is in color, the area I've copied from one photo to another automatically converts to grayscale.

   Also note that the area I've moved from one photo to the other has become a new layer on the childhood picture.

3   Ensuring that Layer 1 (my face) is selected on the childhood picture, I slid the **Opacity** level on the **Layers** panel to about 60%, as illustrated on page 166. This allowed me to see both the background and layer (as sort of a double-exposure) so I can scale and position my new face over my old face.

4   Dragging the corner handles around my face, I sized and positioned my older face over the younger in the childhood picture, as illustrated on page 170.

   Because I was facing to the right in one picture and a bit more to the left in the other, I flipped the "face" layer horizontally by dragging the side handle for my face completely across and over to the other side, turning it into a mirror image.

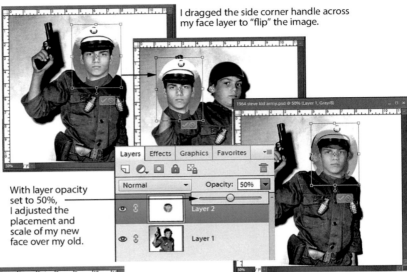

I dragged the side corner handle across my face layer to "flip" the image.

With layer opacity set to 50%, I adjusted the placement and scale of my new face over my old.

With opacity back at 100%, I used the Eraser Tool to remove all but my face from the layer.

(I could also have done this, by the way, by going to the **Image** menu and selecting **Flip Horizontal** from the **Rotate** sub-menu.)

I knew the two faces weren't going to match up perfectly but, by stretching, scaling and rotating, I am able to line up the eyes and the mouths.

Once the layer was in position, I pressed **Enter** to lock in the scaling. Then I set the **Opacity** for the layer back to 100%.

5 Selecting the **Eraser Tool** and setting it to a soft-edged 45 px brush in the **Tool Options Bin**, I erased all the unwanted imagery around my "face" layer.

Because the **Eraser Tool** brush setting had a soft edge to it, the line between the erased and unerased areas on the layer were slightly feathered, creating a softer, more natural edge.

Because my face had changed shape over the years, I can't completely replace my young head with my older head – but, when I erase around the sides of my face, my older face blends in pretty well with my younger head.

The result, at left, is just a bit creepy – but it works!

The final, rather creepy, result

The first step in pasting Sarah into the Monaco scene was using the Magic Wand Tool to select the green background in her photo.

Swap out a background

Swapping in a background uses essentially the same principles as swapping in a head, except that you're trying to create an entire scene from a composite of images.

In the illustration above, I've decided to take Sarah, who was conveniently shot in front of a green screen, and place her in front of the castle wall, overlooking downtown Monaco. (By the way, you can also do this effect using the new **Photomerge Compose** tool, as described on page 52.)

Green screens and blue screens are, of course, great photographic backgrounds for doing this kind of work – as well as for doing Chroma Key and Videomerge, similar background-swapping tricks performed in video.

This is because not only do green and blue screens give you a nice, even color that's easy to select and delete, these bright shades of green and blue don't show up in human skin tones. This makes it easier to separate the human from the background.

1   Using the **Magic Wand Tool**, as illustrated above, I selected the green background, behind Sarah.

The **Magic Wand Tool** is one of the three **Quick Selection Tools**. If the **Magic Wand** doesn't show in your Photoshop Elements **Toolbox**, select the **Quick Selection** or **Selection Brush** and then switch to the **Magic Wand** in the **Tool Options Bin**, as described on page 71.

How much gets selected on a single click of this tool depends on how high the **Tolerance** is set in the **Tool Options**. In order to select the entire green area, I set the **Tolerance** to 25 – and even then needed to hold down the **Shift** key and click on a couple of areas to build the selection until the entire green screen was selected. (At this point, I won't worry about the green showing between her curls.)

Inverse swaps the selection so that Sarah is now selected rather than the background.

2 From the program's **Select** menu, I selected **Inverse**. This swapped the selection area so *Sarah* was selected rather than the green screen background.

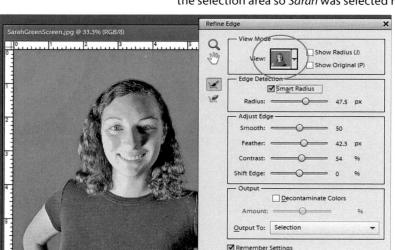

3 From the **Select** drop-down, I then selected the **Refine Edge** tool. This tool allowed me to tweak the edges of my selected area a bit.

By adjusting the **Shift Edge** slider, I ensured that my selection did not include any of the green screen. I also adjusted the **Feather** slider to 3 px so that the selection edge would be softer and more natural.

The Refine Edge tool tightens the edge around the selection and adds some feathering so that the selection blends with its new background. The Overlay View Mode shows unselected areas as overlayed with a red mask.

Finally, using the Adjust Color for Skin Tone tool, Sarah's color temperature is adjusted to more closely match her new background.

4 I then dragged the selected area, Sarah, onto the Monaco photo. Because I had ensured that the photos had similar resolution, Sarah fits nicely onto her new background.

5 Using the 45 px soft-edged brush setting, I dragged the **Eraser Tool** to clean up any stray green left around Sarah. Remember, when you are working with a layer, erasing *cuts transparency through* the layer – revealing the background or layers below.

Using different sized **Eraser Tool** brushes, I removed what I could from between the curls in her hair. Depending on how much detail you're trying to clean up, this part of the process can be the most challenging and time consuming. (I could also have saved myself this clean-up by refining my selection's edge using the **Refine Selection Brush** tool, as described on page 72.)

6 Finally, with **Layer 1** (Sarah) selected, I went to the program's **Enhance** menu, selected the **Adjust Color** sub-menu and then **Adjust Color for Skin Tone**. Using the eye-dropper, I sampled a mid-tone of skin on Sarah's face. Then moving the **Ambient Light** slider (and, to a lesser degree, the **Tan** and **Blush** sliders), I fine-tuned Sarah so she better matched the color tones of someone standing under the Mediterranean sun.

Stray green spots, particularly around the hair, are removed with a soft-edge Eraser Tool brush.

Removing blemishes, spots and other embarassments is easy with the Spot Healing Brush.

Remove warts and blemishes

Nobody's perfect. And neither is any scene. Fortunately, Photoshop Elements makes it easy to dab away the occasional blemish.

In the illustration above, we see Sarah posing with her pet budgies. Unfortunately, Sally, the bird on the left, has left an ugly deposit on Sarah's sweater, marring an otherwise very cute picture.

The **Healing Brush Tool** and **Spot Healing Brush** are both very effective for removing these little flaws and spots.

1   With the photo open in the **Editor**, I selected the **Spot Healing Brush** from the **Toolbox** and, in the **Tool Options Bin**, I set the brush size to 34 px (which is just about the size of the spot I wanted to remove).

2   Dragging the mouse over the area, I "painted" the spot with the **Healing Brush**.

    When I released the mouse button, Photoshop Elements automatically filled in the area with color and texture information borrowed from surrounding pixels.

With the Spot Healing Brush Tool, you merely "paint" over the area you want to remove and, when you release the mouse button, the program blends color and texture information from the surrounding pixels to fill the area and remove the spot!

And we're done! The **Spot Healing Brush** is a terrific, virtually automatic tool that I find all but indispensable.

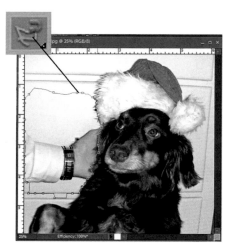

The Magnetic Selection Tool makes it easy to follow the color break along Buddy's fur and hat and create a selection isolating the arm area.

Remove big things from your photos

Sometimes you want to remove something larger than a blemish or spot from your photo. Sometimes you may even want to remove an entire person! This is most easily accomplished by "painting" over the object or person with imagery "cloned" from of another area of your photo – using one of the most powerful and popular Photoshop tools in the program's toolkit.

As illustrated above, my friend Ron dressed up and posed his dog, Buddy, for a photo he plans to use for the cover of his Christmas card. Ron, however, prefers that the final photo not include his arm in the shot so that it looks more like Buddy is standing up on his own.

1   Using the **Magnetic Lasso Selection Tool**, I drew a selection lasso along the edge of Buddy's fur and around the area where Ron's arm appears.

The **Magnetic Lasso** is one of the three **Lasso Selection Tools**. If the **Magnetic Lasso** doesn't show in your Photoshop Elements **Toolbox**, select the **Lasso** or **Polygonal Lasso** and then switch to the **Magnetic Lasso** in the **Tool Options Bin**, as described on page 70.

Selecting an area isolates it so that any changes you make will affect only the selected area, and won't affect Buddy.

The Clone Tool uses imagery from the designated area to paint over the brushed area, while the selection restricts changes to the selected area.

The **Magnetic Selection Tool** made it easy to draw my selection because as I dragged it along Buddy's outline, it followed the color break between Buddy's dark fur and the much lighter background.

2   Switching to the **Clone Stamp Tool**, I **Alt+clicked** to designate the clone source area of my photo – the area of the photo from which I would "borrow" picture information to paint over Ron's arm.

Since I wanted to replace Ron's arm with the color and texture of the painted wall behind it, I held down the **Alt** key (**Option** on a Mac) and clicked to select a spot on the white wall, above Ron's arm. This "source" area is designated with crosshairs, as seen in the illustration on the left.

Once my source spot was selected, I released the **Alt/Option** key.

3   With the **Clone Tool** set to a fairly large brush (200 px in this case) with soft edges (to blend the imagery I'd be adding to the background), I "painted" over Ron's arm, replacing it with the area I'd designated as my clone source.

Because I had created a **selection area**, there was no danger of my accidentally painting the background over Buddy – since he was outside my selection. My painted area was restricted to the area within the "marching ants" dotted lines.

Add things to your photos

Just as the **Clone Tool** can be used to paint over and remove images from your photos, it can also be used to paint new imagery onto a photo – even imagery borrowed from another photo!

For instance, the world may never wonder how I'd look with Jeanne's hair – but it can still be fun to find out.

1   With both photos open (I also ensured both photos were of similar resolution and that our heads were in a similar position), I selected the **Clone Stamp Tool**. I then **Alt+clicked** (**Option+click** on a Mac) on Jeanne's photo to select her hair, at approximately the top center of her scalp. This defined the area of the image I was going to use as my cloning source.

2   I then clicked on the Steve photo (to activate it) and, dragging the **Clone Tool** across it, I painted Jeanne's hair over mine, starting at approximately the same spot on my head as I'd designated for my source on hers.

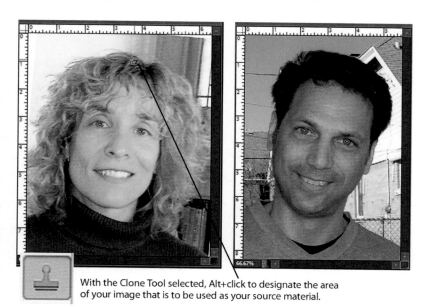

With the Clone Tool selected, Alt+click to designate the area of your image that is to be used as your source material.

175

As you drag the Clone Tool over your destination image file, the destination is "painted" with imagery from your source.

Because I was using such a soft, large brush (100 px, in this case) and because Jeanne has such curly hair, I got a lot of the background from her picture along with the hair.

I could also have created a new layer on the Steve picture and painted the hair onto it – and then used the **Eraser Tool** to clean up the layer, removing the background or other unwanted elements that slipped over from Jeanne's picture.

And, okay. I guess I wouldn't make such an attractive blonde.

Though, if I were, I might have a great career as an aging rock star!

Scanning Photos

Getting Photos from a Digital Camera

Divide Scanned Photos

Photomerge Tools

Process Multiple Files

Creating Premiere Elements Movie Menus

Photoshop Elements Preferences

Chapter 13

Advanced Photo Editing Tools
Photoshop Elements extras

Have you ever scanned in several photos at once and then found yourself cropping and straightening each one individually?

Or have you ever taken several photos of a scene and wondered if there was an easy way to stitch them all together into one big picture?

Photoshop Elements includes tools for doing these things – plus a few more tools worth knowing about, including the ability to interface with a camera or scanner.

In addition to tools for creating and editing graphics and photos, Photoshop Elements includes a number of tools that don't fit into any neat category. These include tools for interfacing with a scanner or camera and tools for processing photo files before you actually bring them into the program. There are also a couple of the program's preferences that are worth knowing about.

Scan your photos

On a Windows PC, your scanner's software can be launched and your scanner can be operated and controlled from within Photoshop Elements.

The scanner's software is launched through WIA (Windows Image Acquisition).

To launch your scanner's software from Photoshop Elements on a Windows PC, go to the **File** menu, select **Import**, then either the name of your scanner or the **WIA** support option;

To launch your scanner's software from the Elements Organizer (on Windows PCs only) go to the **File** menu and select **Get Photos and Videos**, or click on the big **Import** button in the upper left of the interface, then select **From Scanner**.

Launching the scanner tool in the Editor.

On Macs and PCs, you can also simply launch your scanner using your scanner's software.

Whichever you choose, the same scanner software is launched.

As I've said, this software can vary from model to model and from brand to brand of scanner. But the principles are essentially the same:

Many consumer scanners default to an **automatic mode**, which configures the scanner for you and scans your photos at a preset resolution and color setting but which you can customize to some degree. This is the simplest solution – but can produce the most generic results.

If your scanner software includes a **professional mode**, it usually includes options for a number of more advanced settings:

Reflective vs. Film (or Transparency). If your scanner includes the ability to scan slides and film, this setting controls whether your scanner scans a reflection of the photo or shines light through it.

Photo vs. OCR. Some scanners include the ability to scan documents with **Optical Character Recognition**. This OCR function scans your document in as text, which you can later edit in a word processing program. It's not a flawless system, but it *can* save you a lot of retyping.

Resolution. Remember that the size of the document you will get from your scan is a combination of its size and its resolution. In other words, you may only need a 72 dpi image – but if the photo you're scanning is only the size of a postage stamp, you will need to scan it at a much higher resolution to get enough image data to work with.

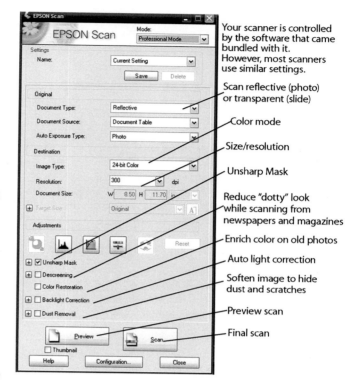

Your scanner is controlled by the software that came bundled with it. However, most scanners use similar settings.

Scan reflective (photo) or transparent (slide)

Color mode

Size/resolution

Unsharp Mask

Reduce "dotty" look while scanning from newspapers and magazines

Enrich color on old photos

Auto light correction

Soften image to hide dust and scratches

Preview scan

Final scan

My scanner software includes a setting for **Target Size**. If I set this, the software automatically configures the scan to the necessary scan resolution. (Remember, you're always better off having too much resolution and having to rez down than not having enough resolution and needing to force your image larger later.)

Color Mode. There are three main color modes:

24-bit Color is standard **RGB color** – 8 bits of data per color channel.

Grayscale is monochrome, often called black & white.

But don't confuse it with **Black & White** (also known as **Bitmap**), which reduces all your colors to either 100% black or 100% white. **Black & White** is a color mode that is generally reserved for things like scanning signatures, which generally don't include shades of gray.

Some scanners also include on-the-fly picture adjustments or scan settings. Here are a couple of valuable adjustments.

Unsharp Mask. This will automatically sharpen your scanned images. It's usually best to have it turned on.

Descreening. When scanning photos from newspapers, magazines and low-end print pieces (like high school yearbooks), you may notice your scanned images have a lot of "dotty-ness." Descreening can help soften those low-quality printing artifacts.

Color Restoration. This feature will automatically enrich the color as you scan a faded, old photo.

Dust Removal. This feature adds a slight blur to your scan, sometimes hiding dust or scratches on a photo.

Scanning is usually done in two steps:

1 **Preview Scan.** A **Preview Scan** gives you a low-resolution preview of everything that's on your scanning table. Your **Preview Scan** will usually include an option for you to define the final scan area by dragging or resizing a marquee, displayed as a moving dotted line outline (the "marching ants").

    The area you designate with this outline will be the only area actually included in your final scan.

After a Preview Scan, you will have the option of designating the area of the Final Scan (indicated by a "marching ants" dotted line marquee outline).

2 **Full Scan.** This final scan will be a scan of your *defined area only*, using the color, resolution and adjustment settings you've configured. It will produce an image file that will open in your Photoshop Elements **Editor** for further editing.

A Photoshop Elements feature that is a great supplement to your scanning tools is **Divide Scanned Photos,** discussed on the facing page.

Screen captures

In addition to scanning and downloading photos, you can add images to Photoshop Elements by essentially "taking a snapshot" of your computer screen. This can be a very helpful function if you're trying to show someone some strange behavior on your computer or if you, like me, regularly create software illustrations for a book. This snapshot is called a **Screen Capture**.

Screen Captures are very easy to do on PCs. To do so, you simply press the **Prt Scr** (short for Print Screen) button on your keyboard. (Holding down the **Alt** key as you press this button captures only the current, active window.) On a Mac, press ⌘+**Ctrl**+**Shift**+**3**.

The image will be copied to your operating system's Clipboard. You can then paste this image into virtually any program (including Microsoft Word) by using the **Edit/Paste** option or by pressing **Ctrl+v** (⌘+v on a Mac).

You can also open the entire captured image as an image file for editing in Photoshop Elements. To do this, go to the program's **File** menu and select **New**, then **Image from Clipboard**.

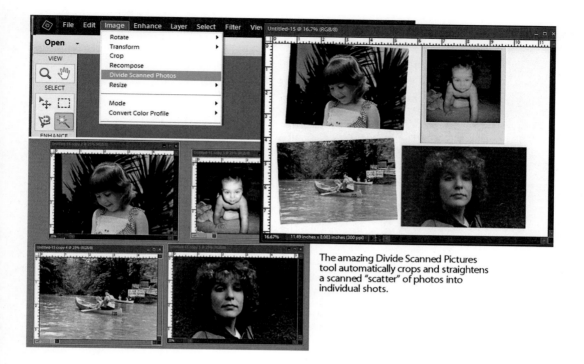

The amazing Divide Scanned Pictures tool automatically crops and straightens a scanned "scatter" of photos into individual shots.

Divide Scanned Photos

If you've ever needed to scan a number of photos in one sitting, you've probably tried to save a little time by scanning several pictures at once. This leaves you with a "scatter" of pictures.

Often, however, it's a such a chore to crop, straighten and save each photo that the time you save scanning several photos at once is traded off in the time it takes to separate and straighten the results!

Thankfully, Photoshop Elements now includes a tool for automatically doing this for you.

To use it:

1   **Scan a group of photos** at once, as described earlier in this chapter. Although the photos don't need to be straight and aligned, they do need to be far enough from each other that Photoshop Elements sees them as separate image files (as illustrated).

2   In Photoshop Elements, go to the program's **Image** menu and select **Divide Scanned Photos**.

The program will automatically separate each photo into a separate image file, cropping and straightening each as needed.

Download photos from your digital camera

As with the scanner, the software that interfaces with your camera can vary from model to model and brand to brand. And your computer probably includes a number of ways for you to get photos from your camera – all of which will produce editable photo files for Photoshop Elements.

The chief advantage to using Photoshop Elements to interface with your camera and download your photos is that your photos will also be automatically added to your Organizer catalog in the process.

There are two ways to launch the Elements Organizer Photo Downloader for your digital camera:

- Unless you've selected the **Always Do This** option, when you plug your camera into your computer and turn the camera on, **Windows or Finder will launch a pop-up screen** offering a number of optional functions. One of these will be to use the Elements Organizer to download your photos; or
- From the **File** drop-down in the Organizer, select **Get Photos and Videos**, then **From Camera or Card Reader.**

Both methods launch the same **Elements Organizer Photo Downloader.** This option screen allows you to designate where the photos are downloading from, what to name the files and where to save them on your computer.

>   **Get Photos From**. From this drop-down menu, select your digital camera, smartphone, iPod or other USB-connected picture-taking device.

Why you should clear your camera's memory regularly

Sometimes, when your camera's storage gets full, you may be tempted to delete just a few photos to make room for a few new ones. There are serious liabilities to doing this.

Your photos are typically stored in your camera or on your camera's storage card as JPEGs. These JPEGs vary slightly in size. Removing a photo or two leaves a "hole" of a certain size on your memory card. When you take a new picture, if it is slightly larger than this hole, your camera's storage may corrupt and you could lose several pictures!

For this reason alone, it's good, safe housekeeping to regularly clear off your digital camera's storage completely to "clean" or reformat the memory card.

Connecting your camera to your computer launches an option screen which offers you a selection of all of the photo software installed on your system.

The Adobe Photoshop Elements Photo Downloader includes options for automatically naming your files and for deleting them from your camera after downloading them.

In Advanced Dialog mode, you have the option of selecting which of the photos stored on your camera are downloaded to your computer.

Import Settings/Location. Click the **Browse** button to browse to a location on your hard drive into which you'd like to save your photos.

Create Subfolder. Automatically creates a new photo storage folder on your hard drive for the photo download, according to the specifications you set in the drop-down menu.

Rename Files. Names your downloaded photos according to the specifications you set in the drop-down menu.

Delete Options. Offers the option of deleting your photos from your camera once you've downloaded them to your computer – an easy way to clean up your camera's photo storage.

Advanced Dialog. Clicking this button opens up an option screen which displays all of the photos in your camera's memory. By checking and unchecking the boxes, you can select which photos are included in your download and which will remain on your camera.

Edit in Camera RAW

Usually, when you take a snapshot with your camera, your photo is delivered to you as a JPEG. This JPEG has been processed by the camera, automatically adjusting its exposure and white balance, and packaged in a convenient, moderately compressed photo format.

Professional cameras, as well as many of the more advanced consumer cameras today, however, also include the option for you to access the photo data in its **Camera RAW** state.

Camera RAW photos are, as the name implies, raw photo data. The files are uncompressed and none of the usual automatic adjustments have been applied. (Think of them as your photo's "negatives." In fact, RAW files are sometimes even called DNG or "digital negative" files.) They can't be printed or used in their **RAW** state. However, their format gives you much more flexibility, when it comes to making adjustments to your photos. You're working with the raw camera data, not undoing adjustments the camera has already made.

Photoshop Elements includes a surprisingly robust **RAW** photo editor.

Also note that, in Photoshop Elements, you can open *any* photo format in the Camera RAW editor by selecting File/Open in Camera RAW!

This means that, as you edit RAW photos, your adjustments to the photos will not be permanent – even if you click **Done** and close the photo file – until you click the **Open Image** button and open the photo in the regular Photoshop Elements Editor workspace.

The Photoshop Elements 2019 **Camera RAW** adjustments panels, organized under the three tabs to the right of the workspace, include a variety of color correction and sharpening tools.

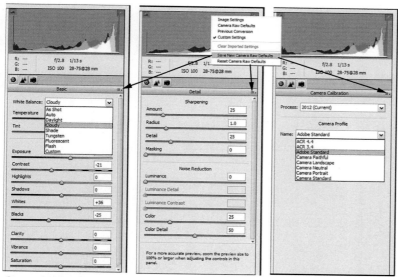

Camera RAW tools for correcting color, sharpening details and selecting a camera profile.

Basic. Under the **Basic** tab are sliders for adjusting your photo's color temperature, white and black balance, brightness, contrast and color saturation. There are also pre-sets for these settings under the **White Balance** drop-down menu at the top of the panel.

Detail. Under the **Detail** tab are adjustments for setting the sharpness and contrast of your individual pixels.

Camera Calibration. Under this tab, you'll find pre-sets that match a number of standard camera settings.

If you click the pop-up menu button in the upper right of any adjustment panel, you'll find the option to save your current settings as your **Camera RAW** default settings, as illustrated above.

Unlike changes you make in the Photoshop Elements Editor, the changes you make to your **RAW** image do not permanently change your file. Even after you've clicked **Done** and closed your **RAW** file, you can re-open it and make further adjustments – or set the adjustments all back to zero.

Once you're satisfied with your adjustments, you can port a copy of the adjusted file to your Photoshop Elements Editor by clicking on the **Open Image** button in the lower right of the **Camera RAW** adjustments panel.

The photo will open in the Editor and you will be able to print it or save it in any of the standard image file formats.

Your original **Camera RAW** image, however, will remain unchanged.

Process Multiple Files

The **Process Multiple Files** feature is a tool for editing or revising a whole batch of photo files in one action. This means that, for instance, you can apply a **Quick Fix** – like **Auto Levels, Auto Contrast, Auto Color** or **Sharpen** – to an entire folder full of photos with just a few clicks! You can also rename an entire batch at once or convert an entire batch to a new file format.

The Process Multiple Files tool (located under the File menu) will process, rename or resize a batch of files in one action.

Creating a separate Destination folder preserves your original files in their original state and size.

A common use of **Process Multiple Files** is to **resize** an entire batch of photos in one action. By properly configuring this tool, you can even send the resized images to another location, preserving your original photos in their original sizes.

1   To launch **Process Multiple Files**, ensure you are in the **Expert** editing workspace and select the option from the Photoshop Elements' **File** menu.

Process Multiple Files can be applied to a folder or to all of the photo files you have open at the time the tool is launched.

2   Select the appropriate option from the drop-down menu at **Process Files From** and, if appropriate, browse to the photo folder at **Source**.

3   Set the **Destination** if you'd like your changed photo files saved to a new location.

4   If you'd like to rename your photo batch, check the **Rename Files** option and set your desired naming conventions. Generally, a batch of photos uses a similar front name followed by a sequence of alphabetic or numeric suffixes.

5   If you'd like to change the **Image Size** for your batch of photo files, check the **Resize Images** option and then set the **Width** or **Height** and **Resolution**.

As long as **Constrain Proportions** is checked, there's no need to set *both* the **Width** and **Height** for your photos. The tool will resize your photos proportionately, based on the single dimension you define.

For instance, if you are resizing your photos for video, you need only to set the **Width** to 1000 pixels. As long as **Constrain Proportions** is ticked, each photo will be resized to the 1000 pixels wide and whatever height is necessary to keep the photo in its correct proportions.

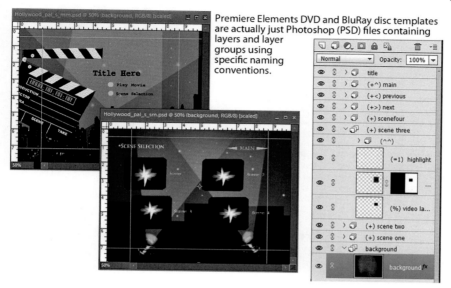

Premiere Elements DVD and BluRay disc templates are actually just Photoshop (PSD) files containing layers and layer groups using specific naming conventions.

Create Premiere Elements Movie Menu templates in Photoshop Elements

You can do a lot of customizing of disc menus right in Premiere Elements.

You can customize the text on the buttons, change the fonts, change the locations of the buttons and titles on the menu pages and even swap out an existing template's background.

But, using Photoshop Elements, you can actually *create your own templates* virtually from the ground up! This template can include your own custom background, your custom graphics, your default fonts, your custom buttons and button frames – with each menu page's elements positioned right where you'd like them.

Menu templates are PSD files

Premiere Elements DVD and BluRay disc menu templates are really just PSD (Photoshop) files. They have a specific structure to them – but they are basically PSD files with layers and Layer Groups laid out in a specific hierarchy.

For a number of reasons, which we'll explain later, we recommend that, when you "create" any new menu template, you begin with an existing menu set.

Just copy and rename **Main Menu** and **Scene Menu** files from an existing template over to a new folder you've created in the DVD TEMPLATES directory.

On a Windows 7, Windows 8 or 10 computer, this directory is located in:

C:/PROGRAM DATA/ADOBE/PREMIERE ELEMENTS/17.0/ONLINE/DVD TEMPLATES/ALL_LANG

(You may need to enable **Show All Files** in your **Folder Options** to see them.)

On a Mac, this directory is located in:

LIIBRARY/APPLICATION SUPPORT/ADOBE/PREMIERE ELEMENTS/17.0/ONLINE/DVD TEMPLATES/ALL_LANG

Anatomy of a Movie Menu
Template File Set

HD Movie Menu template

Standard 4:3 Movie Menu

Widescreen Movie Menu

HD Menu Background Video
Standard 4:3 Menu Background Video
Widescreen Menu Background Video
Downloaded.txt file
Menu Background Music

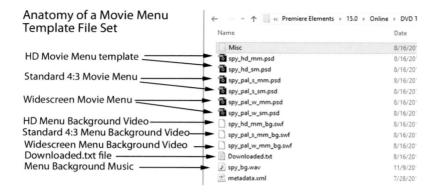

If you see few or no PSD files in these directories, it's because the online content has not been downloaded yet. Premiere Elements DVD templates are downloaded automatically the first time you apply them to a movie.

Studying how these files are named and stored in this folder will help guide you as you create your own.

The illustration above shows the PSD and media files that are combined by Premiere Elements to create a Movie Menu template.

The *names* given to these files are nearly as important as the structure of the files themselves. Each segment of the template file's name has meaning.

In, for instance, **MyTemplate_pal_s_mm.psd**, the "**s**" means that the file is for standard 4:3 video (as opposed to "**w**" for widescreen or "**hd**" for high-definition). The "**mm**" means it is a *main menu* template (as opposed, of course, to an "**sm**" *scene menu* template). We highly recommend you stick with the standard naming conventions when creating your templates.

The "**pal**" designation in the menu templates used to mean that the template was designed for the PAL video system. However, since version 3 of Premiere Elements, both PAL and NTSC have used the same templates. The "**pal**" designation is just an artifact from the days when there were separate templates. *All* current disc templates are "**pal**" templates.

Template folders also include a number of **PNG** files. These files are the thumbnails that appear when you're browsing the Movie Menu templates in Premiere Elements. We'll show you later how to make them for your template.

Create your new template's folder in the sub-folder that best represents the category you'd like your new template to appear under. (GENERAL, for instance. Or ENTERTAINMENT.) **The name you give your folder will be the name that appears as your template's name in Premiere Elements.**

> **Make sure that any new template folders you create or add to the ONLINE/DVD TEMPLATES directory include a file called DOWNLOADED.TXT,** which you can copy from the folder of another template you've already downloaded. This TXT document tells Premiere Elements not to download a new file to this folder – and, if it's not there, Premiere Elements will *erase your new template* the first time you try to use it!

Naming and storing the files

Whenever you create a disc menu template, **you will need to create both a main menu and a scene menu template** – whether you actually intend to use both menu pages or not. This is because, in order for Premiere Elements to recognize your files as a template, two things are required:

- There must be both an "**mm**" (main menu) and an "**sm**" (scene menu) version of the template files. (The names of both menus must be identical, except for the "mm" or "sm" element, as we'll explain below.)

- Each menu set, as well as any accompanying media files (background music, motion background, etc.), must be in *their own, separate folder* on your hard drive in the DVD TEMPLATES directory. The name you give this folder will become the name Premiere Elements uses for your template.

The basic template file structure

We highly recommend that even if you are "creating your Movie Menu template from scratch," you start with a copy of an existing menu template. There are several good reasons for basing your new template on an existing template set.

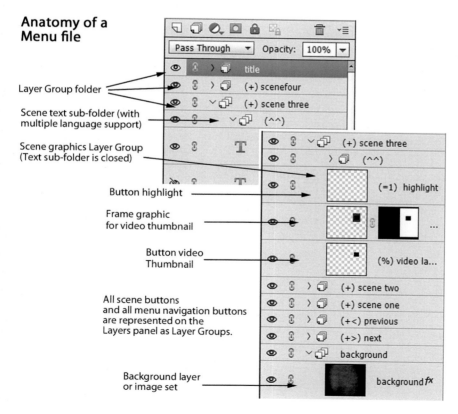

Anatomy of a Menu file

Layer Group folder

Scene text sub-folder (with multiple language support)

Scene graphics Layer Group (Text sub-folder is closed)

Button highlight

Frame graphic for video thumbnail

Button video Thumbnail

All scene buttons and all menu navigation buttons are represented on the Layers panel as Layer Groups.

Background layer or image set

1   Unlike most graphic files you'll create or work with in Photoshop Elements, **disc templates sometimes use non-square video pixels**. And, when you work from an existing template, your working files will already be conformed to this video standard.

2   If you use an existing template, **all the necessary Layer Groups will already be included and named properly.** And it's much easier to discard what you don't want or need (or copy it if you need more) than it is to create a whole tree of Layer Group folders from scratch.

Layer Groups are sub-folders (and sometimes sub-sub-folders) on the **Layers** panel which contain individual layers, as in the illustration at the bottom of page 189.

How these sub-folders are set up and how the elements inside each are arranged plays an important role in how your template functions.

If the Layer Groups aren't set up and named correctly, your template won't work.

Trust us. You'll be way ahead of the game if you start with an existing template set, copied to a new folder.

Replace the background layer of a menu template

Replacing a background of an existing template is relatively easy.

To do this, have both the template you plan to revise and the photo you want to use for your replacement background open.

(If you can not display more than one photo file at once in your Photoshop Elements Editor because they appear as a tabbed set, go to the **Arrange** menu and set it to **All Floating**, as described on page 17.

1   Size your new background photo to around 800x600 pixels. (1920x1080 for a high-definition template.)

Drag this photo from its existing photo file onto the open menu template file that you want to revise, as illustrated on the next page. Your photo will automatically become a layer in your menu template file!

2   The photo will come in with corner handles, which you can drag to size and position the photo until it fits within the menu template.

Once it's all in place, press **Enter** to lock in the size.

3   To move this new layer into position as a background layer, grab the layer in the **Layers** panel and drag it down into position right above the layer currently named **Background** (the current background layer for your menu template), as in the illustration.

Now drag the old current **Background** to the little trash can icon on the **Layers** panel to get rid of it.

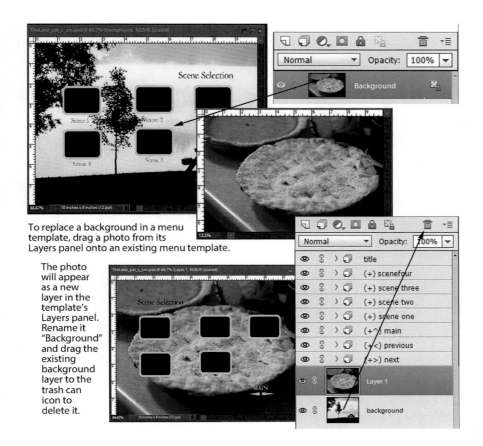

To replace a background in a menu template, drag a photo from its Layers panel onto an existing menu template.

The photo will appear as a new layer in the template's Layers panel. Rename it "Background" and drag the existing background layer to the trash can icon to delete it.

Double-click on the name of the photo layer you have just added so the name becomes editable and rename it "**Background**".

If there are additional layers or Layer Groups of graphics, you can delete them also.

Naming this background layer "**Background**" isn't required in order for the template to work, but it is good housekeeping.

It also identifies the layer in the template as a background layer for Premiere Elements – necessary if you decide to replace the background for this template in the **Movie Menus** authoring workspace of Premiere Elements.

Now sit back and admire your work! Even if you do nothing else, you've essentially created your own custom disc menu template!

Scene Layer Groups

Each of the scene buttons in your disc template file is in a separate folder, or **Layer Group**, on the **Layers** panel, as illustrated to the right.

Inside each **Layer Group**, you'll find graphics for navigation (such as placeholders for the scene menu button thumbnails), a highlight graphic and a sub-folder **Layer Group** containing text and named (^^).

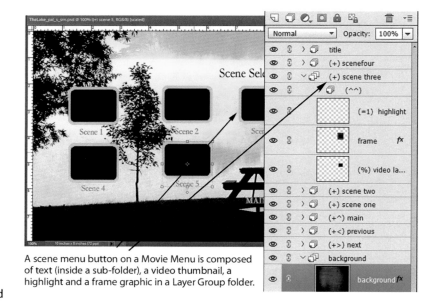

A scene menu button on a Movie Menu is composed of text (inside a sub-folder), a video thumbnail, a highlight and a frame graphic in a Layer Group folder.

Those little symbols inside parentheses on each layer and Layer Group are key elements in your layer and Layer Group naming conventions. They identify the function of each layer for Premiere Elements, and it's very important that you use them correctly.

Along with the text (^^) sub-**Layer Group**, each of these button **Layer Groups** also often contains a layer called (%) **video**. This layer includes a graphic (usually a black square but sometimes the Adobe logo) which serves as a placeholder for the disc navigation scene button, corresponding to your Premiere Elements **Menu Marker**. In other words, the (%) layer is where the menu button's video thumbnail will display.

There is also a layer called (=1). This is your button highlight. The graphic on this layer will serve as the highlight that appears over your scene menu buttons when someone watching your disc navigates from scene button to scene button on your menu page.

You can customize these layers any way you want, as long as you keep them in their current Layer Groups and maintain their names – *as well as their accompanying layer symbols* – so Premiere Elements can find them when it turns your template into disc menu pages.

1   You can manipulate the individual layers within each **Layer Group** or sub-folder by holding down the **Ctrl** key (the ⌘ key on a Mac) as you click on the layer.

    With the **Ctrl** (or ⌘ on a Mac) key held, you can edit, resize and reposition these sub-layers without affecting the other layers in that **Layer Group**.

2   You can also swap in any graphic you'd like as your menu highlight, replacing the current one in the Layer Group. You can even use a hand-drawn image or a photo. Just ensure that it is saved as a layer called (=1).

    We do recommend, however, that you never use white as your highlight graphic's color. White often won't appear as a highlight on the final menu.

Additional graphics

Some menu templates also include a layer or two of graphics between the background and the scene layer set folders. The significance of these layers of graphics is that, if you replace the background (by including a media file background or by selecting a custom background in Premiere Elements' menu workspace), these graphics layers will remain.

You can use this to your advantage, if you'd like. You can include still images as a "foreground" layer to your animated background, for instance, or you can use them to create a frame graphic within which to play your background video.

3   You can change the font, size, color or paragraph alignment for any (^^) text layer, as discussed below.

4   You can also add, remove or revise graphics used in these **Layer Groups**, such as the frames around the video thumbnail placeholders. And you can even remove the thumbnail placeholder itself, if you'd like your template to have text-only scene buttons.

Text Layer Groups

Within each Layer Group folder is a *sub*-**Layer Group** called (^^) (as illustrated on the right), which includes the text for that scene button or text block.

Open this **Layer Group** folder and you'll find 14 layers of text for this button, each in a different language. Each language layer is named with an abbreviation identifying the language and the (-) symbol – as in (**en_US (-)**) **Scene 3**.

You can change the font, font color, font size and paragraph alignment for any of these layers just by double-clicking on the "**T**" icon on the layer.

If your text layer is disabled or turned off, click the eyeball icon to the left of the layer to turn it on. (Which layers are enabled and which are disabled has nothing to do with how the template ultimately functions.)

As with the graphics layers within the **Layer Groups,** you can move the individual layers or the entire (^^) text **Layer Group** to a new position on your menu page – independent of the rest of the Layer Group – by holding down the **Ctrl** (or ⌘) key as you select it.

A scene button's Text sub-Layer Group includes support for 14 languages.

Layer Groups are scene buttons

Each **Layer Group** (folder) on your **Layers** panel – with its text, highlight, scene thumbnail and possibly thumbnail frame – constitutes one menu button.

And, after you're finished customizing the individual elements for each scene button, you can position and scale each button as a single object. To do this, select the Layer Group in the **Layers** panel or click on the button on the PSD file in the Editor workspace, then drag it into position or drag the corner handles to resize it.

Adding scene menu buttons to a template

Perhaps you've come upon the perfect Premiere Elements template – only to find that it includes only four scene buttons on a menu page, but you want six. Or you find a template that has no main menu scene buttons when you want three or four.

Fortunately, adding scene menu buttons to a template page is as easy as adding a photo or layer to a PSD file.

1   **To create additional scene buttons** on a current menu page, drag an existing scene **Layer Group** folder from its position on the **Layers** panel to the **Add Layer** icon at the top of the **Layers** panel. This creates a duplicate of the entire **Layer Group** – and thus creates an additional menu button. Update the text and you're set.

    The duplicate Layer Group and its contents will have the same names as the original set and its contents – except that the word "copy" will be added to its name. Double-click on the necessary layer names and rename them as appropriate.

2   **To add new scene buttons** to a main menu template that doesn't have any, drag one of the **Layer Group** folders from your scene menu template's **Layers** panel, or drag a scene button directly from the scene menu template, and place it onto the main menu image file, as illustrated below.

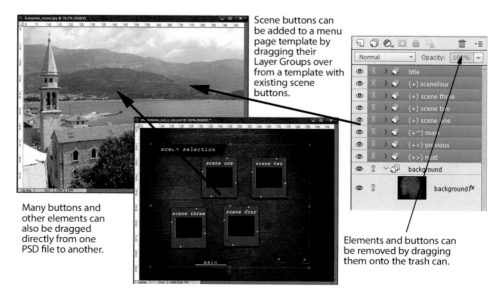

Scene buttons can be added to a menu page template by dragging their Layer Groups over from a template with existing scene buttons.

Many buttons and other elements can also be dragged directly from one PSD file to another.

Elements and buttons can be removed by dragging them onto the trash can.

A copy of this **Layer Group** will appear in the main menu's **Layers** panel and the scene button will appear on your template file, to be customized and positioned as you'd like.

3   By holding down the **Shift** key, you can select several of these **Layer Group** folders at once and drag them all onto your main menu, if you'd like to add several scene buttons in one swoop.

Once there, you can position them and/or their internal elements individually. (Scene Menu buttons link to green **Scene Menu Markers** on your Premiere Elements project timeline. Main Menu buttons link to blue **Main Menu Markers**.)

4   Deleting a scene button from a menu template is as simple as dragging the **Layer Group** folder from its position on the **Layers** panel onto the little trashcan icon at the top right of the panel.

Menu buttons can not overlap!

Note that, as you hover your mouse over a scene button on a template file, Photoshop Elements will indicate the "live" area of your button by highlighting it with a blue box outline. This is a very important feature because *one thing Premiere Elements will not tolerate in a disc menu template is overlapping navigation*.

So, as a final test drive once you've finished revising your templates and positioning your buttons, be sure to hover your mouse over each of the buttons on your template page to make sure none of your navigation areas invades another's live space!

Adding background video and audio

In addition to the PSD files that make up a basic DVD or BluRay disc template, Premiere Elements can use audio and video files in the template's directory folder to add motion or music to the disc menu.

Your video background (optionally including audio) can be AVIs and MPEGs.

Your audio background can be either an MP3 or a WAV file.

The order of the layers in a Disc Menu Template

It is important to note that the *order* of the layer sets in the **Layers** panel – not the *names* of the layer sets – determines the order that Premiere Elements uses them as scene markers. Your first scene, in other words, must be the *bottom*-most scene layer set in the **Layers** panel and the last scene, the top-most.

In other words, even if you call a layer set "Scene Five", if it is stacked below the other layer sets in the **Layers** panel, it will be used for "Scene One" when Premiere Elements uses the template to create its DVD or BluRay disc menu.

To include audio or video backgrounds as part of your templates, you need only *include them in the same directory folder as your disc menu templates* and then name them exactly the same as the template files – except with the letters "**bg**" at the end.

In other words, a video loop background for the main menu

TemplateName_pal_s_mm.psd

would be called

TemplateName_pal_s_mm_bg.avi

A video background file for the scene menu

TemplateName_pal_s_sm.psd

would be called

Template_pal_s_sm_bg.mpg

To apply the same mpeg video to both the main and scene menus, simply omit the "**mm**" or "**sm**" reference in the name as in:

TemplateName_s_pal_bg.mpg

Any AVI, MP4 or MPG video file you include in your template folder and name accordingly will automatically replace the background layer in your menu with video when the template is applied in Premiere Elements.

MP3s and WAV files will play audio or music with your menu.

Each of these will, of course, be over-written if you choose to customize the background video or audio for the template in your Premiere Elements' **Add Movie Menu** workspace.

Naming conventions

Though Premiere Elements is surprisingly forgiving about the names used for its DVD menu template files, I recommend you stick with the "traditional" names whenever possible.

More than once I've helped troubleshoot a custom menu for a client, only to find that the heart of the problem was his naming one of the Layer Groups or template files incorrectly. Using standard names made all the difference.

Stick to these basic naming rules and you should be all set:

1 The template set *must* include both a main menu and a scene menu in order to be recognized by Premiere Elements, even if you ultimately plan to use only a main menu for your DVD.

   This set of menu template files should be in its own folder in a category sub-directory of the DVD TEMPLATES folder. The name you give this folder is what Premiere Elements will use as the name of the menu template.

Anatomy of a Movie Menu Template File Set

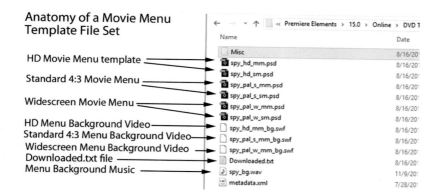

HD Movie Menu template

Standard 4:3 Movie Menu

Widescreen Movie Menu

HD Menu Background Video
Standard 4:3 Menu Background Video
Widescreen Menu Background Video
Downloaded.txt file
Menu Background Music

2 The main menu and scene menu template must have identical names, save for the "**mm**" and "**sm**" designation.

"**s**" templates are for standard 4:3 video

"**w**" templates are for widescreen 16:9

"**hd**" templates are for high-definition BluRay discs

Since version 3, all Premiere Elements disc menu templates, whether to be used in a PAL or NTSC video project, use the same format – the **pal** designation in their names is merely an "artifact". But it must be included in a standard definition template's name in order for the template to work.

That said, the following is the menu template naming convention we recommend you always use, just to stay safe.

> TemplateName_pal_s_mm.psd
> TemplateName_pal_s_sm.psd
>
> TemplateName_pal_w_mm.psd
> TemplateName_pal_w_sm.psd
>
> TemplateName_hd_mm.psd
> TemplateName_hd_sm.psd

For background video or audio, tag the letters "**_bg**" onto the ends of the files names.

If the name includes "**sm**" or "**mm**," the media file will function as background for only the scene menu or main menu page, as in:

> TemplateName_pal_s_mm_bg.avi
> TemplateName_pal_s_mm_bg.mp3

A media file without "**sm**" or "**mm**" in the name will function as background for *both* the main menu and scene menu.

> TemplateName_pal_s_bg.avi

Movie Menu Thumbnails

In every Movie Menu template folder included with the program, you will find a number of PNG files. These little files are the thumbnail images that Premiere Elements uses as previews when you select and lay out your **Movie Menus**.

It's not necessary to create a thumbnail for your movie menu – but if you don't, you may see only your template's name and not a thumbnail preview in the **Movie Menus** workspace in Premiere Elements.

If you browse to the directory folder for a default **Movie Menu** template with Windows Explorer or Finder, you'll see thumbnail images (PNG files) in several languages. You need only create one each for your scene and main menu in whatever language your program is set up for.

To create English thumbnails:

1 With your main menu template open in the Photoshop Elements Editor, select **Save For Web** from the **File** menu.

   A **Save For Web** option panel will open, as illustrated below.

2 Select the **PNG-24** preset in the upper right of the panel

3 Set the **Image Size/New Size** to 160 px **Width**. (The **Height** will auto-fill.)

4 Click **Save**. A browse screen will open.

5 Browse to the directory folder where your new menu templates are saved.

   Name your file **en_US_TemplateName_pal_s_prv_mm.png**.

Repeat this process for your scene menu template, except replace the "**mm**" in the file's name with "**sm**".

When you next start Premiere Elements, the program should recognize the new template and its thumbnails should appear in your **Movie Menu** workspace.

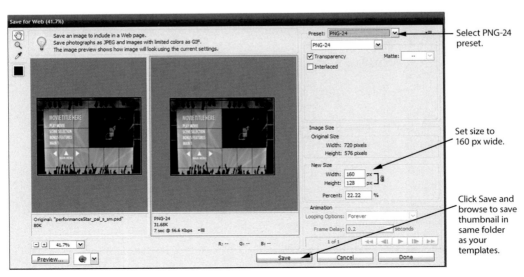

Select PNG-24 preset.

Set size to 160 px wide.

Click Save and browse to save thumbnail in same folder as your templates.

Photoshop Elements Preferences and Presets

The Photoshop Elements **Preferences** are accessed under the program's **Edit** menu (or, on a Mac, under the program's name). Many of these settings are pretty self-explanatory. But here are a few that I think are worth noting:

Saving Files. By default, the program is set to **Always Ask** whenever you try to save or overwrite a file. This drives me crazy! When I want to save my work, *I want to save my work!*

Unless you want to save versions of your photos as you work, I recommend setting **On First Save** to **Save Over Current File**.

File Extensions. For most of your work, it won't matter if your **File Extensions** (.jpg, .gif, .psd) are saved in upper case or lower case. However, in some environments – particularly if you're creating images for the Internet, it can make a big difference. HTML sees upper case letters as different names than lower case. There is no right or wrong setting here, but you do want to be aware of how the program is naming your files so you can maintain some consistency and control.

File Compatibility. I recommend checking the option to **Prefer Adobe Camera Raw for Supported Raw Files**. RAW is a function of higher-end digital cameras that stores images unprocessed and uncompressed, giving you more control over how the imagery is interpreted and adjusted (as discussed on page 180). If your camera supports it, you'll probably want access to it.

Floating Windows. As discussed on page 16, open files in Photoshop Elements are displayed by default filling the editing workspace. To release your photo files from the interface and have them "float" over the program, check the **Enable Floating Documents** option on the **General preferences** screen.

High-Density Monitor Support. To make Photoshop Elements' menus readable on a wider range of higher density monitor resolutions, the program includes preferences for controlling the size of the text on the program's interface. You'll find these settings (on PCs only) on the **Display & Cursor** page, under **High Density Displays**. In most cases, you can simply leave the **IU Scale Factor** set to **Automatic**. However, it can also be set to manually to **Small (100%)** or, for higher resolution monitors , to **Large (200%)**. (You'll need to restart the program in order for the new settings to take effect.)

Transparency. Transparency in an image file is usually represented in Photoshop and Photoshop Elements by a gray and white checkerboard pattern (as seen in **Create non-square graphics** on page 133 of **Chapter 9, Work With Photoshop Elements Layers**). This preference screen allows you to customize the pattern or turn it off completely.

Units & Rulers. This preference screen sets the default measurements that are displayed on your image files in the Editor workspace. For most online work or for editing graphics and photos for video, you may want to set your **Rulers** to **Pixels**, a more relevant measurement than inches or centimeters.

Type. This one is just a personal preference, a peeve left over from my years as a layout artist. If you're planning to work with type in your image files, select the option to use **Smart Quotes**. **Smart Quotes** are the difference between quotation marks and plain old tick marks. The difference, for instance, between " (which are tick marks, used for measurements) and the slightly curved " (true quotation marks). Using true quotation marks can mean the subtle difference between a layout looking "typewritery" and one looking truly designed.

The Organizer has its own set of **Preferences**, also located under the **Edit** menu (on a PC). Among them are settings for configuring how the program interfaces with your scanner and camera.

You'll find information for setting up a **Contact Book** in the Organizer preferences on page 252 and information on setting up **E-mail Sharing** on page 249.

New File presets

Although much of the work you'll be doing in Photoshop Elements will involve working on existing files and photos, occasionally you'll want to create graphics from scratch. To that end, the program comes bundled with a number of **New File** presets, available under **File/New/Blank File**.

The **Preset** drop-down menu on the New File panel includes presets for standard paper sizes, web sizes, video graphics and, under **Web, Mobile App Design** or **Iconography** you'll even find a number of presets under the **Size** menu for creating graphics for icons for mobile device and phone apps.

The Info Bar

The Status Bar

The Info Panel

Chapter 14

Learn About Your Photoshop Elements File

Important information on your Photoshop Elements file window

There is a lot more to a PSD, or an image file, than meets the eye!

In this chapter, we'll take a close look at an image file, what Photoshop Elements has to tell us about it and, ultimately, what it all means.

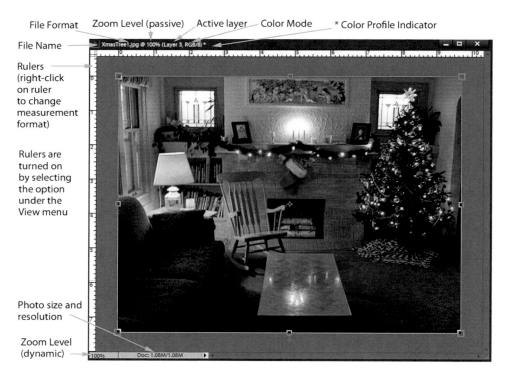

File Format Zoom Level (passive) Active layer Color Mode * Color Profile Indicator

File Name

Rulers (right-click on ruler to change measurement format)

Rulers are turned on by selecting the option under the View menu

Photo size and resolution

Zoom Level (dynamic)

The Info Bar

Whenever you open a photo or an image file in Photoshop Elements' Editor workspace, it appears with a frame around it. This frame includes a lot of useful information about the file.

Along the top of the frame, you'll see:

> **File Name**. This is the name of the file, of course – including the suffix, which defines the file's format (PSD, TIF, JPG, etc.).
>
> **Zoom Level (Passive)**. Displayed both after the **File Name**, at the top of the image frame, and in the lower left corner of the image frame, this number, a percentage, tells the scale of the image, as currently displayed in your Editor workspace. You can zoom in or out by pressing **Ctrl++** (the Ctrl and plus key) or **Ctrl+-** (the Ctrl and minus key) on your keyboard (or ⌘++ or ⌘+- on a Mac) .

This **Zoom Level** number can be a bit misleading, however. This is because it is measuring the scale of the picture's size in *pixels* rather than in linear numbers, such as inches or centimeters.

This means that, if you're looking at an image file with a resolution of 300 ppi at 100% zoom, the picture is going to look about *four times larger* on your computer monitor than it will when it is printed.

But, for most of the images you're working on for video or for the web, at 100% zoom, your image should appear at just about its actual size.

Layer. If you have a layered PSD file open in your **Editor** workspace, the layer that is currently selected will appear in parentheses, following the **Zoom Level**.

Color Mode. Following the **Layer** notation, or alone in the parentheses, is the **Color Mode** of your image file. In most cases, this mode will be **RGB/8**. However, if you are editing a monochrome (black & white) photo, this mode will read **Gray/8**.

RGB mode means that the pixels in your image are composed of combinations of red, green and blue. Each of these three colors can be set to any of 256 levels (0-255).

Why 256? Well, this seemingly arbitrary number is actually a very *real* number, with its origins in binary code, the base 2 numbering system that is at the heart of all computer programming. Every instruction written into every computer program is based on some base 2 number.

256 is 2^8 (2 to the 8th power, or 2x2x2x2x2x2x2x2). Hence, the red, green and blue color levels are each 8-bit settings (with 256 possibilities) – which is why the number 8 appears after the RGB **Color Mode** listing.

By the way, there are other, even deeper RGB modes. (16-bit color, for instance.) However, 8-bit color is the standard for video and online graphics, and it is the only RGB color mode that Premiere Elements can work with. Besides, the 256 levels of red, green and blue yields 16,777,216 possible color combinations, which is probably more than enough colors for most photo and video purposes.

Photoshop Elements can work in three additional color modes, which can be selected for your image files under the **Image** drop-down on the Menu Bar.

Grayscale, or black and white, which is actually 256 levels of a single color: black. (White is merely the color black set to the level 0.)

Indexed Color is a system for limiting the number of colors in an image. If you've worked on graphics for the Web, you likely already know how reducing colors on a GIF file can reduce its file size. (Although, because it provides a limited color range, **Indexed Color** is also probably not the best **Color Mode** in which to work with photos.)

Bitmap is a **Color Mode** made up of pixels that are only either pure black and pure white – with no shades of gray in between.

Why does a "100% zoom" video fill only part of my computer screen?

Remember, a standard NTSC video frame is only the equivalent of a 640x480 pixel image. Most likely your computer monitor is set to a resolution of between 1024x768 pixels and 1920x1080 pixels. This means that a full-screen video image at 100% zoom may take up only one-fourth of your computer screen! (A high-definition 1920x1080 video, however, will more than likely fill your screen.)

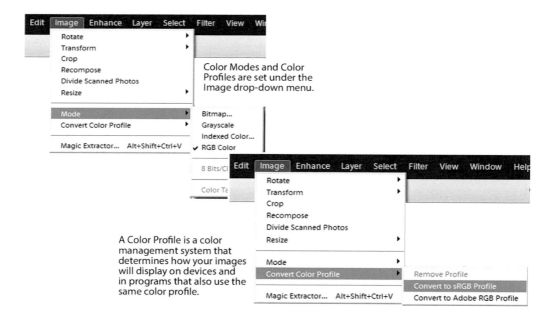

Color Modes and Color Profiles are set under the Image drop-down menu.

A Color Profile is a color management system that determines how your images will display on devices and in programs that also use the same color profile.

The professional version of Photoshop includes additional color modes, which are useful for preparing files, for instance, for production on an offset press. However, for our purposes – and particularly as you produce graphics and imagery for use in Premiere Elements or for the Web – you'll usually be working with **RGB** or **Grayscale** mode only.

> * (**Color Profile**). An asterisk appearing after the Color Mode listing is an indication that a **Color Profile** has been assigned to the image.

A **Color Profile** is a standardization system for color that can be applied across several programs and hardware devices. This ensures that the image's colors appear the same on every device, and in every application, that's using that same profile. There are two color profiles available in Photoshop Elements: **sRGB** and **Adobe RGB**, both of which are standard enough that either one should produce excellent results.

Many graphics cards and monitors will allow you to set them to a color profile. If it is available on your computer, you'll usually find it listed under **Color Management**, under **Settings/Advanced** for your display. (On a PC you can access these settings in your **Color Management** controls. On a Mac, open your **System Preferences** and click on **Display**.)

Using the same color profile for all of your programs and hardware is the best way to ensure that what you see on your computer is ultimately what you get, image-wise.

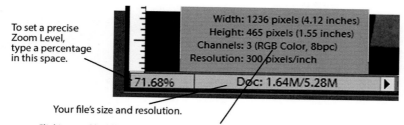

To set a precise Zoom Level, type a percentage in this space.

Width: 1236 pixels (4.12 inches)
Height: 465 pixels (1.55 inches)
Channels: 3 (RGB Color, 8bpc)
Resolution: 300 pixels/inch

Your file's size and resolution.

Clicking and holding on the size/resolution bar displays a pop-up info panel.

The Status Bar

There's even more information about your file on the **Status Bar,** which appears at the bottom left of your image frame, as illustrated above.

Zoom Level (Dynamic). Although this number, a percentage, is the same as the information displayed at the top of the panel, the **Zoom Level** displayed at the bottom left of an image frame is *dynamic*. In other words, you can click on it and type any number in this space and, when you press **Enter,** Photoshop Elements will jump to that precise zoom view.

Size/Resolution. Along the bottom of your image panel, to the right of the **Dynamic Zoom Level** indicator, is a display listing, by default, your image file's size and resolution. As illustrated above, when you click and hold on this indicator, a pop-up panel will display additional information about your file.

Additionally, as illustrated below, clicking the black arrow button to the right of the **Status Bar** allows you to set this area to display a number of other facts about your image, including the name of the tool that you currently have selected, the size of your image file and even how long it would take your image file to download from a Web site!

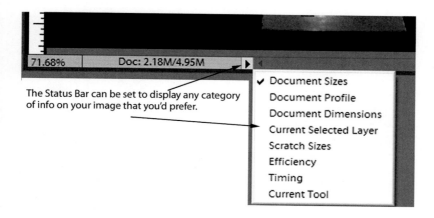

The Status Bar can be set to display any category of info on your image that you'd prefer.

✓ Document Sizes
Document Profile
Document Dimensions
Current Selected Layer
Scratch Sizes
Efficiency
Timing
Current Tool

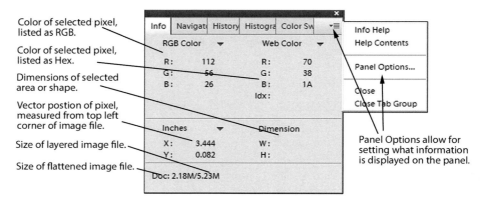

Color of selected pixel, listed as RGB.

Color of selected pixel, listed as Hex.

Dimensions of selected area or shape.

Vector postion of pixel, measured from top left corner of image file.

Size of layered image file.

Size of flattened image file.

Panel Options allow for setting what information is displayed on the panel.

The Info panel provides a variety of information about your image file.

The Info panel

Another tool for getting information about your image file is the **Info** panel – which is launched from the program's **Window** menu or by clicking the arrow next to the **More** button in the lower right of the program's interface. As illustrated above, this panel displays color and location information about specific pixels you have selected in your image as well as measurements of selected areas.

Color Info. As you hover your mouse over your image, you'll see numbers appearing next to the R, G and B listings in the upper left panel of this panel. These numbers are the color level settings for the individual pixels your cursor is currently over.

The R, G and B listings on the upper right of the panel display as an alpha-numeric combination.

The six number and letter combinations from these three colors are called the pixel color's **Hex** code, a common system for identifying colors on Web files.

In Hex code, for instance:

Black is 000000
White is ffffff
A medium gray is 808080

If you click on the down arrow next to the **RGB** or **Web Color** listing, you can set that panel to display this information using other color definitions, including **HSB** (hue, saturation and brightness).

Vector Position. The current position of your mouse cursor over your image file is listed in the lower left panel of this panel, as measured in pixels from the top left corner of your photo or image file.

By clicking on the down arrow to the right of the *Inches* listing, you can set this information panel – as well as the information panel on the **Dimensions** panel, to the right – to display these measurements as pixels, inches, metric measurements, percentages or even picas.

Dimensions. If you are working with one of the **Marquee Selection Tools** or one of the **Shape** drawing tools (see **Chapter 5, Get to Know the Photoshop Elements Toolbox**), the lower right panel of this panel will display the dimensions of the area you are selecting or drawing. (Professional designers sometimes use this **Info** panel, along with the **Rectangular Marquee** tool, to select and measure areas of their image files.)

Doc Size. The size of the image file you're currently editing is displayed along the bottom of the Info panel.

If you're working on a layered image file, you'll see two numbers listed. The first is the size of the image file once all of the layers in your image file have been flattened; the second is the size of the image file if saved as a layered PSD file.

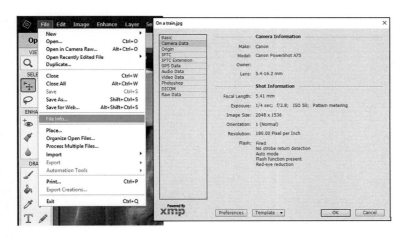

File Info

Photoshop Elements includes a detailed **File Information** window which lists an amazing amount of metadata about your photos including data on the lens your photo was shot with, the GPS location of the picture, if a flash was used and detailed RAW data. Additionally, many fields on this panel (on the **Basic** and **DICOM** pages, for instance) are dynamic and can be filled in by you, permanently saving detailed information about the photo file to the file itself.

To access this panel, go the program's **File** menu and select **File Info**.

This metadata, by the way, can be used by the Elements Organizer to catalog and manage your photo. For more information on metadata, see page 218 of **Chapter 15, Manage Your Files with the Organizer**.

Part V

The Elements Organizer

File Management with the Organizer

The Media Browser

Keyword Tags and Metadata

Smart Tags and the Media Analyzer

Storing Your Media in Albums

Identifying People, Places and Events

Chapter 15

Manage Your Files with the Organizer

Getting to Know the Media Browser

The Elements Organizer, which comes bundled with both Photoshop Elements and Premiere Elements, is Adobe's media file management tool.

It's a way to organize and search your media files and to create search criteria for your audio, video and photo files.

It also includes a number of great tools for creating everything from slideshows to DVD case covers from your media files!

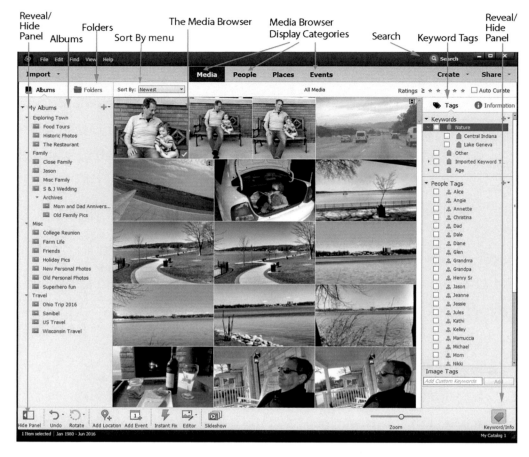

A companion program to both Premiere Elements and Photoshop Elements, the Elements Organizer is primarily a media file management system. It includes several interesting ways for you to organize and search your still photo, video, music and audio files

Additionally, the Organizer includes a number of tools for working with your media files to create photo projects, like calendars, scrap books and slideshows, as we discuss in **Chapter 16, Create Fun Pieces** and **Chapter 17, Share Your Photos and Videos**.

The Elements Organizer links directly to both Premiere Elements and Photoshop Elements and it can be launched from the **Elements Hub** of either program – or by clicking the **Organizer** button on the bar along the bottom left of either program's interface.

Think of your Elements Organizer as a giant search engine that can be programmed to store and retrieve the audio, video and still photo files on your computer, based on a wide variety of criteria – some of which you assign, some of which are assigned automatically and some of which are inherently a part of your photo, sound and video files when they're created.

These search criteria aren't limited to obvious details – such as the type of media or the date it was saved to your computer.

Adaptive Grid vs. Details View

The **Media Browser** in the Organizer displays your files by default in **Adaptive Grid View,** an efficient way to view and browse the media files on your system. Unfortunately, it doesn't give you easy access to information about your media files or even display the file names.

To display more detailed information about your media files, go to the program's View menu and select **Details.** (**File Names** can also be displayed in **Details** view by checking the option under the **View** menu.)

You can also toggle between **Details View** and **Adaptive Grid View** by pressing **Ctrl+d** on your keyboard (⌘**+d** on a Mac).

Search criteria can include **Keyword Tags** – or it can be minute technical details, such as the type of camera that was used to shoot a photo or whether the photo was shot with a flash or natural light.

Additionally, the Organizer includes features that support other tools and functions in both Premiere Elements and Photoshop Elements. The **Media Analyzer/Auto Analyzer**, discussed on page 220, for instance, prepares your video files for use with the **Smart Fix** and **Smart Mix** tools in Premiere Elements.

Your Elements Organizer's media files can also be assigned **Tags**, categorized according to the **People** in them or the **Places** they were shot, or identified by the **Events** they represent.

Video file

The Media Browser area

The main area of the Organizer's interface, in which your media files are displayed as thumbnails and which dominates the Organizer workspace, is called the **Media Browser**.

There are several types of media files, and they are each represented by slightly different thumbnail images in the **Media Browser**, as illustrated to the right:

Photo file

Video files are represented as image thumbnails with a filmstrip icon on the upper right corner.

Photo files are represented by a plain thumbnail of the image file.

Audio files are represented by gray thumbnails with a speaker icon on them.

The size of these thumbnail images in the **Media Browser** is controlled by the slider at the bottom right of the interface.

Audio file

Auto Curate

Auto Curate automatically analyzes the photos in your catalog and picks what it believes are the best.

To activate **Auto Curate**, check the option on the upper right of the **Media Browser**. To increase or decrease the quantity of images it selects, move the slider right or left.

The Back or All Media buttons

Whatever tags or filters you've applied, you can always work your way back to a display of all the media in your **Catalog** by clicking the **Back** or **All Media** button in the upper left of the **Media Browser**.

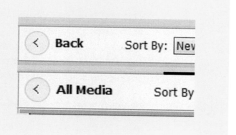

Under the **View** drop-down on the Organizer menu bar, in the **Media Types** sub-menu, you can filter which file types are displayed in the **Media Browser**.

Using the tabs along the top of the interface, you can set whether the **Media Browser** displays your files as categories of **People, Places** or **Events** – categories we'll show you how to build later in this chapter.

In **Detail View** (see page 213) media file **Details** (such as the date the file was created or its **Star Rating**) as well as its **File Name** can be displayed under its thumbnail in the **Media Browser**.

Although by default the files are listed according to the date they were created – most recent to oldest – you can display them in a couple of different orders. To change the order your files are displayed in, select an option from the **Sort** menu at the top left of the **Media Browser**.

Oldest or **Newest** lists your files according to the date they were saved to your computer, either most recent or oldest first.

Name lists your files alpha-numerically, according to their names.

Import Batch lists only the files added recently to your Elements **Organizer Catalog**.

The Organizer Catalog

The media files that the Organizer manages and displays, as well as the metadata that defines them, are said to be in the Organizer's **Catalog**. Some files and information are added to this **Catalog** automatically, while others may be added to the **Catalog** manually.

The Elements Organizer's **Catalog** is a file that includes data and metadata on all of the video clips, audio clips and photo files in your computer's **managed** folders (see page 218) as well as any media files that you've edited with Premiere Elements or Photoshop Elements.

If you download or capture video or photos to your computer using any of the tools in Premiere Elements or Photoshop Elements, they too are automatically added to your Organizer's **Catalog**.

Manually add to and update your Organizer Catalog

The first time you launch the Elements Organizer, it will offer to search your computer for media files in order create to your initial **Catalog**. (If you've had a previous version of the Organizer installed, the program will offer to simply update your existing **Catalog**.) If you're running the program on a Mac, it may even offer to build its initial **Catalog** from the data in your iPhoto catalog.

Import media files into your Catalog

You can manually add files to your **Catalog** by clicking the **Import** button in the upper left of the interface.

- To manually add files, and folders full of files, to your Organizer's **Catalog**, select **From Files and Folders**. Browse to the folder or files you would like to add and then click **Get Media**.

- To download media **From a Camera or Card Reader** or (on a Windows PC) to add images **From a Scanner**, select the respective option.

- When you select the option to import **In Bulk**, a panel will open in which you can designate folders to search. The program will locate any unlisted files in these directories and offer you the option of adding them to your catalog.

Your **Catalog**, by the way, does not actually *contain* your media files. It's merely a data file with links to your media files and their metadata. A **Catalog** file is actually a relatively small file – and, in fact, you can create several catalogs and manage them under the program's **File** menu.

Resync media in or remove media from your Catalog

If you move, delete or change files using Windows Explorer, Finder or a program other than one of the Elements programs, you may find your Organizer's **Media Browser** will indicate some thumbnails as having broken or outdated links to the **Catalog**.

To update these connections manually or to remove the thumbnail of a deleted file from the Organizer **Catalog**, go to the **File** menu and select the option to **Reconnect/All Missing Files**.

The Organizer will update your links and indicate for you all of the thumbnails in the **Media Browser** that do not have files linked to them, offering you the options of re-connecting the links or of deleting these dead thumbnails.

To avoid the program losing track of the links to your media, it's best to use the Elements Organizer to move or remove files from your computer:

- To delete a file using the Organizer, **right-click** on the file(s) and select **Delete from Catalog**. You will then be given the option of merely removing the file from the **Catalog** or removing it completely from your hard drive.

- To move a file to a new location on your computer using the Organizer, click to select the file(s) in the **Media Browser** and, from the **File** drop-down, select the option to **Move,** then browse to the new location.

Switch between Album and Folder Views

By default, the **Media Browser** displays your files according to the dates they were saved, from most recent to oldest.

The panel along the left side of the interface displays, by default, a list of the "**managed**" folders on your computer's hard drive(s). (For information on managing your computer's folders, see page 218.)

The **Folders** panel will display your managed folders as a **List** or, if you select the **Tree** option, it will display your computer's entire file directory.

If you click the **Albums** tab, the panel will display a list of **Albums** you've created and added your media to. If you click on an **Album**, the **Media Browser** will display only the media in that **Album**. (For more information on creating and managing **Albums**, see page 223.)

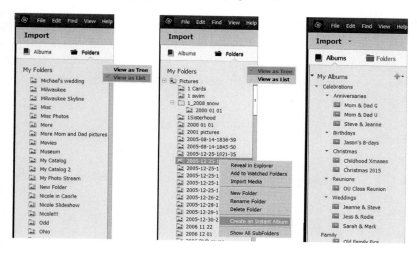

Managed, Unmanaged and Watched Folders

As far as your Organizer's **Catalog** is concerned, there are three types of folders on your hard drive. These folders are listed when the left side panel is in **Folder** view (see the bottom of page 217).

Unmanaged Folders are folders whose contents do not have any links to the Organizer. The folder either does not contain any media files or the media files have not yet been added to the **Catalog**.

Unmanaged Folder

Managed Folders are folders whose contents have been added to the **Catalog** and whose media files can be viewed and searched by the Organizer.

Managed Folder

Watched Folders have a dynamic link to the Organizer's **Catalog**. As media files are added to a **Watched Folder**, they are automatically added to the **Catalog**.

Watched Folder

(Note that any media files which are used in a Premiere Elements project or are edited and saved in Photoshop Elements are *automatically* added to the **Catalog**, regardless of where they are stored.)

The very first time you launch the Organizer, it will search your computer for media files and automatically convert a number of folders into **Managed Folders**.

You can also manually designate a folder as a **Managed Folder** or a **Watched Folder** by setting the left side panel to **Folder** view (see the bottom of page 217) and selecting the **Tree** display option (to view your computer's entire file directory). **Right-click** on any folder you'd like to manage and select either **Import Media** (which will convert the folder into a **Managed Folder**) or **Add to Watched Folders**.

What is metadata?

Metadata is the hidden information embedded into virtually every computer file, including when the file was saved, who modified it last, what program created the file, etc.

The Elements Organizer uses metadata to manage, order and search your media files.

All of your media files carry some metadata. By default, your files are displayed in the Organizer's **Media Browser** according to the date created – most recent first. (To see the file's title, created date, etc., go to the **View** menu and select **Details**.)

"**Date saved**" is the simplest display of metadata and the most basic way to manage your media files – but it's far from the only way. Virtually any metadata can be used to search, organize or gather your media.

You might be surprised to learn how much metadata is added to your photos and video files by your camera or camcorder automatically.

If the **Keyword Tags/Information** panel isn't displayed to the right of the **Media Browser**, click the **Tags/Info** button in the lower-right corner of the interface. Select the **Information** tab at the top of the panel and select a photo that you've downloaded from a digital camera in the **Media Browser**.

If you open the **Metadata** section of this panel, as illustrated on the right, and then click on the button in the upper right of this panel to display the **Complete** metadata, you'll see an amazing amount of information – from the date and time the photo was shot to the photo dimensions, the make, model and serial number of camera that was used to take the photo, the shutter speed, if a flash was used, what settings and F-stop setting was used, if it was shot with manual or automatic focus and so on.

All of this is metadata. And it can be used – along with any additional metadata you assign to your photos and video manually – as search and sort criteria in the Elements Organizer.

To search by metadata, go to the **Find** drop-down on the Organizer Menu Bar and select the option to search **By Details (Metadata)** as illustrated below.

In the option screen that opens, you can set up a search to find, for instance, all photos shot on a specific date or at a specific time, at certain camera settings – in fact, you can search by pretty much any of the metadata attached to your photo or other media file!

Also under this **Find** drop-down menu, you'll find many more search methods for your files. One of the most amazing search functions, in my opinion, is the Organizer's ability to locate files that contain **Visual Similarity with Selected Photo(s) and Video(s)** (under **Visual Searches**).

That's right: If you have a picture of the beach or the mountains or even of an individual, the Organizer will find for you all of the other photos in your collection that have similar color schemes and visual details!

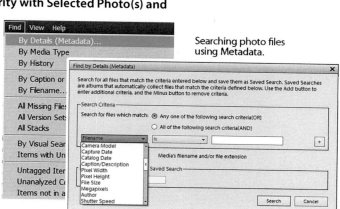

Searching photo files using Metadata.

Add your own Metadata

There are a number of ways to add searchable metadata to your media files. You can, for instance:

Your media files can be categorized by keyword, date, people, place or event.

> Place your media in an **Album** (as discussed on page 223).
>
> Add **Keyword Tags** (as discussed on page 224).
>
> Apply one to five **star ratings** to your clips by dragging across the stars that appear under the thumbnail in the **Media Browser**. (If you don't see stars under your clips, go under the **View** menu and select **Details** and/or zoom into the displayed thumbnail using the slider in the program's lower right.)
>
> Identify your photos by the **People** in them (a process the program does semi-automatically, as discussed on page 225).
>
> Tag your photos and videos with the **Place** they were shot (as discussed on page 227) . (This data is automatic if your camera has a GPS.)
>
> Associate your media with a **Date** or an **Event** (as discussed on page 229).

Using both metadata that you supply and metadata supplied automatically by the camera or other device you've recorded your media with, the Organizer provides you with a wide variety of ways to organize and search your media files – including applying **Search** filters, as discussed on page 222.

Auto Analyze your media

The **Media Analyzer** (also called the **Auto Analyzer**) is a key feature of the Organizer that works silently in the background, analyzing and logging information about your photos, video and audio files.

As it analyzes your media files, it records metadata about a number of your media files' qualities, including information on the content of your video or photos (for instance, if there are close-ups, if your photos or video includes faces), information on flaws in your media files (for instance, if your picture is too dark or too light or if your video includes a lot of jiggle) and even, amazingly, information on the content or subject matter in your photos. This metadata is saved as **Smart Tags**.

These **Smart Tags** can be used, along with your manually added metadata, as **Search** filter criteria, as discussed on page 222.

Auto/Media Analyzer metadata is used by various "**Smart**" tools in Premiere Elements to make automatic corrections to your video or photos:

Premiere Elements' **Smart Fix** tool uses data gathered by the **Analyzer** to make automatic adjustments to your video's brightness or contrast or to automatically apply video stabilization.

The **Smart Trim** tool uses data gathered by the **Analyzer** to recommend cuts to remove poorer quality sequences.

The **Motion Tracking** tool uses data gathered by the **Analyzer** to build motion tracks based on objects in your video.

The **InstantMovie** tool and **Video Story** tool use information provided by the **Analyzer** to make editing decisions.

The **Analyzer** also identifies and gathers media for the **Auto Creations** that appear on the **Elements Hub** (see page 14).

The **Analyzer** includes **Face Recognition** technology, identifying faces in your photos and, when possible, identifying the people based on their faces.

This technology not only plays a role in helping you manage and search your files based on the **People** in the pictures (see page 225), but it also provides **Face Recognition** metadata to the Premiere Elements' **Pan & Zoom** tool so it can automatically generate a motion path from one face to another in your photos.

To disable the **Analyzer's Face Recognition** feature, go to the Organizer's **Preferences** (under the **Edit** menu on a PC) and, on the **Media Analysis** page, uncheck **Run Face Recognition Automatically**.

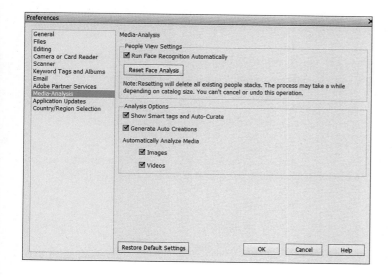

Search your catalog using Filters

The **Search** system for locating media in the Organizer is extremely sophisticated.

When you click the **Search** button in the upper right of the Organizer's interface, the program opens into a **Search** workspace.

Along the left side of this workspace, you'll find several icons. These icons represent **Filters** for determining which media files are displayed in the **Media Browser.**

These filters include: **Smart Tags** (page 220), **People** (page 225), **Places** (page 227), **Dates** (page 229), **Folders** (page 217), **Keyword Tags** (page 224), **Albums** (page 223), **Events** (page 230), **Media Type** (page 214), and the **Star Rating** you've assigned the media file.

As you click to select specific **Albums, Tags, People,** etc., these filter criteria will appear in the **Search Bar** along the top of this workspace, as illustrated above.

By clicking on the symbols between each filter listed, you can set your search to display your media based on whether the files include one metadata element **AND** another, **OR** another or **WITHOUT** another.

In the search illustrated below, I have set my filters to find pictures in either the **Dale's Old Slides** or **Florida** albums that include **Dad** but do not include **Diane**.

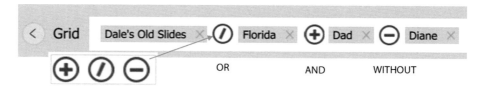

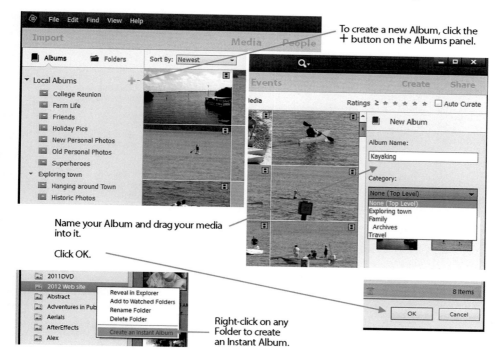

To create a new Album, click the + button on the Albums panel.

Name your Album and drag your media into it.

Click OK.

Right-click on any Folder to create an Instant Album.

Assign your media files to Albums

Albums are collections of media files that you create and assign your photos and videos to.

When an **Album** is selected in the panel to the left of the **Media Browser**, only the files assigned to that **Album** appear in the **Media Browser**.

Albums are a simple way to gather photos, for instance, for creating slideshows or to gather media for a photo or video project.

To create an **Album**:

Select the media files you'd like to add to your **Album** in the **Media Browser** (by holding down the **Shift, Ctrl** or, on a Mac, the ⌘ key as you click on the files). Click the green **Create Album** button at the top right of the **Albums** panel, as illustrated above. An **Edit Album** panel will open to the right of the **Media Browser**, from which you can name your **Album**, select a sub-category for it and add files to it or remove files from it. When you're done, click **OK**.

If you switch to **Folder** view (see page 217), you can also turn any **Folder** into an **Album** just by **right-clicking** on it and selecting the **Instant Album** option.

Additional media files can be added to an **Album** by dragging the photo or video from the **Media Browser** onto that **Album's** green folder icon in the **Albums** panel on the left. To re-open an **Album** in the **Edit Album** panel, **right-click** on it and select **Edit**. (And, yes, a media file can be in more than one **Album** at the same time.)

To delete an **Album, right-click** on it and select **Delete**.

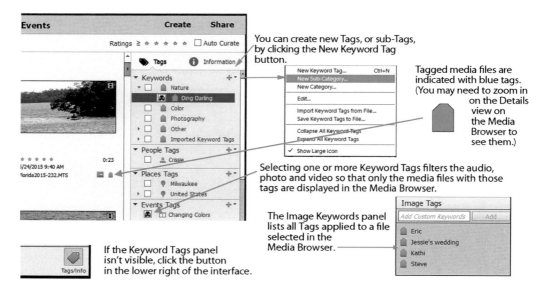

You can create new Tags, or sub-Tags, by clicking the New Keyword Tag button.

Tagged media files are indicated with blue tags. (You may need to zoom in on the Details view on the Media Browser to see them.)

Selecting one or more Keyword Tags filters the audio, photo and video so that only the media files with those tags are displayed in the Media Browser.

The Image Keywords panel lists all Tags applied to a file selected in the Media Browser.

If the Keyword Tags panel isn't visible, click the button in the lower right of the interface.

Manage your files with Keyword Tags

Tagging is a way to manually add custom search metadata to your media files.

At first adding **Keyword Tags** to hundreds of accumulated digital photos and videos may seem like a lot of housekeeping – but the payoff is great!

Creating a new **Tag** is as simple as clicking on the **+** symbol at the top right of this panel. You can create as many **Tags** and as many **Categories** – and **Sub-Categories** under them – as you'd like. You can, for instance, create a **Sub-Category** under Places and name it France. Then, within that **Sub-Category**, create **Tags** for Cousin Pierre, Landmarks, The Louvre, etc. (You can also drag your **Keyword** sub-categories in and out of categories on the **Keyword Tags** panel!)

To assign a **Tag** to a media file, drag the **Tag** from the **Keyword Tags** panel onto the selected file or files in the **Media Browser** (or drag selected media files onto the **Keyword Tag**). You can assign as many **Tags** as you'd like to a file. And you can assign the same **Tag** to as many files as you'd like.

In addition to **Keyword Tags**, the Organizer also includes **People, Places** and **Events Tags**. As you assign a media file to a person, place or event (as discussed on the following pages of this chapter) your file will automatically be tagged in the corresponding category.

And, as the **Auto Analyzer** works its way through your photo library, it will add its own **Smart Tags** (see page 220) to your media. These **Smart Tags** include information about the content of your photos including the presence of children and seniors, if the photos show celebrations or religious ceremonies and if the photos are portraits or pictures of scenery. These **Smart Tags** will appear under **Smart Tags** in the **Tags** panel.

If you check a checkbox next to a **Tag** in the **Tags** panel, only the photos, video or audio files assigned to that **Tag** to will appear in the **Media Browser**. If you checkbox a major category of **Tags**, the files assigned to all of that category's sub-categories of **Tags** will appear.

To further refine your search, you can check several **Tags** at once.

Find People in your files

One of the most powerful tools for managing and searching your photo files in the Elements Organizer – and one which Adobe has clearly invested a lot of effort into developing – is **Face Recognition**.

Face Recognition and the **People Finder** will work with you to identify the people in your photos (identifying as many as it can on its own) so you can easily locate all of the photos that include one or several individuals.

Once you've identified the faces in your photos, you'll be able to retrieve any photos identified with any name or names by using the **Keyword Tag** filter, as discussed on the facing page.

It can take a while to work through all of your photos, but it's actually kind of fun – and the program does a lot of the work for you!

To begin the process:

1 Click the **People** tab at the top of the **Media Browser**.

Under the **Named** tab, the **Media Browser** will display photos grouped by people you've identified.

Under the **Unnamed** tab, the **Media Browser** will display photos grouped by faces the Organizer thinks are similar. (If faces are not displayed, uncheck the **Hide Small Stacks** option in the upper left of the workspace.)

2 Identify **Unnamed** people.

To identify a face in the **Unnamed** workspace, click on **Add Name** below the photo and type in a name.

If the name you are typing has already been tagged to photos in your catalog, the program will offer it to you has an option. Select the name from the list offered.

If you type a name and then click the check mark (or press **Enter** on your keyboard), the name will be added to your list of **People**. If you type in a name of someone already in your **People** list and click the check mark rather than selecting the name from the list the Organizer offers, an additional instance of that name will appear in your **People**.

If you'd like this face not to be added to your list of **People**, **right-click** on the face displayed and select **Ignore This Person**.

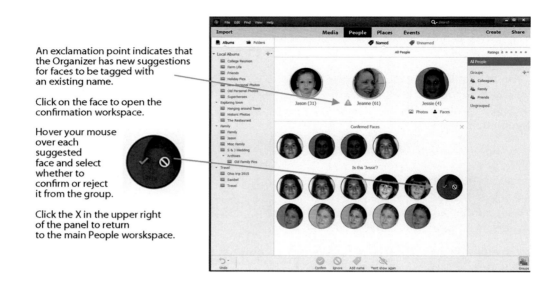

An exclamation point indicates that the Organizer has new suggestions for faces to be tagged with an existing name.

Click on the face to open the confirmation workspace.

Hover your mouse over each suggested face and select whether to confirm or reject it from the group.

Click the X in the upper right of the panel to return to the main People worskspace.

Unnamed people in photos are continually "discovered" by the Organizer's **Auto Analyzer** (see page 220) as it works in the background while you're not using your computer.

The Organizer will "suggest" photos of faces that it thinks belong to a named person.

3 Confirm **Named** people.

As you add **People** to your **Named** files, you may notice that occasionally the **Media Browser** will display an exclamation point inside an orange triangle next to a name, as illustrated above.

This is an indication that the Organizer has found more faces that it thinks should be tagged with an existing name.

Double-click on the face above the name and a workspace will open up in which you can confirm or reject the Organizer's selections.

To remove faces from this list, hover your mouse over each face and click the **Remove** indicator.

When you're happy with the faces that appear under a given name, click the **X** in the upper corner of the confirmation workspace to return to the main **People** workspace.

The Organizer actually "learns" from its mistakes, and it gets more accurate the more you help it identify **People**.

You can begin or end a work session at any time. The Organizer always saves all your work.

Add People to Groups

Your **People** stacks are listed in alphabetic order. But, to make them a bit easier to manage (especially if you've got dozens of them!) you can also arrange them into **Groups.**

The groups **Colleagues, Family** and **Friends** are listed by default. To add someone to an existing **Group**, drag the **Group** onto his or her face.

To create a new **Group**, click the **Add Group** button at the top right of the **Groups** panel.

An option panel will open in which you can name your new **Group** and select whether it will be a main **Group** (select **None**) or a sub-category of an existing **Group**.

To see the **People** in a specific **Group**, click the **Group's** name in the **Groups** panel.

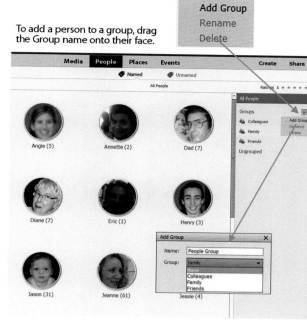

To add a person to a group, drag the Group name onto their face.

Manage your photos by Place

Just as you can manage your photo files using **Albums, Keyword Tags** and the **People** in them, you can also manage your photos or video by the location at which they were shot. Locating media shot at a given location is as simple as clicking on a pin on a map.

Even cooler, if your camera has a built-in GPS (and virtually all smartphone cameras do, if **Location Services** is turned on!), the Elements Organizer will read this metadata and add the photos to your map automatically!

To tag photos or video with a **Place**:

1   Click the **Places** tab at the top of the interface.

A map will be displayed on the right side of the **Media Browser.**

If you select the **Pinned** tab, media files already tagged with **Place** metadata will appear on the map as thumbnails. The number on each thumbnail indicates the number of photos tagged to a given **Place**.

The more you zoom in on the map, the more precise their placement will be displayed.

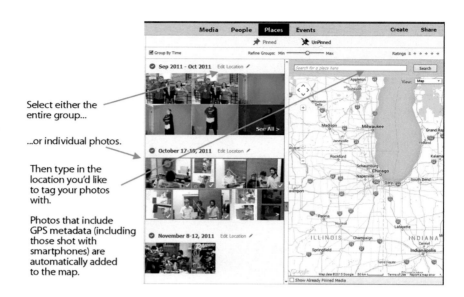

Select either the entire group...

...or individual photos.

Then type in the location you'd like to tag your photos with.

Photos that include GPS metadata (including those shot with smartphones) are automatically added to the map.

If you click on the **Unpinned** tab, you'll have option to tag either a group or specific media files to a **Place**.

2 Select photos or videos you'd like to assign to a **Place**.

Under the **Unpinned** tab, the **Media Browser** will display media files not yet assigned to **Places**, grouped by the date they were shot.

To assign an entire **Time Group** of photos or video to a **Place**, click on the **Add Location** link above the group.

To assign individual photos or video files in a **Time Group** to a **Place**, uncheck the **Group by Time** box in the upper left of the interface. All unassigned media files will be displayed in the **Media Browser**. (You can switch between the **Adaptive Grid** and **Details** view of these media files [see page 201] by pressing **Ctrl+d** on a PC or ⌘**+d** on a Mac.)

Select the photos or video files you'd like to assign to a **Place**. A checkmark will appear on your selected media files. To select several files, hold down the **Shift** or **Ctrl** key (the ⌘ key on a Mac) as you click.

3 Indicate a **Place**.

Enter the name of the location you'd like to assign to your media files in the **Search For A Location** box above the map – then click **Search** (or press **Enter** on your keyboard). You can enter the name of a city, a zip code or even a specific street address!

As you type, the search box will suggest locations. Click to select the correct location.

Your photo(s) will be added to that location and tagged with that **Place** metadata.

Alternatively, you can simply drag your selected photos onto a location on the map – although this may not be as precise as typing in the location information manually.

Once you've tagged your photos with **Place** metadata, you can locate all photos shot at that location by zooming in on the map or by filtering the location **Keyword Tags**, as described on page 224.

Manage your media files by Date or Event

Finally, you can manage your media files according to specific dates or events.

1 Click the **Events** tab at the top of the interface.

   If you have media files tagged to **Events**, they will appear as stacks under the **Named** tab.

   Under the **Suggested** tab, the **Media Browser** will display media files not yet assigned to **Events**, grouped by date.

By adjusting the **Number of Groups** slider or by selecting options from the **Calendar** menu to the right, you can adjust how precisely the **Suggested** media files are displayed by date.

To tag **Suggested** media files by **Event**:

2 Select the media files you'd like to add to an **Event**.

   To add an entire group of media files to an **Event**, click on the **Add Event** link above the group.

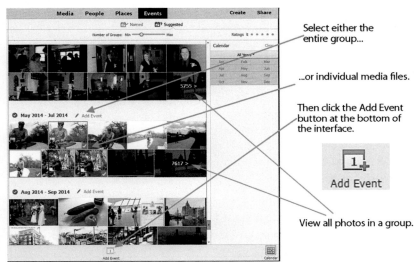

Select either the entire group...

...or individual media files.

Then click the Add Event button at the bottom of the interface.

Add Event

View all photos in a group.

To add an individual media file or files to a location, click on the thumbnail(s) displayed or click on the **000>** thumbnail to view all of the photos in a group.

A checkmark will appear on your selected media file(s). To select several files, hold down the **Shift** or **Ctrl** key (the ⌘ key on a Mac) as you click.

3 Name the **Event**.

Once you've selected the media files, click the **Name Event(s)** button at the bottom of the interface.

In the **Name Event** option panel that opens, you can add the name of the event, the range of dates the event represents and a description of the event.

Once you've tagged your media files with **Event** metadata, you can gather all photos related to that event by clicking on the stack under the **Named** tab or by filtering the **Event Keyword Tags**, as described on page 224.

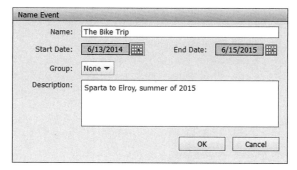

Instant Fix a photo

In addition to all of the file management tools built into the program, the Organizer also includes a fairly powerful **Instant Fix** workspace for cleaning up and adding effects to your photos.

To open this workspace, select a photo or several photos in the Organizer's **Media Browser** and then click the **Instant Fix** button along the bottom of the program.

If you've selected more than one photo, you can apply effects or adjustments to one photo in the selected group or all of the photos at once. (Some fixes – **Flip, Crop** and **Red-Eye Removal** – can only be applied to one photo at a time.)

When you have a group of photos open in the workspace, you can toggle between group and individual views by selecting the option at the top of the program. You can switch back and forth between applying effects and adjustments to the group or individual photos at any time.

Effects and adjustments can be undone by clicking the **Undo** button in the lower left of the workspace or by pressing **Ctrl+z** (⌘+d on a Mac) on your keyboard.

Instant Fixes include:

Flip Photo Horizontal (Available only for one photo at a time).

Crop (Available only for one photo at a time), when selected, will display a library of pre-set crop sizes as well as the option to create a custom crop.

Red-Eye Removal (Available only for one photo at a time) is a fully automatic fix.

Effects/FX, when selected, will display a library of photo effects which can be added to one photo or the group with a single click.

Smart Fix will apply instant color, light and sharpness fixes to one photo or to the group.

Light, when selected, will display previews of lighting adjustments which can be added to one photo or the group with a single click.

Color, when selected, will display previews of color level adjustments which can be added to one photo or the group with a single click.

Clarity, when selected, will display previews of sharpness/softness adjustments which can be added to one photo or the group with a single click.

To save your changes, click the **Save** button in the lower right of the program. Your original photo(s) will not be overwritten. Rather, your photo will appear in the Organizer's **Media Browser** as a **Version Set**.

To access previous versions of your photo, including the original photo, **double-click** on it in the **Media Browser** to open it in a photo preview window. **Right-click** on the photo and select the **Version Set** sub-menu.

In the **Version Set** sub-menu, you'll find options to **Flatten** the versions into one photo, **Convert the Version Set Into Individual** photos and to **Revert to the Original** photo.

Printing Your Photos
Creating a Photo Book
Creating a Photo Greeting Card
Creating a Photo Calendar
Creating a Photo Collage
Creating Other Photo Pieces

Chapter 16

Create Fun Pieces
The Organizer's project templates

The Elements Organizer includes a number
of tools for creating everything from a
photo scrapbook to a greeting card, DVD
cover or a CD or DVD disc label.

When you use the templates and
wizards in the Organizer (and sometimes
Photoshop Elements), creating these
photo pieces is as simple as selecting your
artwork and following the prompts.

The **Create** tab on the upper right of the Elements Organizer's interface gives you access to an array of tools for creating projects from your media files.

A number of these options are actually links to tools in Premiere Elements or Photoshop Elements, and selecting them will launch the workspace in that program.

Create an Organizer Slideshow

There are actually several ways to create a slideshow in Premiere Elements and Photoshop Elements. But the Organizer's new and improved **Slideshow creator** is perhaps the most intuitive option – and includes some very nice looking themes to give your slideshow a real professional look!

1   Select the photos and/or video clips you'd like to include in your slideshow in the **Media Browser**. (You can add and remove these media clips later.)

2   Select the **Slideshow** creator tool.

As illustrated below left, the **Slideshow Creator** can be launched by selecting the option from under the **Create** button or by clicking the **Slideshow** button on the **Action Bar** along the bottom of the Organizer. You can also **right-click** on your selected clips and choose **Create a Slideshow**.

A **Preview** of your slideshow will be generated.

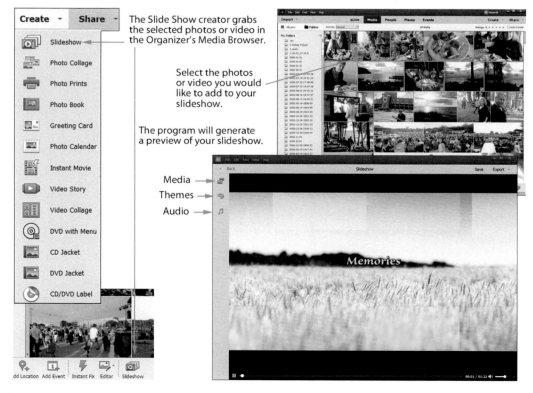

The Slide Show creator grabs the selected photos or video in the Organizer's Media Browser.

Select the photos or video you would like to add to your slideshow.

The program will generate a preview of your slideshow.

Add a Text Slide.   Add Photos or Video.

Add Captions to Slides.

3   Add media to your slideshow.

To add media to your slideshow, click the **Media** button to the left of your preview.

To add a text slide to your slideshow, click the button in the upper right of the **Media** panel. The text slide will appear as an editable title template.

To add clips to your slideshow, click the **Add Photos and Video** button. Under this button you'll find the option to locate your media using the Organizer's **Media Browser** or by browsing your hard drive.

To add captions to your slides, check the option to **Add Captions**. The text you add as captions will appear as animated text overlays on your slides.

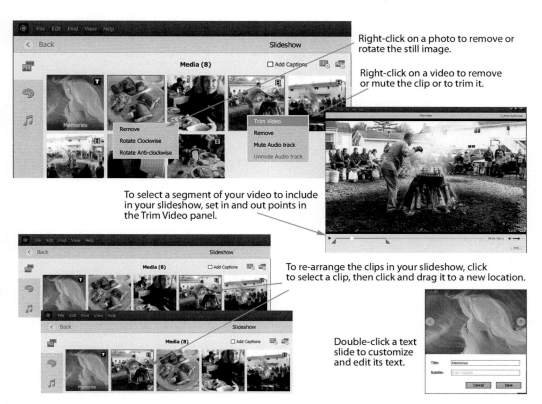

Right-click on a photo to remove or rotate the still image.

Right-click on a video to remove or mute the clip or to trim it.

To select a segment of your video to include in your slideshow, set in and out points in the Trim Video panel.

To re-arrange the clips in your slideshow, click to select a clip, then click and drag it to a new location.

Double-click a text slide to customize and edit its text.

4   Edit your slides.

As illustrated at the bottom of the previous page, there are a number of ways to edit your slides in the **Media** panel.

To rotate a still photo, right-click on the thumbnail and select the rotation option.

To trim a video clip, right-click on the thumbnail and select **Trim Video.** Set your video's in and out points on the panel that opens.

To re-order your slides, click first to select the slide you want to move, then click on it again and drag it to its new position.

5   Modify your slideshow.

As illustrated below, you can access other slideshow templates by clicking the **Themes** button.

Additionally, you can select your own custom music for your slideshow by clicking on the **Audio** button.

6   Output your slideshow.

Click **Save** to save your slideshow in a format that will allow you to re-open it and re-edit it later.

Click **Export** to upload your slideshow to YouTube or Vimeo or to output it as an MP4. MP4s can be played on your computer, uploaded to a web site or used in a Premiere Elements project.

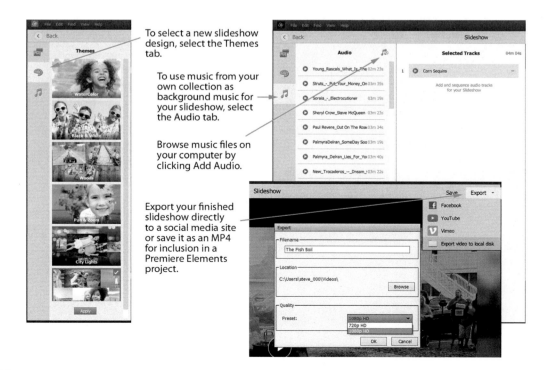

To select a new slideshow design, select the Themes tab.

To use music from your own collection as background music for your slideshow, select the Audio tab.

Browse music files on your computer by clicking Add Audio.

Export your finished slideshow directly to a social media site or save it as an MP4 for inclusion in a Premiere Elements project.

The Print preview panel includes settings for printing your photos in a variety of sizes and layouts as well as options for adding cool custom frames.

Create Photo Prints

The **Photo Prints** option under the **Create** tab gives you access to several ways to output your photos.

Print Individual Prints on your local printer

As you'd expect, this option sends your selected photo(s) to your printer. But you may be surprised at the number of possible print layouts this option screen includes!

1   Select the photo or photos you'd like to print in the **Media Browser** and click to select the **Photo Prints** option under the **Create** tab.

Then, on the **Photo Prints** option panel that appears, select **Local Printer,** as illustrated to the left.

The **Prints** preview panel will open. The program will automatically arrange the photos you've selected so it can print as many as possible on each page printed out.

How many photos it fits on a page depends on the **Print Size** you've selected for photos (as in **Step 2**, below).

The complete set of photos you've selected to print are displayed as thumbnails along the left side of the panel, and you may add or remove photos from this list.

2   Select your photo print-out options.

As illustrated on the previous page, the **Select Print Size** drop-down allows you to set how large each photo prints. You can also select from this menu the option to print each photo at its **Actual Size**.

Whenever you print any photo, it's important to consider the resolution of the image. Printing photos smaller than their actual size will usually not be a problem. However, if you set your photo to print at a size in which its final output resolution is less than 150-200 ppi, you will likely see reduced quality and fuzziness in your output. This could definitely be a problem if you selected the **Individual Print** option and you then selected a print size much larger than the actual photo.

Select Type of Print

The **Type of Print** menu on the **Prints** option panel arranges the photos in your print-out page in one of three patterns.

Individual Prints prints photos to your printer at the size you designate.

Picture Package sends an arrangement of photos to your printer based on the number of photos you designate per page. This **Type of Print** also gives you the option of printing these photos with a **Frame** around each.

Contact Sheet prints proof-style thumbnails of your photos, according to the layout settings you provide.

Print a Picture Package or Contact Sheet on your local printer

The main difference between the **Picture Package** and the **Individual Prints** print-out options is in how you set the size and number of photos that will appear on your print-out page.

When **Type of Print** is set to **Individual Prints**, you will have the option

Printing a contact sheet.

of selecting the *size* your photos will print out at. When you set the **Type of Print** option to **Picture Package** (or **Contact Sheet**), you will have the option of selecting the *number* of photos you want to print on each page.

Create a Photo Book

A **Photo Book** is a collection of photos laid out in 20 to 80 custom-designed pages. The wizard takes you through the basic steps of setting up the book. Once the book is initially set up, you can add more photos to it and tweak the design and layout.

The Photo Book option panel.

1   Select the photos in the **Media Browser** you'd like to include in your **Photo Book.** Then select the **Photo Book** button under the **Create** tab.

    (You can add, swap out and delete photos later.)

    The **Photo Book** option panel will open in Photoshop Elements.

2   Select a size and output options for your book from the **Photo Book** option panel (illustrated above).

3   On this same panel, select a **Theme** for your book.

    You can assign any number of pages to your book and you can add and remove pages later as needed.

    Click **OK**

The photos you have selected when you launch this tool will automatically be loaded into your **Photo Book** in the order that they appear in the **Media Browser.**

The first of your selected photos will become your **Title Page Photo.**

The program will fill as many pages as possible with the photos you've selected.

You can add pages to or remove pages from your book by clicking the icons in the top left of the **Page Bin.**

You may also change the theme and/or frames for the individual pages or add graphics by selecting options at the bottom right.

Click a block of text to customize it.

Right-click on photo to modify or replace it.

Select a page for editing from the Page bin.

Add or remove pages.

Click to finish and send to printer.

Select graphics and page layouts.

To add, edit or replace photos, **right-click** on the photo frame:

- If the frame is blank, you'll be prompted to browse for a photo on your hard drive.
- If a photo is already in the frame, options will be displayed to resize the photo or **Position Photo Within Frame**, rotate it or replace it.

By dragging on their corner handles, photos and their frames can be resized and repositioned on the page.

To send your finished book to your home printer, click the **Print** button along the bottom of the workspace.

On the **Print Preview** page, you will also find the option to **Print** (save) your **Photo Book** as an Adobe PDF file under **Select Printer**.

Rotate photo

Zoom in /out photo

Replace photo

Accept/ Cancel

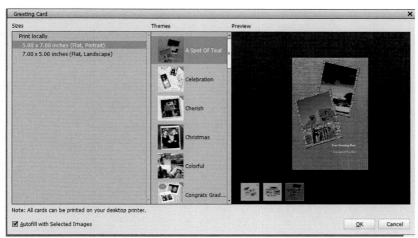

The Greeting Card option panel.

Create a Greeting Card

Once completed, your **Greeting Card** can be printed on your home printer. (This tool is available only if you have Photoshop Elements.)

1 Select the **Greeting Card** button under the **Create** tab.

The photos you have in your **Project Bin** – whether because they are open in the **Editor** or selected in the **Organizer** – will automatically be loaded into your **Greeting Card.** Photos may also be added or removed after the book is created.

2 Select a size and output option for your book from the **Greeting Card** option screen (illustrated above).

3 On this same panel, select a **Theme** for your card. (These features can be modified later.)

Click **OK**.

The program will generate your card.

As with the **Photo Book**, you may swap out photos and modify your **Greeting Card's** layout, graphics or text, as described on page 240.

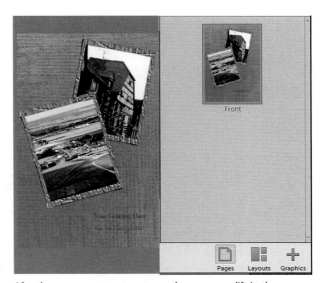

After the program generates your card, you can modify its theme, text, photos and effects.

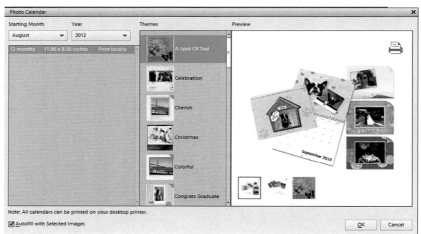

The Calendar option panel.

Create a Photo Calendar

Once completed, your **Photo Calendar** can be printed on your home printer. (This tool is only available if you have Photoshop Elements.)

1 Select the photos you'd like to use in your calendar in the **Media Browser**.

2 Select the **Photo Calendar** button under the **Create** tab.

3 Select a starting date, size and output options for your book from the **Photo Calendar** option screen (illustrated above).

4 On this same panel, select a **Theme** for your card. (These features can be modified later.)

The photos you have in your **Media Browser** will automatically be loaded into your **Photo Calendar**.

Photos may also be added or removed after the book is created.

The program will generate your card.

As with the **Photo Book**, you may swap out photos and modify your **Photo Calendar's** layout, graphics or text, as described on page 240.

After the program generates your calendar, you can modify its layout, graphics, text and photos.

Create a Photo Collage

Adobe has re-designed the **Photo Collage** tool in version 2019, making it less automatic, more powerful and more like the **Video Collage** tool in Premiere Elements. As with many of the **Create** tools in the Organizer, you will need to have Photoshop Elements installed in order to use this tool.

1   Select the seven photos you'd like to use in your collage in the **Media Browser.**

2   Select the **Photo Collage** option under the **Create** tab. Photoshop Elements will launch and up to seven of the photos you've selected will appear in the default **Photo Collage** template.

3   Select a template for your **Photo Collage** from the option screen on the right. Templates are divided into categories like **Landscape, Portrait, Facebook Cover** and **Instagram**. Double-click to apply a new template to your collage.

4   To replace a photo in your collage, select the photo in the grid and click the **Add Photo** button at the top right of the interface.

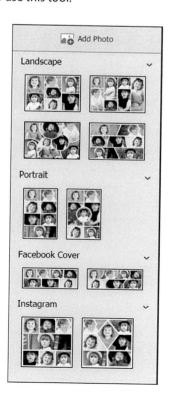

As with the **Photo Book**, you may swap out photos and modify your **Photo Calendar's** layout, graphics or text, as described on page 240.

Click **Save** to save the collage or select an export option under the **Share** button in the upper right of the program.

Create an InstantMovie

If you have Premiere Elements installed, selecting the option to create an **InstantMovie** gathers the photos and video clips you've selected in the Organizer's **Media Browser** and ports them to Premiere Elements, where an **InstantMovie Theme** is applied.

Create a Video Story

If you have Premiere Elements installed, selecting the option to create a **Video Story** gathers the photos and video clips you've selected in the Organizer's **Media Browser** and ports them to Premiere Elements and into the **Video Story** workspace.

Create a Video Collage

If you have Premiere Elements installed, selecting the option to create a **Video Collage** gathers the photos and video clips you've selected in the Organizer's **Media Browser** and ports them to Premiere Elements and into the **Video Collage** workspace.

Create a DVD with Menu

If you have Premiere Elements installed, selecting the option to create a **DVD With Menu** gathers the photos and video clips you've selected in the Organizer's **Media Browser** and ports them to a Premiere Elements project for further editing.

Create a CD Jacket

This tool creates a 9¾" x 4¾" image that you can print out and fit into a CD or DVD "jewel case." (Note that disc jewel cases are 4¾" x 4¾", so this artwork is designed to wrap around the case and includes a ¼" spine.)

Create a DVD Jacket

This tool creates an 11" x 7½" label for a DVD case. This template is made to fit a 5¼" x 7½" case with a ½" wide spine.

Print a CD/DVD Label

This tool creates 4¾", circular-shaped artwork for printing onto discs. It includes the necessary spindle hole through the center.

At Muvipix, we recommend never using glue-on labels for your DVDs and CDs. They can cause a number of problems. This tool is best used with printable discs and inkjet printers designed to print on them.

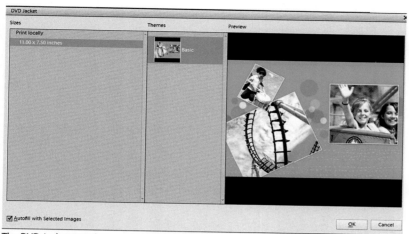

The DVD Jacket template creates an image that wraps around a DVD case that has 5.25" x 7.50" faces and a 0.5" spine.

The CD/DVD Label template creates art that can be printed onto a 4.75" disc.

Sharing Your Photos as E-mail Attachments

Sharing to Flickr, Vimeo and Twitter

Sharing Your Photos or Videos to a CD or DVD

Sharing Your Photos to a PDF Slideshow

Chapter 17

Share Your Photos and Videos

The Organizer's output tools

The Elements Organizer includes a number
of tools for outputting your photo and
video files – from posting them online or
e-mailing them to creating a DVD or PDF
slideshow.

In addition to tools for creating photo and video projects, the Elements Organizer includes a number of tools for sharing your photos and videos.

Share your photos via e-mail

The **E-mail sharing** option optimizes your selected photo files and then sends them off, with a brief note, to the person or group of people you designate as **Recipients**.

As with any **Share** tool, you can pre-select your media files before starting the tool or add your media files later.

1   Select the photo(s) you want to attach to your e-mail in your **Media Browser**.

2   Select the **E-mail** option under the **Share** tab in the Organizer.

   The **E-mail** share panel will open.

3   Drag any more photo(s) you'd like to add to your e-mail attachments from the Organizer's **Media Browser** into the **E-mail Attachments Items** bin.

   Remove any photos you'd like to delete by selecting them in the panel and clicking the **trashcan** button below the photos.

   You can add photos in any file format. The program will convert whatever you add to this bin into a JPEG for e-mailing.

   Set the **Photo Size** and **Quality** by using the slider and selecting a photo size from the **Maximum Photo Size** drop-down menu.

   Naturally, the more photos you're including in your e-mail, the more you'll need to decrease the photo size or quality.

The panel displays an **Estimated Size** and, in order to ensure your e-mail doesn't choke your recipients' e-mail services, you'll probably want to keep your total e-mail size below 1 megabyte or so.

When you are happy with your settings for this panel, click **Next**.

4   Create a message to accompany your photos and then **Select Recipients** from your list of contacts.

(See the sidebar on page 251 – **Create an Elements Organizer Contact Book** – for information on creating your **Contacts** list.)

When you are happy with your settings for this panel, click **Next**.

Your e-mail and optimized attachments will be sent to your selected recipients.

Share your photos on Flickr

When you select photos in your **Media Browser** and select the **Flickr** option under the **Share** tab, your photos will be prepared, then uploaded to your account at www.flickr.com.

The first time you use the tool, you will need to log in to Flickr and **Authorize** the upload:

1   Click **Authorize**.

After you click the **Authorize** button, your web browser will open to your Flickr page. If you are already logged into Flicker, you're done with the authorization. You can close your web browser now. If not, you will need to log in first.

2   Back in the Organizer, click the **Complete Authorization** button.

The program will finish preparing your file(s). An option panel will then open, asking you to name your file(s) and set who can see them.

3   Once you've set your options, as illustrated on the facing page, click **Upload**. Your file(s) will load to your Flickr account.

Set up e-mail sharing for the Elements Organizer

In order to use the Elements Organizer's e-mail **Share** options, you must have an active e-mail profile and address listed on the **Email** page of the Organizer's **Preferences** (under the **Edit** drop-down on the Organizer Menu Bar on a PC).

On this **Email Preferences** page, under **Configure Email Client**, select a name for your **Email Profile**, then fill in your e-mail address and password.

Click the **Validate** button. The program will indicate if your validation was successful.

E-mails sent directly from the Organizer will use this e-mail address as their output path.

Share your photos on Twitter

When you select photos in your **Media Browser** and select the **Twitter** option under the **Share** tab, your photos will be prepared, then uploaded to your account at www.Twitter.com – much like the process described in **Share Your Videos and Photos on Flickr** on page 249.

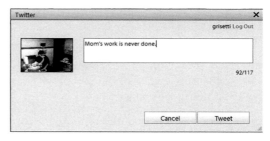

The first time you use the tool, you will need to **Authorize** the upload, as described in **Share Your Videos and Photos on Flickr**.

Share your video on Vimeo

When you select a video in your **Media Browser** and select the **Vimeo** option under the **Share** tab, your video will be prepared, then uploaded to your account at www.vimeo.com – much like the process described in **Share Your Videos and Photos on Flickr** on page 249.

The first time you use the tool, you will need to **Authorize** the upload, as described in **Share Your Videos and Photos on Flickr**.

Share your video on YouTube

When you select a video in your **Media Browser** and select the **YouTube** option under the **Share** tab, your video will be prepared, then uploaded to your account at YouTube – much like the process described in **Share Your Videos and Photos on Flickr** on page 249.

The first time you use the tool, you will need to **Authorize** the upload, as described in **Share Your Videos and Photos on Flickr**.

If you have Premiere Elements installed, videos can also be uploaded to YouTube using Premiere Elements' **Export & Share/Online** option.

Burn a Video DVD

If you have Premiere Elements installed, when you click on the **Share** option to **Burn Video DVD**, the program will launch Premiere Elements and the files you have selected in the Organizer's **Media Browser** will be ported to a Premiere Elements project.

Share as a PDF Slide Show

Selecting the **PDF Slide Show** option under the **Share** tab creates a dynamic slideshow of the photo files you have selected in the **Media Browser** and outputs them in the PDF (Portable Document File) format, which it then e-mails to your selected recipients.

The slideshow can be viewed on any computer using the free utility Acrobat Reader.

Create an Elements Organizer Contact Book

In order to have the options to **Select Recipients** for your **E-mail Attachments,** you will need to have these potential recipients listed in your Elements Organizer's **Contact Book**.

To create and add your contacts to this book, go to the **Edit** drop-down on the Organizer Menu Bar and select **Contact Book**:

Click **New Contacts** to manually add your contacts' names and e-mail addresses.

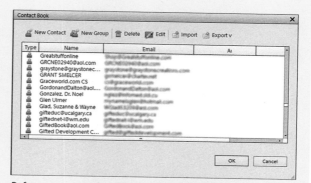

Before you can send out Photo Mail or an e-mail using Adobe's services, you'll need to build a Contact Book, an option available under the Organizer's Edit menu.

Or export your selected contacts from your e-mail program as a **Vcard**, or .vcf file, then click the **Import** button on the Organizer **Contact Book** panel.

Once they have been added to your **Contact Book, these names** will be listed under **Select Recipients** whenever you select the **E-mail Attachment** or **Photo Mail** option.

A

Actions Panel, The 59
Add to Selection 100
Adjustment Layers (Photo) 77, 129–132
Adjust Color 121
Adjust Color Curves 123
Adjust Color for Skin Tone 123, 172
Adjust Facial Features 128
Adjust Hue/Saturation 122
Adjust Lightness 124
Adjust Sharpness 126, 127
Albums, in the Organizer 20, 220
All Layers (Select option) 101
Alpha and transparency 10, 141, 143
Anti-aliasing 75, 149
Artistic Filters 159
Aspect ratio, video 5
Auto-Analyzer 14. See Media Analyzer
Auto Color Correction 118
Auto Contrast 118
Auto Creations 14, 221
Auto Curate pictures in Organizer 214
Auto Fixes 118
Auto Levels 118
Auto Red Eye Fix 118
Auto select object. See Smart Selection tool
Auto Sharpen 118
Auto Smart Fix 118
Auto Smart Tone, for photos 118, 120

B

B&W Color Pop Guided Edit 36
B&W Selection Guided Edit 36
Background Color 65–96
Background Eraser Tool 83
Background layer 142, 190–200
Basic Training tutorials 23
Bevel Layer Style 163
Bicubic Sharper 113
Bicubic Smoother 113
Bitmap 203
Black & White Guided Edit 36

Blending layers 137
Blur Filter 159
Blur Tool 79
Brightness/Contrast 124
Brush settings and options 82, 84
Brush Strokes filter 161
Burn Tool 80

C

Calendar, create. See Photo Calendar, create
Camera RAW editing 52–53
Canvas Size 8, 109, 114–115
Catalog, Organizer. See Organizer Catalog
CD/DVD Label, create 244
Chrome Filter 161
Clone Stamp Tool 78, 174, 175
Cloning areas of photos 174–176
Clouds 160
Color, adjust 121
Color correcting photos 30, 117–132, 131
Color Curves 123
Color Management 204
Color Mode 203
Color Picker 65
Color Profile 204
Color Replacement Brush 81
Color Sampler. See Sampler Tool
Color Swatch panel 66–96
Complex Layer Styles 163
Constrain Proportions 106, 113
Contact Book, for the Elements Organizer 251
Contact Sheet, printing 238
Content Aware Fill 29, 76, 95
Content Aware Move Tool 94
Convert to Black and White 126
Cookie Cutter Tool 90
Copying layers 139
Correct Camera Distortion 155
Correct Skin Tones Guided Edit 35
Create workspace 233–246
Crop Photo Guided Edit 35
Crop pre-selections. See Crop suggestions
Crop Tools 29, 88-90

Custom Shape Tool 86
Cutting from photos, pasting and layers 104–107

D

Dates, finding files based on 229
Decontaminate Color in Refine Edge Tool 103
Defringe Layer 106, 123
Depth of Field Guided Edit 49–50, 50–51
Desaturate color 122
Deselect 100
Details Smart Brush Tool 77
Difference Clouds 160
Digital Cameras, Get Media from 182–183
Distort filter 161
Distort text 151
Distort Transform 151
Divide Scanned Photos 181
Doc Size. (Document size in Photoshop Elements) 207
Dodge Tool 80
Double Exposure Guided Edit 36, 38–39, 39–40, 40–41
Downloading photos from your camera 181
Draw Tools in Photoshop Elements 81–88
Drop Shadow 164
DVD Jacket, create 244

E

E-mail, share your photos as attachments 248
E-mail sharing, setting up in the Organizer 250
Edge Contrast setting 70
Edge Detection with Refine Edge Tool 101–102
Edge Selector mode for Refine Selection Brush 73
Editing text in PSD 147
Editor workspace 15
Effects, Photoshop Elements 153–164
Effects Layer 157
Elements Hub, the 14, 21

Index

Elements Organizer, manually updating and adding files 216
Ellipse Tool 87
Elliptical Marquee Tool 69, 98, 169
Emboss Filters 161
Enhance Colors Guided Edit 36
Enhance Tools in Photoshop Elements 74–79
EPS graphics file 142
Equalize filter 154
Eraser Tool 83, 106, 170, 172
Events, finding files based on 229
Events Tags 224
Expert Editing in Photoshop Elements 16–19
Export video. See Share your movie
Eyedropper 66

F

Face Recognition, Auto Analyzer 221, 225
Facial Features adjustments. See Adjust Facial Features
Faded Photo effect 159
Faux Styles for text 149
Feathering 69, 99, 101
Feather (Refine Edge) 103
Fibers 160
File extensions for Photoshop Elements files 199
File Info for photos 207
Fill with color or pattern 85, 107–108
Filters, Photoshop Elements 153–164
Filters panel 159
Filter Gallery 156
Find Organizer files based on metadata 219
Flattening layers 138
Flickr, uploading to 249
Flip Horizontal 170
Floating photo files in Editor 16–17, 199
Folder Views, switching in the Organizer 217
Font Size 149
Font Style 148
Foreground/Background Colors 65–67, 85, 107
Frame, add to photo 32
Frame Creator Guided Edit 48

G

GIFs 141
Glass Buttons Layer Styles 164
Glow Photo Effect 159
Gradient Map 154
Gradient Tool 85, 107
Graphics 164
Grayscale 179, 203
Greeting card, creating 241
Groups of People, in the Organizer 227
Grow (selection) 101
Guided Editing for photos 33–60
Guides, in Photoshop Elements Editor 18

H

Hand Tool 29, 67
Haze Removal for photos 126
Healing Brush Tool 76, 173
HEIF (heic) support 22
High-Density monitor settings 199
High-Pass Filter 161
High Key Guided Edit 36
High resolution monitor settings. See High-Density monitor settings
Horizontal Type Mask Tool 146
Horizontal Type Tool 146
Hue/Saturation 122

I

Image Effects 164
Image from Clipboard 180
Image Size 8, 109–113
Image Size vs. Canvas Size 8, 110
Import files into the Organizer 216
Impressionist Brush 81
Indexed Color 203
Info Bar 202
Info Panel 206
Inner Glows 164
Inner Shadows 164
InstantMovie 244
Instant Fixes in the Organizer 31
Instant Fix photo in the Organizer 230–231
Intersect with Selection 100
Inverse (selection) 100
Invert Effect 154
iPhoto catalog, importing into Organizer 216

J

Jiggly playback. See Reduce Interlace Flicker
Jigsaw Puzzle Layer Style 164

L

Lasso Tool 70, 98
Layers, in Photoshop Elements files 9, 119, 133–144, 169, 203
Layers panel 136–144, 189–200
Layer Groups 137, 192–198
Layer Masks 140
Layer Sets. See Layer Groups
Layout settings in Photoshop Elements 16–17
Leading 149
Lens Effects Guided Edit 49, 50
Lens Flare Effect 160
Levels 125
Levels Guided Edit 35
Lighten and Darken Guided Edit 35
Lighting, adjust 124
Lightness, adjust in photos 124
Line Drawing Guided Edit 48
Line Drawing photo effect 36
Line Tool 87
Liquify Filter 161
LOMO Effect, Guided Edit 36
Low Key Guided Edit 36

M

Magic Eraser Tool 84
Magic Wand Tool 71, 98, 105, 171
Magnetic Lasso Tool 70, 98, 174
Managed Folders in the Organizer 218
Map, finding files based on place. See Place, organizing your files based on
Marquee Selection Tools 69, 98
Media Analyzer 220–221
Media Browser in the Organizer 214
Meme Creator Guided Edit 22, 37, 38
Metadata 218–232
Modify Tools in Photoshop Elements 88–96
Monotone Color Photo Effect 159
Motion Blur 159
Move Tool 67, 169
Movie Menu templates, creating and customizing. See Disc

menus, custom creating in Photoshop Elements
Multi-Photo Text Guided Edit 22, 37, 39

N

New Project presets for Photoshop Elements 200
Night Vision Layer Style 164
Noise Filter 161
Non-square graphics, creating 141–144
Non-square pixels 4

O

OCR (Optical Character Recognition) 179
Offset Filter 161
Old Fashioned Photo Guided Edit 37
Opacity in Layers panel 169
Open Closed Eyes in photos 74–75
Open Type font 148
Organizer, cleaning up 216
Organizer, The 209–232
Organizer, the, Create projects 233–246
Organizer, the, media file management with 211–232
Organizer, the, Publish & Share options 247–252
Organizer, the; search media. See Search media with the Organizer
Organizer, updating and adding files 215
Orton Effect Guided Edit 48
Outer Glows 164
Output selection as layer or new document 103
Out of Bounds effect, Guided Edit 37–39

P

Painterly Guided Edit 37, 42–43
Painting Photo Effect 159
Paint Bucket (Fill) Tool 85, 107
Panels Photo Effect 159
Panel Bin, The 18–19
Paragraph Alignment 149
Partial Sketch Guided Edit 22, 37
Patterns Layer Styles 164
Pattern Stamp Tool 78
PDF Slideshow, Share 251

Pencil Tool 88
People, finding files based on people in them 225
People Finder 225. See People, finding files based on people in them
People Tags 224
Perfect Portrait Guided Edit 48
Perspective Crop Tool 91
Perspective Transform 151
Pet Eyes red-eye removal tool 74
Photocopy Filter 161
Photographic Effects Layer Styles 164
Photomerge 52–58
Photomerge Compose feature 52–54
Photomerge Exposure feature 54–56
Photomerge Faces feature 52
Photomerge Group Shot feature 52
Photomerge Panorama feature 57–58
Photomerge Scene Cleaner feature 52
Photoshop Elements Toolbox 18, 63–96, 98
Photoshop file. See PSD file
Photo Bin, The 20
Photo Book, create 238–239
Photo Calendar, create 242
Photo Collage, create 22, 243
Photo Filter 155
Photo Text Guided Edit 37
Picture Package, printing 238
Picture Stack Guided Edit 37, 46
Pixelate Filter 161
Pixels 4, 6, 111
Pixel Dimensions 4, 112
Place, organizing your files based on 227
Places Tags 224
Plastic Wrap Filter 159
PNGs 141
Polygonal Lasso Tool 70, 98
Polygon Tool 87
Pop Art effect, Guided Edit 37
Posterize effect 155
Preferences in Photoshop Elements 199
Preview changes 121
Printing options 237–238
Process Multiple Files 186
Project settings for Photoshop Elements. See New Project

presets for Photoshop Elements
PSD file 12, 141, 201
Puzzle Effect Guided Edit 46, 46–47

Q

Quick Fixes 27–32, 186
Quick Fix Preview Tool 31
Quick Fix Toolbox 29
Quick Frames for photos 32
Quick Selection Tool 29, 71, 98
Quick Textures for photos 32

R

Radial Blur 159
Rain Layer Style 164
Raster graphics 7
Recompose Guided Edit 48
Recompose Tool 48, 92–94
Rectangle Tool 87
Rectangular Marquee Tool 69, 98
Red Eye Removal Tool 74
Refine Edge of Selection 99, 101–103, 105, 172
Refine Selection Brush Tool 71, 72, 73
Reflection Effect, Guided Edit 37
Remove Color 122
Remove Color Cast 121
Removing areas from your photos 174
Removing blemishes from photos 173
Render Filter 160, 161
Replace Background Guided Edit 48
Replace Color 122
Replacing background in photo 171
Resample Image 111, 113–114
Reselect 100
Resize a photo 109–116
Resize photo batch 186
Resizing text layers 150
Resolution 5, 111
Restore Old Photo Guided Edit 48
Resync Organizer catalog 216
RGB Color Mode 10, 179, 203
Rotate and Straighten Guided Edit 35
Rounded Rectangle Tool 87
Rule of Thirds (Crop Tool overlay) 90

Index

S

Sampler Tool 66
Saturated Slide Film Guided Edit 48
Save for Web, graphics formats 143
Saving files preferences in Photoshop Elements 199
Scale Styles 113
Scanning photos 178–180
Scratches and Blemishes Guided Edit 49
Screen captures 180
Search media with the Organizer 222
Seasons Photo Effect 159
Selected Layers/All Layers 101
Selections, working with in Photoshop Elements 9, 68–71, 97–108, 119
Selection Brush Tool 71
Select All 100
Select drop-down menu 100, 172
Select Tools in Photoshop Elements 68–71
Setting Foreground/Background Colors to black/white 67–96
Shadows/Highlights 124
Shake Reduction for photos 129
Shapes in Photoshop Elements 7, 86
Shape Overlay Guided Edit 37
Shape Tools, in Photoshop Elements 86–87
Sharpen Filter 161
Sharpen Guided Edit 35
Sharpen Tool 79, 80
Sharpness, adjust 127
Similar (selection) 101
Simplifying layers 138
Sketch Filters 161
Skin Tone, adjust color for 35, 123
Slideshow, creating in the Organizer 234–237
Smart Brush Tools 77
Smart Detect Selection Edge. See Edge Detection with Refine Edge Tool
Smart Fix 30
Smart Quotes setting for Photoshop Elements type 200
Smart Selection tool 73
Smooth (Refine Edge) 102
Smudge Tool 79
Snow Image Effect 164

Speed Effect Guided Edit 38
Speed Pan Guided Edit 38
Sponge Tool 80
Spot Healing Brush Tool 75, 173
Square pixel equivalents to video frames 5
Stained Glass Filter 162
Straighten Tool 29, 95
Stroke (outline) selection 107–108
Stroke layer 164
Styles panel in Photoshop Elements 162–163
Stylize Filters 161
Subtract from selection 68, 100
Swapping background in photo 171
Swapping faces 168
Swapping Foreground and Background Colors. 67

T

Tabbed set, displaying photos as in Editor 16–17
Tags in the Organizer. See Keyword Tags
Text, creating in Photoshop Elements 145–152
Text, sizing and transforming 150–151
Textures Photo Effect 159
Texture Filters 162
Text and Border Overlay Guided Edit 22, 49, 50
Text Color 149
Text on Custom Path Tool 152
Text on Selection Tool 151
Text on Shape Tool 152
Threshold Effect 155
Tilt-Shift Guided Edit 49
Tolerance 83, 171
Tone, Color. See Auto Smart Tone, for photos
Toolbox, in Photoshop Elements. See Photoshop Elements Toolbox
Tool Options Bin 11, 64, 69, 71, 77, 79, 80, 81, 83, 85, 86, 94, 106, 170, 173
Tool Options for Type Tools 148
Tool Option Bar. See Tool Options Bin
Transform 106, 151
Trick photography 167–176
True Type font 148
Twitter, uploading to 250

Type on Path. See Text on Custom Path Tool
Type on Selection. See Text on Selection Tool
Type on Shape. See Text on Shape Tool
Type Tool Options 148–149
Typing Tools 146–147

U

Undo 100
Unmanaged folders in the Organizer 218
Unsharp Mask 126, 161

V

Vector graphics 7
Vertical Type Mask Tool 146
Vertical Type Tool 146
Video resolution, square pixel equivalents 5
Vignette Guided Edit 35
Vimeo, uploading to 250
Vintage Photo Effect 159
Visibility Layer Style 164
Visual Similarity, finding media files by 219

W

Warp Text 149
Watched Folders in the Organizer 218
Watercolor Effect Guided Edit 49
What's new in Photoshop Elements 2018? 21
Wow Chrome Layer Style 164
Wow Neon Layer Style 164
Wow Plastic Layer Style 164

Y

YouTube, uploading to 250

Z

Zoom Burst Effect Guided Edit 38
Zoom Tool, Photoshop Elements Toolbox 67

51944851R00150

Made in the USA
Columbia, SC
24 February 2019